LEAN AND GREEN COOKBOOK 2021

An Exhaustive Lean and Green Cookbook
With 300+ Super Tasty Recipes To Losing Weight
By Harnessing The Power Of "Fueling Hacks Meals"

TABLE OF CONTENTS

INTRODUCTION 7

LEAN & GREEN RECIPES - POULTRY RECIPES 9

Chicken & Zucchini Pancakes	9
Chicken & Veggie Quiche	9
Chicken & Asparagus Frittata	9
Chicken & Veggie Frittata	10
Chicken & Zucchini Muffins	10
Chicken & Bell Pepper Muffins	11
Chicken & Kale Muffins	11
Chicken & Zucchini Muffins	12
Chicken & Orange Salad	12
Chicken & Strawberry Salad	13
Chicken & Fruit Salad	13
Chicken, Tomato & Arugula Salad	14
Chicken, Cucumber & Tomato Salad	14
Chicken, Kale & Olives Salad	15
Chicken, Kale & Cucumber Salad	15
Turkey & Veggie Salad	16
Ground Turkey Salad	16
Chicken & Kale Soup	16
Chicken & Spinach Stew	17
Turkey Meatballs & Kale Soup	17
Turkey & Spinach Stew	18
Turkey & Mushroom Stew	18
Chicken Stuffed Avocado	19
Chicken Lettuce Wraps	19
Chicken & Strawberry Lettuce Wraps	20
Ground Chicken Lettuce Wraps	20
Chicken Burgers	20
Chicken & Avocado Burgers	21
Chicken Meatballs with Mash	21
Chicken & Veggie Skewers	22
Stuffed Chicken Breast	22
Balsamic Chicken Breast	23
Lemony Chicken Thighs	23
Spicy Chicken Drumsticks	23
Baked Chicken & Bell Peppers	24
Orange Chicken	24
Chicken Breast with Asparagus	25
Chicken with Zoodles	25
Chicken with Yellow Squash	26
Chicken with Bell Peppers	26
Chicken with Mushrooms	27
Chicken with Broccoli & Mushrooms	27
Chicken & Veggies Stir Fry	28
Chicken & Broccoli Bake	28
Cheesy Chicken & Spinach	28
Chicken & Cauliflower Curry	29
Chicken & Veggies Casserole	29
Chicken & Green Veggies Curry	30
Turkey & Avocado Lettuce Wraps	30
Turkey Burgers	31
Turkey, Apple & Veggies Burgers	31
Turkey Stuffed Zucchini	31
Turkey Stuffed Acorn Squash	32
Turkey & Spinach Meatballs	32
Turkey Meatballs Kabobs	33
Turkey with Peas	33
Turkey & Veggie Casserole	34
Turkey Chili	34

RED MEAT RECIPES 35

Steak & Tomato Salad	35
Steak, Egg & Veggies Salad	35
Steak & Kale Salad	36
Steak & Veggie Salad	36
Beef & Bok Choy Soup	37

Beef & Cabbage Stew	37
Beef & Carrot Stew	38
Baked Beef Stew	38
Beef Lettuce Wraps	39
Simple Beef Burgers	39
Beef & Spinach Burgers	40
Spicy Beef Burgers	40
Spiced Beef Meatballs	40
Beef & Veggie Meatballs	41
Spicy Beef Koftas	41
Beef Kabobs	42
Garlicky Beef Tenderloin	42
Simple Steak	42
Rosemary Steak	43
Spiced Flank Steak	43
Simple Flank Steak	43
Steak with Green Beans	44
Veggie & Feta Stuffed Steak	44
Beef & Broccoli Bowl	45
Beef Taco Bowl	45
Veggie Stuffed Steak	46
Steak with Broccoli	46
Beef with Mushrooms	47
Steak with Carrot & Kale	47
Ground Beef with Veggies	48
Beef Chili	48
Beef Stuffed Bell Peppers	48
Garlicky Pork Tenderloin	49
Pork Stuffed Avocado	49
Pork Burgers	50
Pork & Veggie Burgers	50
Rosemary Pork Tenderloin	51
Pork with Veggies	51
SEAFOOD RECIPES	**52**
Salmon & Arugula Omelet	52
Tuna Omelet	52
Salmon & Veggie Salad	52
Tuna Salad	53
Shrimp & Greens Salad	53
Shrimp, Apple & Carrot Salad	54
Shrimp & Green Beans Salad	54
Shrimp & Olives Salad	55
Shrimp & Arugula Salad	55
Shrimp & Veggies Salad	55
Scallop & Tomato Salad	56
Fish Stew	56
Shrimp Stew	57
Salmon Lettuce Wraps	57
Spicy Salmon	58
Lemony Salmon	58
Zesty Salmon	58
Stuffed Salmon	59
Salmon with Asparagus	59
Salmon Parcel	60
Salmon with Cauliflower Mash	60
Salmon with Salsa	61
Walnut Crusted Salmon	61
Garlicky Tilapia	62
Tilapia Piccata	62
Cod in Dill Sauce	62
Cod & Veggies Bake	63
Cod & Veggie Pizza	63
Garlicky Haddock	64
Haddock in Parsley Sauce	64
Halibut with Zucchini	65
Roasted Mackerel	65
Herbed Sea Bass	65
Lemony Trout	66
Tuna Burgers	66
Tuna Stuffed Avocado	66
Fish & Spinach Curry	67
Crab Cakes	67
Shrimp Lettuce Wraps	68

Shrimp Kabobs	68
Shrimp with Zucchini Noodles	68
Shrimp with Spinach	69
Shrimp with Broccoli & Carrot	69
Shrimp, Spinach & Tomato Casserole	70
Prawns with Bell Pepper	70
Prawns with Broccoli	70
Prawns with Asparagus	71
Prawns with Kale	71
Scallops with Broccoli	72
Scallops with Asparagus	72
Scallops with Spinach	72
Shrimp & Scallops with Veggies	73

VEGETARIAN RECIPES — 74

Avocado Toast	74
Baked Eggs	74
Eggs in Bell Pepper Rings	74
Eggs in Avocado Halves	75
Broccoli Waffles	75
Cheesy Spinach Waffles	75
Kale Scramble	76
Tomato & Egg Scramble	76
Tofu & Spinach Scramble	76
Tofu & Veggie Scramble	77
Apple Omelet	77
Mushroom & Tomato Omelet	77
Veggie Omelet	78
Veggies Quiche	78
Zucchini & Carrot Quiche	79
Green Veggies Quiche	79
Kale & Mushroom Frittata	80
Kale & Bell Pepper Frittata	80
Bell Pepper Frittata	80
Broccoli Frittata	81
Zucchini Frittata	81
Eggs with Spinach	82
Eggs with Kale & Tomatoes	82
Eggs with Veggies	83
Tofu & Mushroom Muffins	83
Fruit Salad	84
Strawberry, Orange & Rocket Salad	84
Strawberry & Asparagus Salad	84
Blueberries & Spinach Salad	85
Mixed Berries Salad	85
Kale & Citrus Fruit Salad	85
Kale, Apple & Cranberry Salad	86
Rocket, Beat & Orange Salad	86
Cucumber & Tomato Salad	86
Mixed Veggie Salad	86
Eggs & Veggie Salad	87
Tofu & Veggie Salad	87
Kale & Carrot Soup	87
Cheesy Mushroom Soup	88
Spinach & Mushroom Stew	88
Veggie Stew	89
Tofu & Mushroom Soup	89
Tofu & Bell Pepper Stew	90
Carrot Soup with Tempeh	90
Vegetarian Burgers	90
Cauliflower with Peas	91
Broccoli with Bell Peppers	91
3-Veggies Medley	92
3 Veggies Combo	92
Cauliflower with Peas	92
Bok Choy & Mushroom Stir Fry	93
Broccoli with Bell Peppers	93
Stuffed Zucchini	93
Zucchini & Bell Pepper Curry	94
Zucchini Noodles with Mushroom Sauce	94
Squash Casserole	95
Veggies & Walnut Loaf	95
Tofu & Veggie Burgers	96
Tofu & Veggie Lettuce Wraps	96

Tofu with Kale	97
Tofu with Broccoli	97
Tofu with Peas	98
Tofu with Brussels Sprout	98
Tofu with Veggies	99
Tofu & Mushroom Curry	99
Tofu & Veggies Curry	100
Tempeh with Bell Peppers	100
Tempeh with Brussel Sprout & Kale	101
Tempeh with Veggies	101

FUELING HACKS RECIPES 102

Berry Mojito	102
Coconut Smoothie	102
Tiramisu Shake	102
Vanilla Shake	102
Shamrock Shake	103
Chocolate Shake	103
Peppermint Mocha	103
Pumpkin Frappe	103
Vanilla Frappe	104
Chocolate Frappe	104
Caramel Macchiato Frappe	104
Eggnog	104
Pumpkin Spiced Latte	105
Hot Chocolate	105
Cherry Mocha Popsicles	105
Yogurt Cookie Dough	106
Chocolate Coconut Pie	106
Caramel Crunch Parfait	106
Chocolate Berry Parfait	106
Brownie Pudding	107
Brownie Peanut Butter Pudding	107
Chia Seed Pudding	107
Chocolate Cake Fries	107
French Toast Sticks	108
Fudge Balls	108
Peanut Butter Bites	108
Yogurt Cereal Bark	109
Chocolate Crunch Cookies	109
Oatmeal Cookies	109
Peanut Butter Cookies	110
Mint Cookies	110
Gingersnap Cookies	110
Crunch Sandwich Cookies	111
Sandwich Cookies	111
Snickerdoodles	111
Chocolate Whoopie Pies	112
Brownie Bites	112
Chocolate Haystacks	113
Peanut Butter Bites	113
Marshmallow Cereal Treat	113
Blueberry Scones	114
Gingerbread Biscotti	114
Yogurt Berry Donuts	114
Chocolate Donuts	115
Blueberry Muffins	115
Mocha Muffin	115
Sweet Potato Muffins	116
Sweet Potato & Cheese Muffins	116
Peanut Butter Cream Cupcakes	117
Meringue Cups	117
Peanut Butter Cups	118
Mini Chocolate Cakes	118
Mocha Cake	118
Shake Cake	119
Marshmallow Cereal Cake	119
Cinnamon Buns	119
Chocolate Crepe	120
Pumpkin Waffles	120
Oatmeal Waffles	120
Chocolate Waffles	121
Mac & Cheese Waffles	121
Maple Pancakes	121

Mashed Potato Pancake	122
Mini Biscuit Pizza	122
Pizza Bread	122
Mashed Potato Tortilla	123
Potato Bagels	123
Noodle Soup Chips	123
Mac & Cheese Chips	124
Tortilla Chips	124
Mac & Cheese Doritos	124
Chicken Nuggets	125
Smashed Potato Grill Cheese	125
Buffalo Cauliflower Poppers	126
Parmesan Chicken Bites	126
Mozzarella Pizza Bites	126
Taco Salad	127
Snack Mix	127
Sriracha Popcorn	127
Pumpkin Pie Trail Mix	127
SHOPPING LIST	**128**
Meat	128
Egg & Dairy	128
Fruit	128
Vegetables & Fresh Herbs	128
Seasoning & Dried Herbs	128
Fueling Hacks Products	129
MEAL PLAN 1	**129**
MEAL PLAN 2	**130**
CONCLUSION	**131**

INTRODUCTION

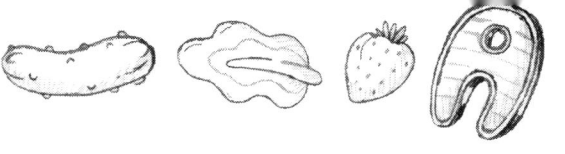

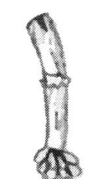

Are you searching for a weight loss program that would guarantee you good and effective results? Do you want to try something different and logical to achieve good health? Then here comes the Lean and Green diet- a perfect weight loss program for all. This dietary regime takes a whole new approach to mixing different weight loss measures in a single diet plan. The diet is basically restrictive, and it promotes the use fueling meals to meet all the nutritional needs. And if you want to learn more about this diet, how to adjust Fuelings with daily meals then continue reading as you are going to get several easy and healthy recipes in this cookbook that will let you control your caloric intake and reduce weight in just a few weeks.

What is Lean and Green Diet

Lean and Green diet is basically a weight loss or weight maintenance program that suggests the use of a lean and green meal along with processed food called "fueling." And here is the concept of fueling is organized around the whole Lean and Green Diet:

The diet says to add nutritional Fuelings to the diet while controlling the overall caloric intake.

- The fueling is actually powdered food, which is mixed with liquid like water and then added to the diet as a part of routine meals.
- Besides consuming these fueling, the dieters are also suggested to exercise 30 minutes daily to lose their weight.
- By trying fueling as a substitute for real food, you can curb the carb and sugar intake and can manage your caloric intake as well.

How much Fuelings to consume, how much food to eat, and what to eat on this dietary regime depends on the type of weight loss plan you are going for. However, on this diet, the overall calorie intake for adults is reduced to 800 to 1000 per day, which lets you lose about 12 lbs. of weight per 12 weeks on average.

Weight-loss Benefits of Lean and Green Diet

Our caloric intake should be around 1000 calories per day in order to initiate weight-loss fat burning in the body. But cutting down your calories just by avoiding food is not the solution. A dieter needs help to maintain his low-caloric intake and meet all the nutritional needs as well. The Lean and Green Diet thus provides a perfect solution- the food Fuelings. A fueling is made specially to keep the calories low and provide all the essential nutrients that are required to carry out the normal metabolic activities in the body. Each fueling is created to have only 100 to 110 calories, which is low enough to keep the daily caloric intake to 1000 calories.

Eating on Lean and Green Diet

The lean and green meal must have the following essential ingredients to keep it healthy and safe:

- **Seafood:**

Seafood is best to have on any weight loss regime because it is free from saturated fats and brings a lot of nutritional value to the table. You can have all types of fishes and seafood on this diet, including halibut, salmon, trout, lobster, tuna, shrimp, crab, and scallops, etc.

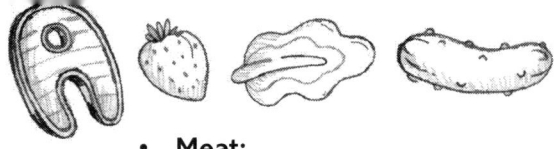

- **Meat:**

The lean and green diet only allows 85 percent of lean meat on a diet; whether it is chicken, beef, turkey, lamb, pork, and ground meat, it all has to be lean. Lean meat has lower fat content, which makes it great to keep the caloric intake in control.

- **Eggs:**

Eggs are rich in protein, and they are low in carbs; that's what makes eggs the right for this diet.

- **Soy products:**

In soy products, tofu is the only product that is allowed on the diet because it is processed, and the caloric content is suitable for the lean diet.

- **Fats:**

Not all fats are healthy, and there are a handful of options that you must try on this diet, which includes most of the vegetable olive oil, walnut oil, canola oil, flaxseed oil.

- **Low carb vegetables:**

Focus on all the green veggies for this diet. Except for potatoes, yams, sweet potatoes, yellow squash, and beetroots, you can try every other vegetable on this diet, including cabbage, spinach, cucumbers, etc.

- Sugar-free snacks:
- Sugar-free beverages:
- Condiments and seasonings:

Foods to Avoid

As the Lean and Green diet is restrictive in approach, there is a certain food that is not allowed on this diet. The following food must be avoided.

- All fried foods
- High carb refined grain items
- Saturated fats
- Milk
- All varieties of alcohol
- All sweetened beverages

 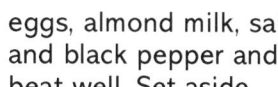 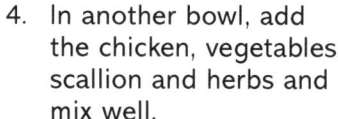 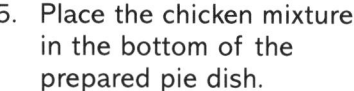

LEAN & GREEN RECIPES

POULTRY RECIPES

CHICKEN & ZUCCHINI PANCAKES

Servings: 4
Preparation Time: 15 minutes
Cooking Time: 32 minutes

INGREDIENTS:

- 4 cups zucchini, shredded
- Salt, as required
- ¼ cup cooked chicken, shredded
- ¼ cup scallion, chopped finely
- 1 egg, beaten
- ¼ cup coconut flour
- Salt and ground black pepper, as required
- 1 tablespoon extra-virgin olive oil

INSTRUCTIONS:

1. In a colander, place the zucchini and sprinkle with salt.
2. Set aside for about 8-10 minutes.
3. Squeeze the zucchinis well and transfer into a bowl.
4. In the bowl of zucchini, add the remaining ingredients and mix until well combined.
5. In a large nonstick wok, heat the oil over medium heat.
6. Add ¼ cup of zucchini mixture into the preheated wok and spread in an even layer.
7. Cook for about 3-4 minutes per side.
8. Repeat with the remaining mixture.
9. Serve warm.

NUTRITIONAL INFORMATION PER SERVING:

Calories: 109
Fat: 5.8g
Carbohydrates: 9.4g
Fiber: 4.4g
Sugar: 2.2g
Protein: 6.4g
Sodium: 72mg

CHICKEN & VEGGIE QUICHE

Servings: 4
Preparation Time: 15 minutes
Cooking Time: 20 minutes

INGREDIENTS:

- 6 eggs
- ½ cup unsweetened almond milk
- Freshly ground black pepper, as required
- 1 cup cooked chicken, chopped
- ½ cup fresh baby spinach, chopped
- ½ cup fresh baby kale, chopped
- ¼ cup fresh mushrooms, sliced
- ¼ cup green bell pepper, seeded and chopped
- 1 scallion, chopped
- ¼ cup fresh cilantro, chopped
- 1 tablespoon fresh chives, minced

INSTRUCTIONS:

1. Preheat your oven to 400 degrees F.
2. Lightly grease a pie dish.
3. In a large bowl, add the eggs, almond milk, salt and black pepper and beat well. Set aside.
4. In another bowl, add the chicken, vegetables, scallion and herbs and mix well.
5. Place the chicken mixture in the bottom of the prepared pie dish.
6. Place the egg mixture over chicken mixture evenly.
7. Bake for approximately 20 minutes or until a toothpick inserted in the center comes out clean.
8. Remove from the oven and set aside to cool for about 5-10 minutes before slicing.
9. Cut into desired size wedges and serve.

NUTRITIONAL INFORMATION PER SERVING:

Calories: 162
Fat: 8.1g
Carbohydrates: 2.9g
Fiber: 0.6g
Sugar: 1.1g
Protein: 19.3g
Sodium: 145mg

CHICKEN & ASPARAGUS FRITTATA

Servings: 4
Preparation Time: 15 minutes
Cooking Time: 12 minutes

INGREDIENTS:

- ½ cup cooked chicken, chopped
- 1/3 cup low-fat Parmesan cheese, grated
- 6 eggs, beaten lightly

- Salt and ground black pepper, as required
- 1 teaspoon coconut oil
- ½ cup boiled asparagus, chopped
- 1 tablespoon fresh parsley, chopped

INSTRUCTIONS:

1. Preheat the broiler of oven.
2. In a bowl, add the cheese, eggs, salt and black pepper and beat until well combined.
3. In a large ovenproof wok, melt coconut oil over medium-high heat and cook the chicken and asparagus for about 2-3 minutes.
4. Add the egg mixture and stir to combine,
5. Cook for about 4-5 minutes.
6. Remove from the heat and sprinkle with the parsley.
7. Now, transfer the wok under broiler and broil for about 3-4 minutes or until slightly puffed.
8. Cut into desired sized wedges and serve immediately.

NUTRITIONAL INFORMATION PER SERVING:

Calories: 156
Fat: 9.9g
Carbohydrates: 1.3g
Fiber: 0.4g
Sugar: 0.8g
Protein: 15.4g
Sodium: 270mg

CHICKEN & VEGGIE FRITTATA

Servings: 8
Preparation Time: 45 minutes
Cooking Time: 15 minutes

INGREDIENTS:

- 1 teaspoon olive oil
- ½ cup yellow onion, sliced
- 2 garlic cloves, minced
- 2 cups fresh spinach, chopped
- 1 cup red bell pepper, seeded and chopped
- 2 cups cooked chicken, chopped
- 2 large eggs
- 4 large egg whites
- 1¼ cups unsweetened almond milk
- 1 cup low-fat cheddar cheese, shredded
- Freshly ground black pepper, as required
- 1 tablespoon Parmesan cheese, shredded

INSTRUCTIONS:

1. Preheat your oven to 350 degrees F.
2. Grease a 9-inch pie plate.
3. In a wok, heat oil over medium heat and sauté onion and garlic for about 2-3 minutes.
4. Add spinach and bell pepper and sauté for about 1-2 minutes.
5. Stir in chicken and transfer the mixture into the prepared pie dish evenly.
6. Add eggs, egg whites, almond milk, cheddar cheese, salt, and black pepper in a mixing bowl and beat until well combined.
7. Pour egg mixture over the chicken mixture evenly and top with Parmesan cheese.
8. Bake for approximately 40 minutes or until top becomes golden brown.
9. Remove the pie dish from oven and set aside for about 5 minutes.
10. Cut into 8 equal-sized wedges and serve.

NUTRITIONAL INFORMATION PER SERVING:

Calories: 161
Fat: 2.4g
Carbohydrates: 3.1g
Fiber: 0.7g
Sugar: 1.4g
Protein: 17.9g
Sodium: 317mg

CHICKEN & ZUCCHINI MUFFINS

Servings: 4
Preparation Time: 15 minutes
Cooking Time: 15 minutes

INGREDIENTS:

- 4 eggs
- ¼ cup olive oil
- ¼ cup water
- 1/3 cup coconut flour
- ½ teaspoon baking powder
- ¼ teaspoon salt
- ¾ cup cooked chicken, shredded
- ¾ cup zucchini, grated
- ½ cup low-fat Parmesan cheese, shredded
- 1 tablespoon fresh oregano, minced

- 1 tablespoon fresh thyme, minced
- ¼ cup low-fat cheddar cheese, grated

INSTRUCTIONS:

1. Preheat your oven to 400 degrees F.
2. Lightly grease 8 cups of a muffin pan.
3. In a bowl, add eggs, oil and water and beat until well combined
4. Add the flour, baking powder, and salt, and mix well.
5. Add the remaining ingredients and mix until just combined.
6. Place the muffin mixture into the prepared muffin cup evenly.
7. Bake for approximately 13-15 minutes or until tops become golden brown.
8. Remove muffin pan from oven and place onto a wire rack to cool for about 10 minutes.
9. Invert the muffins onto a platter and serve warm.

NUTRITIONAL INFORMATION PER SERVING:

Calories: 321
Fat: 24.2g
Carbohydrates: 8.1g
Fiber: 4.3g
Sugar: 1.5g
Protein: 19.2g
Sodium: 484mg

CHICKEN & BELL PEPPER MUFFINS

Servings: 4
Preparation Time: 15 minutes
Cooking Time: 20 minutes

INGREDIENTS:

- 8 eggs
- Salt and ground black pepper, as required
- 2 tablespoons water
- 8 ounces cooked chicken, chopped finely
- 1 cup green bell pepper, seeded and chopped
- 1 cup onion, chopped

INSTRUCTIONS:

1. Preheat your oven to 350 degrees F.
2. Grease 8 cups of a muffin tin.
3. In a bowl, add eggs, black pepper and water and beat until well combined.
4. Add the chicken, bell pepper and onion and stir to combine.
5. Transfer the mixture in prepared muffin cups evenly.
6. Bake for approximately 18-20 minutes or until golden brown.
7. Remove the muffin tin from oven and place onto a wire rack to cool for about 10 minutes.
8. Carefully invert the muffins onto a platter and serve warm.

NUTRITIONAL INFORMATION PER SERVING:

Calories: 232
Fat: 10.6g
Carbohydrates: 5.6g
Fiber: 1g
Sugar: 3.4g
Protein: 28.1g
Sodium: 161mg

CHICKEN & KALE MUFFINS

Servings: 4
Preparation Time: 15 minutes
Cooking Time: 20 minutes

INGREDIENTS:

- 8 eggs
- Freshly ground black pepper, as required
- 2 tablespoons water
- 7 ounces cooked chicken, chopped finely
- 1½ cups fresh kale, tough ribs removed and chopped
- 1 cup onion, chopped
- 2 tablespoons fresh parsley, chopped

INSTRUCTIONS:

1. Preheat your oven to 350 degrees F.
2. Grease 8 cups of a muffin tin.
3. In a bowl, add eggs, black pepper and water and beat until well combined.
4. Add chicken, kale, onion and parsley and stir to combine.
5. Transfer the mixture in prepared muffin cups evenly.
6. Bake for approximately 18-20 minutes or until golden brown.

7. Remove the muffin tin from oven and place onto a wire rack to cool for about 10 minutes.
8. Carefully invert the muffins onto a platter and serve warm.

NUTRITIONAL INFORMATION PER SERVING:

Calories: 225
Fat: 10.3g
Carbohydrates: 6.1g
Fiber: 1.1g
Sugar: 1.9g
Protein: 26.6g
Sodium: 168mg

CHICKEN & ZUCCHINI MUFFINS

Servings: 4
Preparation Time: 15 minutes
Cooking Time: 15 minutes

INGREDIENTS:

- 4 eggs
- ¼ cup olive oil
- ¼ cup water
- 1/3 cup coconut flour
- ½ teaspoons baking powder
- ¼ teaspoons salt
- ¾ cup cooked chicken, shredded
- ¾ cup zucchini, grated
- ½ cup low-fat Parmesan cheese, shredded
- 1 tablespoon fresh oregano, minced
- 1 tablespoon fresh thyme, minced
- ¼ cup low-fat cheddar cheese, grated

INSTRUCTIONS:

1. Preheat your oven to 400 degrees F.
2. Lightly grease 8 cups of a muffin pan.
3. In a bowl, add eggs, oil, and water, and beat until well combined.
4. Add the flour, baking powder, and salt, and mix well.
5. Add the remaining ingredients and mix until just combined.
6. Place the muffin mixture into prepared muffin cups evenly.
7. Bake for approximately 13–15 minutes or until tops become golden brown.
8. Remove muffin pan from oven and place onto a wire rack to cool for about 10 minutes.
9. Invert the muffins onto a platter and serve warm.

NUTRITIONAL INFORMATION PER SERVING:

Calories: 270
Fat: 20g
Carbohydrates: 3.5g
Fiber: 1.4g
Sugar: 0.9g
Protein: 18g
Sodium: 229mg

CHICKEN & ORANGE SALAD

Servings: 5
Preparation Time: 15 minutes
Cooking Time: 16 minutes

INGREDIENTS:

For Chicken:

- 4 (6-ounce) boneless, skinless chicken breast halves
- Salt and ground black pepper, as required
- 2 tablespoons extra-virgin olive oil

For Salad:

- 8 cups fresh baby arugula
- 5 medium oranges, peeled and sectioned
- 1 cup onion, sliced

For Dressing:

- 2 tablespoons extra-virgin olive oil
- 2 tablespoons fresh orange juice
- 2 tablespoons balsamic vinegar
- 1½ teaspoons shallots, minced
- 1 garlic clove, minced
- Salt and ground black pepper, as required

INSTRUCTIONS:

1. *For chicken:* season each chicken breast half with salt and black pepper evenly.
2. Place chicken over a rack set in a rimmed baking sheet.
3. Refrigerate for at least 30 minutes.
4. Remove the baking sheet

  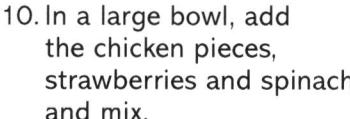 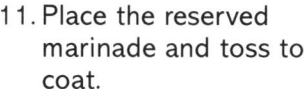

from refrigerator and pat dry the chicken breast halves with paper towels.

5. Heat the oil in a 12-inch sauté pan over medium-low heat.
6. Place the chicken breast halves, smooth-side down, and cook for about 9-10 minutes without moving.
7. Flip the chicken breasts and cook for about 6 minutes or until cooked through.
8. Remove the sauté pan from heat and let the chicken stand in the pan for about 3 minutes.
9. Transfer the chicken breasts onto a cutting board for about 5 minutes.
10. Cut each chicken breast half into desired-sized slices.
11. *For Salad:* place all ingredients in a salad bowl and mix.
12. Add chicken slices and stir to combine.
13. *For Dressing:* place all ingredients in another bowl and beat until well combined.
14. Place the salad onto each serving plate.
15. Drizzle with dressing and serve.

NUTRITIONAL INFORMATION PER SERVING:

Calories: 360
Fat: 15.1g
Carbohydrates: 26g
Fiber: 5.4g
Sugar: 18g
Protein: 31.8g
Sodium: 111mg

CHICKEN & STRAWBERRY SALAD

Servings: 8
Preparation Time: 20 minutes
Cooking Time: 16 minutes

INGREDIENTS:

- 2 pounds boneless, skinless chicken breasts
- ½ cup olive oil
- ¼ cup fresh lemon juice
- 2 tablespoons Erythritol
- 1 garlic clove, minced
- Salt and ground black pepper, as required
- 4 cups fresh strawberries
- 8 cups fresh spinach, torn

INSTRUCTIONS:

1. For marinade: in a large bowl, add oil, lemon juice, Erythritol, garlic, salt and black pepper and beat until well combined.
2. In a large resealable plastic bag, place chicken and ¾ cup marinade.
3. Seal bag and shake to coat well.
4. Refrigerate overnight.
5. Cover the bowl of remaining marinade and refrigerate before serving.
6. Preheat the grill to medium heat. Grease the grill grate.
7. Remove the chicken from bag and discard the marinade.
8. Place the chicken onto grill grate and grill, covered for about 5-8 minutes per side.
9. Remove chicken from grill and cut into bite-sized pieces.
10. In a large bowl, add the chicken pieces, strawberries and spinach and mix.
11. Place the reserved marinade and toss to coat.
12. Serve immediately.

NUTRITIONAL INFORMATION PER SERVING:

Calories: 336
Fat: 17.2g
Carbohydrates: 11g
Fiber: 2.2g
Sugar: 8g
Protein: 34.3g
Sodium: 143mg

CHICKEN & FRUIT SALAD

Servings: 4
Preparation Time: 15 minutes

INGREDIENTS:

For Vinaigrette:

- 2 tablespoons apple cider vinegar
- 2 tablespoons extra-virgin olive oil
- Salt and freshly ground black pepper, as required

For Salad:

- 2 cup cooked chicken, cubed
- 4 cup lettuce, torn
- 1 large apple, peeled, cored and chopped
- 1 cup fresh strawberries, hulled and sliced

INSTRUCTIONS:

1. **For vinaigrette:** in a small bowl, add all ingredients and beat well.
2. **For Salad:** in a large salad bowl, mix together all ingredients.
3. Place vinaigrette over chicken mixture and toss to coat well.
4. Serve immediately.

NUTRITIONAL INFORMATION PER SERVING:

Calories: 215
Fat: 9.4g
Carbohydrates: 12g
Fiber: 2.4g
Sugar: 8g
Protein: 20.9g
Sodium: 87mg

CHICKEN, TOMATO & ARUGULA SALAD

Servings: 4
Preparation Time: 15 minutes
Cooking Time: 15 minutes

INGREDIENTS:

For Chicken:

- 3 (6-ounce) skinless, boneless chicken breast halves
- 2 teaspoons orange zest, grated finely
- 1/3 cup fresh orange juice
- 4 garlic cloves, minced
- 2 tablespoons maple syrup
- 1½ teaspoons dried thyme, crushed

For Salad:

- 6 cups fresh baby arugula
- 2 cups cherry tomatoes, quartered
- 3 tablespoons extra-virgin olive oil
- 2 tablespoons fresh lime juice
- Salt and ground black pepper, as required

INSTRUCTIONS:

1. **For chicken:** in a zip lock bag, all the ingredients.
2. Seal the bag and shake to coat well.
3. Refrigerate to marinate for about 6-8 hours, flipping occasionally.
4. Preheat your oven to broiler.
5. Line a broiler pan with a piece of foil.
6. Arrange the oven rack about 6-inch away from heating element.
7. Remove the chicken breasts from bag and discard the marinade.
8. Arrange the chicken breasts onto the prepared pan in a single layer.
9. Broil for about for 15 minutes, flipping once halfway through.
10. Remove the chicken breasts from oven and place onto a cutting board for about 10 minutes.
11. Cut the chicken breasts into desired sized slices.
12. **For Salad:** in a bowl, add all ingredients and toss to coat well.
13. Add chicken slices and stir to combine.
14. Serve immediately.

NUTRITIONAL INFORMATION PER SERVING:

Calories: 316
Fat: 15.6g
Carbohydrates: 15g
Fiber: 1.9g
Sugar: 10g
Protein: 30.4g
Sodium: 99mg

CHICKEN, CUCUMBER & TOMATO SALAD

Servings: 4
Preparation Time: 15 minutes
Cooking Time: 16 minutes

INGREDIENTS:

- 4 (6-ounce) boneless, skinless chicken breast halves
- Salt and freshly ground black pepper, as required
- 2 tablespoons olive oil
- 1 tomato, chopped
- 1 cucumber, chopped
- 3 cup fresh baby greens
- 3 cup lettuce, torn

INSTRUCTIONS:

1. Season each chicken breast half with salt and black pepper evenly.
2. Place chicken over a rack set in a rimmed baking sheet.
3. Refrigerate for at least 30 minutes.
4. Remove from refrigerator and with paper towels, pat dry the chicken breasts.
5. In a 12-inch wok, heat the oil over medium-low heat.
6. Place the chicken breast

halves, smooth-side down, and cook for about 9-10 minutes without moving.

7. Flip the chicken breasts and cook for about 6 minutes or until cooked through.
8. Remove the wok from heat and let the chicken stand in the pan for about 3 minutes.
9. Divide greens, lettuce, cucumber and tomatoes onto serving plates.
10. Top each plate with 1 breast half and serve.

NUTRITIONAL INFORMATION PER SERVING:

Calories: 376
Fat: 14.8g
Carbohydrates: 5.1g
Fiber: 1.1g
Sugar: 2.3g
Protein: 53.7g
Sodium: 177mg

CHICKEN, KALE & OLIVES SALAD

Servings: 4
Preparation Time: 15 minutes

INGREDIENTS:

For Dressing:

- 2 tablespoons fresh orange juice
- 2 tablespoons fresh lemon juice
- 3 tablespoons extra-virgin olive oil
- 1 tablespoon red wine vinegar
- 1 tablespoon honey
- 1 tablespoon fresh orange zest, grated
- ¾ tablespoon Dijon mustard
- Salt and ground black pepper, as required

For Salad:

- 3 cups cooked chicken, chopped
- 2 cups mixed olives, pitted
- 1 cup red onion, chopped
- 6 cups fresh kale, tough ribs removed and torn

INSTRUCTIONS:

1. *For Dressing:* in a small bowl, add all ingredients and beat well.
2. *For Salad:* in a large salad bowl, mix together all ingredients.
3. Place dressing over salad and toss to coat well.
4. Serve immediately.

NUTRITIONAL INFORMATION PER SERVING:

Calories: 412
Fat: 21.1g
Carbohydrates: 20g
Fiber: 4.6g
Sugar: 6.4g
Protein: 34.6g
Sodium: 771mg

CHICKEN, KALE & CUCUMBER SALAD

Servings: 4
Preparation Time: 15 minutes
Cooking Time: 18 minutes

INGREDIENTS:

For Chicken:

- 1 teaspoon dried thyme
- ½ teaspoon garlic powder
- ½ teaspoon onion powder
- ¼ teaspoon cayenne pepper
- ¼ teaspoon ground turmeric
- Salt and ground black pepper, as required
- 2 (7-ounce) boneless, skinless chicken breasts, pounded into ¾-inch thickness
- 1 tablespoon extra-virgin olive oil

For Salad:

- 5 cups fresh kale, tough ribs removed and chopped
- 1 cup cucumber, chopped
- ½ cup red onion, sliced
- ¼ cup pine nuts

For Dressing:

- 1 small garlic clove, minced
- 2 tablespoons fresh lemon juice
- 2 tablespoons extra-virgin olive oil
- 1 teaspoon maple syrup
- Salt and ground black pepper, as required

INSTRUCTIONS:

1. Preheat your oven to 425 degrees F. Line a baking dish with parchment paper.
2. For chicken: in a bowl, mix together the thyme, spices, salt and black pepper.
3. Drizzle the chicken breasts with oil and then rub with spice mixture generously and drizzle with the oil.
4. Arrange the chicken breasts onto the prepared baking dish.
5. Bake for approximately 16-18 minutes.
6. Remove pan from oven and place the chicken breasts onto a cutting board for about 5 minutes.

7. *For Salad:* place all ingredients in a salad bowl and mix.
8. *For Dressing:* place all ingredients in another bowl and beat until well combined.
9. Cut each chicken breast into desired sized slices.
10. Place the salad onto each serving plate and top each with chicken slices.
11. Drizzle with dressing and serve.

NUTRITIONAL INFORMATION PER SERVING:

Calories: 398
Fat: 23.8g
Carbohydrates: 13g
Fiber: 2.3g
Sugar: 2.7g
Protein: 32.9g
Sodium: 164mg

TURKEY & VEGGIE SALAD

Servings: 4
Preparation Time: 15 minutes

INGREDIENTS:

For Salad:

- 3 cups cooked turkey meat, chopped
- 2 cups, cucumber, chopped
- 1 cup cherry tomatoes, halved
- 1 cup radishes, trimmed and sliced
- 6 cups fresh baby arugula
- 4 tablespoons scallion greens, chopped
- 4 tablespoons fresh parsley leaves, chopped

For Dressing:

- 1 garlic clove, minced
- 3 tablespoons extra-virgin olive oil
- 1 tablespoon balsamic vinegar
- 1 tablespoon fresh lemon juice
- Salt and ground black pepper, as required

INSTRUCTIONS:

1. *For Salad:* in a large serving bowl, add all the ingredients and mix.
2. *For Dressing:* in another bowl, add all the ingredients and beat till well combined.
3. Pour dressing over salad and gently toss to coat well.
4. Serve immediately.

NUTRITIONAL INFORMATION PER SERVING:

Calories: 302
Fat: 16.2g
Carbohydrates: 6g
Fiber: 2.2g
Sugar: 3.2g
Protein: 33.5g
Sodium: 140mg

GROUND TURKEY SALAD

Servings: 6
Preparation Time: 20minutes
Cooking Time: 13 minutes

INGREDIENTS:

- 1 pound ground turkey
- 1 tablespoon olive oil
- Salt and ground black pepper, as required
- ¼ cup water
- ½ of English cucumber, chopped
- 4 cups green cabbage, shredded
- ½ cup fresh mint leaves, chopped
- 2 tablespoons fresh lime juice
- ¼ cup walnuts, chopped

INSTRUCTIONS:

1. Heat oil in a large wok over medium-high heat and cook the turkey for about 6-8 minutes, breaking up the pieces with a spatula.
2. Stir in the water and cook for about 4-5 minutes or until almost all the liquid is evaporated.
3. Remove from the heat and transfer the turkey into a bowl.
4. Set the bowl aside to cool completely.
5. In a large serving bowl, add the vegetables, mint and lime juice and mix well.
6. Add the cooked turkey and stir to combine.
7. Serve immediately.

NUTRITIONAL INFORMATION PER SERVING:

Calories: 219
Fat: 13.8g
Carbohydrates: 4.8g
Fiber: 2.2g
Sugar: 2g
Protein: 22.9g
Sodium: 120mg

CHICKEN & KALE SOUP

Servings: 4
Preparation Time: 15 minutes
Cooking Time: 15 minutes

INGREDIENTS:

- 2 tablespoons extra-virgin olive oil
- ½ of medium onion, chopped
- 3 garlic cloves, minced

 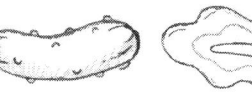   

- 4 cups low-sodium chicken broth
- 1 cup cooked chicken, cubed
- 1 bunch fresh kale, tough ribs removed and chopped
- 2 tablespoons fresh lemon juice
- Salt and ground black pepper, as required

INSTRUCTIONS:

1. In a soup pan, heat olive oil over medium-high heat and sauté the onion and garlic for about 2-3 minutes.
2. Stir in the cooked chicken and broth and bring to a gentle boil.
3. Now, adjust the heat and to low and simmer for about 3 minutes.
4. Stir in the kale and simmer for 5 minutes or until kale is tender.
5. Stir in the lemon juice, salt and black pepper and remove from the heat.
6. Serve hot.

NUTRITIONAL INFORMATION PER SERVING:

Calories: 194
Fat: 8.1g
Carbohydrates: 15g
Fiber: 2.1g
Sugar: 0.8g
Protein: 15.9g
Sodium: 182mg

CHICKEN & SPINACH STEW

Servings: 8
Preparation Time: 15 minutes
Cooking Time: 30 minutes

INGREDIENTS:

- 2 tablespoons olive oil
- 1 yellow onion, chopped
- 1 tablespoon garlic, minced
- 1 tablespoon fresh ginger, minced
- 1 teaspoon ground turmeric
- 1 teaspoon ground cumin
- 1 teaspoon ground coriander
- 1 teaspoon paprika
- 1 teaspoon cayenne pepper
- 6 (4-ounce) boneless, skinless chicken thighs, trimmed and cut into 1-inch pieces
- 4 tomatoes, chopped
- 1 (14-ounce) can unsweetened coconut milk
- Salt and ground black pepper, as required
- 3 cups fresh spinach, chopped

INSTRUCTIONS:

1. In a large heavy-bottomed pan, heat the oil over medium heat and sauté the onion for about 3-4 minutes.
2. Add the ginger, garlic, and spices, and sauté for about 1 minute.
3. Add the chicken and cook for about 4-5 minutes.
4. Add the tomatoes, coconut milk, salt, and black pepper, and bring to gentle simmer.
5. Now, adjust the heat to low and simmer, covered for about 10-15 minutes.

6. Stir in the spinach and cook for about 4–5 minutes.
7. Remove from the heat and serve hot.

NUTRITIONAL INFORMATION PER SERVING:

Calories: 293
Fat: 17g
Carbohydrates: 5.7g
Fiber: 1.6g
Sugar: 3.6g
Protein: 26.5g
Sodium: 122mg

TURKEY MEATBALLS & KALE SOUP

Servings: 6
Preparation Time: 20 minutes
Cooking Time: 25 minutes

INGREDIENTS:

For Meatballs:

- 1 pound lean ground turkey
- 1 garlic clove, minced
- 1 egg, beaten
- ¼ cup low-fat Parmesan cheese, grated
- Salt and ground black pepper, as required

For Soup:

- 1 tablespoon olive oil
- 1 small yellow onion, chopped finely
- 1 garlic clove, minced
- 6 cups low-sodium chicken broth
- 8 cups fresh kale, trimmed and chopped
- 2 eggs, beaten lightly
- Salt and ground black pepper, as required

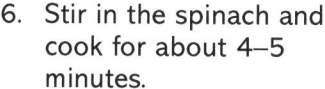 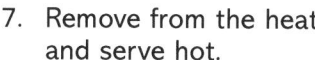 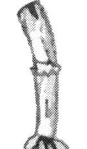 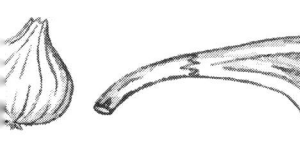   

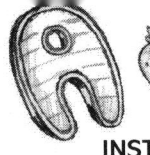

INSTRUCTIONS:

1. *For meatballs:* in a bowl, add all ingredients and mix until well combined.
2. Make equal-sized small balls from mixture.
3. In a large soup pan, heat oil over medium heat and sauté onion for about 5-6 minutes.
4. Add the garlic and sauté for about 1 minute.
5. Add the broth and bring to a boil.
6. Carefully place the balls in pan and bring to a boil.
7. Reduce the heat to low and cook for about 10 minutes.
8. Stir in the kale and bring the soup to a gentle simmer.
9. Simmer for about 2-3 minutes.
10. Slowly, add the beaten eggs, stirring continuously.
11. Cook for about 1-2 minutes, stirring continuously.
12. Season with the salt and black pepper and remove from the heat.
13. Serve hot.

NUTRITIONAL INFORMATION PER SERVING:

Calories: 288
Fat: 14g
Carbohydrates: 12g
Fiber: 1.6g
Sugar: 1.4g
Protein: 29.3g
Sodium: 117mg

TURKEY & SPINACH STEW

Servings: 4
Preparation Time: 15 minutes
Cooking Time: 35 minutes

INGREDIENTS:

- 2 tablespoons extra-virgin olive oil
- 1 medium onion, chopped
- 2 cups carrots, peeled and chopped
- 2 large tomatoes, peeled, seeded and chopped final
- 1 teaspoon ground cumin
- ½ teaspoon red pepper flakes, crushed
- 2 cups low-sodium vegetable broth
- 2 cups cooked turkey meat, chopped
- 3 cups fresh spinach, chopped
- 1 tablespoon fresh lemon juice
- Salt and ground black pepper, as required

INSTRUCTIONS:

1. Heat olive oil in a large soup pan over medium heat and sauté the onion and carrot for about 6-8 minutes.
2. Add the tomatoes, cumin and red pepper flakes and cook for about 2-3 minutes.
3. Add the broth and bring to a boil.
4. Adjust the heat to low and simmer for about 10 minutes.
5. Stir in the chickpeas and simmer for about 5 minutes.
6. Stir in the kale and simmer for 4-5 minutes more.
7. Stir in the lemon juice, salt and black pepper and remove from the heat.
8. Serve hot.

NUTRITIONAL INFORMATION PER SERVING:

Calories: 24
Fat: 11g
Carbohydrates: 12g
Fiber: 3.7g
Sugar: 6.5g
Protein: 23.8g
Sodium: 147mg

TURKEY & MUSHROOM STEW

Servings: 10
Preparation Time: 15 minutes
Cooking Time: 3 hours 10 min.

INGREDIENTS:

- 2 pounds turkey thigh and leg meat, chopped
- 2 tablespoons olive oil
- 1 garlic clove, crushed
- 12 ounces fresh button mushrooms
- 2 scallions, sliced
- 2 tablespoons fresh thyme leaves
- Salt and ground white pepper, as required
- 1 cup full-fat coconut milk
- 2 tablespoons whole grain mustard
- 1 teaspoon xanthan gum
- ½ cup fresh parsley, roughly chopped

INSTRUCTIONS:

1. Heat a non-stick wok over high heat and cook the turkey meat for about 4-5 minutes or until browned completely.

2. Transfer the turkey meat into a slow cooker.
3. In the same wok, heat the oil and sauté the mushrooms and scallion for about 3-5 minutes.
4. Transfer the mushroom mixture into the slow cooker alongside the thyme, salt and black pepper.
5. In a bowl, add the coconut milk, mustard and xanthan gum and beat until well combined.
6. Add the coconut milk mixture into the slow cooker and stir to combine well.
7. Set the slow cooker on High and cook, covered for about 3 hours.
8. Uncover and sir in the parsley.
9. Serve hot.

NUTRITIONAL INFORMATION PER SERVING:

Calories: 304
Fat: 16g
Carbohydrates: 3.6g
Fiber: 1.4g
Sugar: 0.9g
Protein: 32.9g
Sodium: 357mg

CHICKEN STUFFED AVOCADO

Servings: 2
Preparation Time: 15 minutes

INGREDIENTS:

- 1 cup cooked chicken, shredded
- 1 avocado, halved and pitted
- 1 tablespoon fresh lime juice
- ¼ cup yellow onion, chopped finely
- ¼ cup low-fat plain Greek yogurt
- Pinch of cayenne pepper
- Salt and ground black pepper, as required

INSTRUCTIONS:

1. With a small scooper, scoop out the flesh from the middle of each avocado half and transfer into a bowl.
2. In the bowl of avocado flesh, add the lime juice and with a fork, mash until well blended.
3. Add remaining ingredients and stir to combine.
4. Divide the chicken mixture into avocado halves evenly and serve immediately.

NUTRITIONAL INFORMATION PER SERVING:

Calories: 281
Fat: 15g
Carbohydrates: 9g
Fiber: 5g
Sugar: 3.2g
Protein: 23.7g
Sodium: 176mg

CHICKEN LETTUCE WRAPS

Servings: 6
Preparation Time: 15 minutes
Cooking Time: 35 minutes

INGREDIENTS:

- 1 pound chicken thighs
- 1 tablespoon olive oil
- ¼ **teaspoon garlic** powder
- Salt and ground black pepper, as required
- 10 romaine lettuce leaves
- ¾ **cup carrot**, peeled and julienned
- ¾ **cup cucumber**, julienned
- ¼ cup scallion (green part), chopped

INSTRUCTIONS:

1. Preheat your oven to 390 degrees F. Line a baking sheet with parchment paper.
2. In a bowl, add the chicken, oil, garlic powder, salt and black pepper and mix well.
3. Arrange the chicken thigh onto the prepared baking sheet in a single layer.
4. Bake for approximately 20-30 minutes or until desired doneness.
5. Remove from the oven and set aside to cool for about 20 minutes.
6. Cut the cooled chicken thighs into bite-sized pieces.
7. In a bowl, add the chicken pieces, celery, parsley, mayonnaise, salt and black pepper and mix until well combined.
8. Arrange the lettuce leaves onto serving plates.
9. Place about ¼ cup of chicken mixture over each lettuce leaf evenly.
10. Top with carrot, cucumber and scallion and serve.

NUTRITIONAL INFORMATION PER SERVING:

Calories: 209
Fat: 9.6g
Carbohydrates: 3g
Fiber: 0.7g
Sugar: 1.3g
Protein: 26.7g
Sodium: 122mg

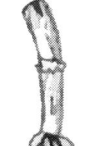

CHICKEN & STRAWBERRY LETTUCE WRAPS

Servings: 2
Preparation Time: 15 minutes

INGREDIENTS:

- 6 ounces cooked chicken breast, cut into strips
- ½ cup fresh strawberries, hulled and sliced thinly
- 1 English cucumber, sliced thinly
- 1 tablespoon fresh mint leaves, minced
- 4 large lettuce leaves

INSTRUCTIONS

1. In a large bowl, add all ingredients except lettuce leaves and gently toss to coat well.
2. Place the lettuce leaves onto serving plates.
3. Place the chicken mixture over each lettuce leaf evenly and serve immediately.

NUTRITIONAL INFORMATION PER SERVING:

Calories: 165
Fat: 2.9g
Carbohydrates: 8.8g
Fiber: 1.7g
Sugar: 4.4g
Protein: 26g
Sodium: 58mg

GROUND CHICKEN LETTUCE WRAPS

Servings: 5
Preparation Time: 15 minutes
Cooking Time: 15 minutes

INGREDIENTS:

For Chicken:

- 2 tablespoons avocado oil
- 1 small onion, chopped finely
- 1 teaspoon fresh ginger, minced
- 2 garlic cloves, minced
- 1¼ pounds ground chicken
- Salt and ground black pepper, as required

For Wraps:

- 10 romaine lettuce leaves
- 1½ cups carrot, peeled and julienned
- 2 tablespoons fresh parsley, chopped finely
- 2 tablespoons fresh lime juice

INSTRUCTIONS:

1. In a wok, heat the oil over medium heat and sauté the onion, ginger, and garlic for about 4-5 minutes.
2. Add the ground chicken, salt, and black pepper, and cook over medium-high heat for about 7-9 minutes, breaking up the meat into smaller pieces with a wooden spoon.
3. Remove from the heat and set aside to cool.
4. Arrange the lettuce leaves onto serving plates.
5. Place the cooked chicken over each lettuce leaf and top with carrot and cilantro.
6. Drizzle with lime juice and serve immediately.

NUTRITIONAL INFORMATION PER SERVING:

Calories: 246
Fat: 9.2g
Carbohydrates: 5.8g
Fiber: 1.5g
Sugar: 2.4g
Protein: 33.5g
Sodium: 154mg

CHICKEN BURGERS

Servings: 4
Preparation Time: 15 minutes
Cooking Time: 10 minutes

INGREDIENTS:

For Burgers:

- 1¼ pounds ground chicken
- 1 egg
- ½ yellow onion, grated
- Salt and ground black pepper, as required
- 1 teaspoon dried thyme
- 2 tablespoons olive oil

For Serving:

- 4 cups lettuce, torn
- 1 cucumber, chopped

INSTRUCTIONS:

1. In a bowl, add all the ingredients and mix until well combined.
2. Make 8 small equal-sized patties from the mixture.
3. In a large frying pan, heat the oil over medium heat and cook the patties for about 4-5 minutes per side or until done completely.
4. Divide the lettuce and cucumber onto serving

plates and top each with 2 burgers.

5. Serve hot.

NUTRITIONAL INFORMATION PER SERVING:

Calories: 370
Fat: 18g
Carbohydrates: 5.9g
Fiber: 1.1g
Sugar: 2.5g
Protein: 43.3g
Sodium: 181mg

CHICKEN & AVOCADO BURGERS

Servings: 4
Preparation Time: 15 minutes
Cooking Time: 10 minutes

INGREDIENTS:

- ½ of ripe avocado, peeled, pitted and cut into chunks
- ½ cup low-fat Parmesan cheese, grated
- 1 garlic clove, minced
- Freshly ground black pepper, as required
- 1-pound lean ground chicken
- Olive oil cooking spray
- 6 cups fresh baby greens

INSTRUCTIONS:

1. In a bowl, add the avocado chunks, Parmesan cheese, garlic and black pepper and toss to coat well.
2. Add the ground chicken and gently stir to combine.
3. Make 4 equal-sized patties from the chicken mixture.
4. Heat a greased grill pan over medium heat.
5. Place the patties into grill pan and cook for about 5 minutes per side.
6. Divide the greens onto serving plates and top each with 1 burger.
7. Serve immediately.

NUTRITIONAL INFORMATION PER SERVING:

Calories: 271
Fat: 15.5g
Carbohydrates: 3.5g
Fiber: 2.2g
Sugar: 0.7g
Protein: 27.6g
Sodium: 268mg

CHICKEN MEATBALLS WITH MASH

Servings: 4
Preparation Time: 20 minutes
Cooking Time: 10 minutes

INGREDIENTS:

For Meatballs:

- 1 pound ground chicken
- 2 garlic cloves, minced
- 1 large egg, beaten
- ½ cup low-fat Parmesan cheese, grated freshly
- 2 tablespoons fresh parsley, chopped
- Salt and ground black pepper, as required
- 2 tablespoons olive oil

For Broccoli Mash:

- 1½ cups broccoli florets
- 2 tablespoons fresh basil, chopped finely
- 1 tablespoon coconut oil, softened
- 1 garlic clove, minced
- Salt and ground black pepper, as required

For Serving:

- ¼ cup black olives
- 1 cup fresh baby spinach leaves
- ½ of lemon, cut into slices

INSTRUCTIONS:

1. For meatballs: in a large bowl, add all ingredients except for oil and sesame seeds and with your hands, mix until well combined.
2. Make small equal-sized balls from the mixture.
3. In a non-stick wok, heat oil over medium heat and cook the meatballs for about 10 minutes or until done completely.
4. With a slotted spoon, transfer the meatballs onto a paper towel-lined plate to drain.
5. Meanwhile, for broccoli mash: in a pan of the lightly salted boiling water, add the broccoli and cook for about 2-3 minutes.
6. Remove from the heat and drain the broccoli completely.
7. In a food processor, add the broccoli and remaining ingredients and pulse until smooth.
8. Divide the broccoli mash onto serving plates and top with meatballs, olives, spinach and lemon slices.
9. Serve immediately.

    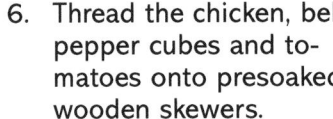

NUTRITIONAL INFORMATION PER SERVING:

Calories: 333
Fat: 24.6g
Carbohydrates: 4.5g
Fiber: 1.6g
Sugar: 0.8g
Protein: 25.4g
Sodium: 369mg

CHICKEN & VEGGIE SKEWERS

Servings: 6
Preparation Time: 15 minutes
Cooking Time: 8 minutes

INGREDIENTS:

- ¼ cup low-fat Parmigiano Reggiano cheese, grated
- 3 tablespoons olive oil
- 2 garlic cloves, minced
- 1 cup fresh basil leaves, chopped
- Salt and ground black pepper, as required
- 1¼ pounds boneless, skinless chicken breast, cut into 1-inch cubes
- 1 large green bell pepper, seeded and cubed
- 24 cherry tomatoes

INSTRUCTIONS:

1. Add cheese, butter, garlic, basil, salt, and black pepper in a food processor and pulse until smooth.
2. Transfer the basil mixture into a large bowl.
3. Add the chicken cubes and mix well.
4. Cover the bowl and refrigerate to marinate for at least 4-5 hours.
5. Preheat the grill to medium-high heat. Generously, grease the grill grate.
6. Thread the chicken, bell pepper cubes and tomatoes onto presoaked wooden skewers.
7. Place the skewers onto the grill and cook for about 6-8 minutes, flipping occasionally.
8. Remove from the grill and place onto a platter for about 5 minutes before serving.

NUTRITIONAL INFORMATION PER SERVING:

Calories: 201
Fat: 10.6g
Carbohydrates: 4.3g
Fiber: 1.1g
Sugar: 2.6g
Protein: 22.3g
Sodium: 99mg

STUFFED CHICKEN BREAST

Servings: 4
Preparation Time: 15 minutes
Cooking Time: 25 minutes

INGREDIENTS:

- 1 tablespoon olive oil
- 1 small onion, chopped
- 1 pepperoni pepper, seeded and sliced thinly
- ½ of red bell pepper, seeded and sliced thinly
- 2 teaspoons garlic, minced
- 1 cup fresh spinach, trimmed and chopped
- ½ teaspoon dried oregano
- Salt and ground black pepper, as required
- 4 (5-ounce) skinless, boneless chicken breasts, butterflied and pounded

INSTRUCTIONS:

1. Preheat your oven to 350 degrees F.
2. Line a baking sheet with parchment paper.
3. In a saucepan, heat the olive oil over medium heat and sauté onion and both peppers for about 1 minute.
4. Add the garlic and spinach and cook for about 2-3 minutes or until just wilted.
5. Stir in oregano, salt and black pepper and remove the saucepan from heat.
6. Place the chicken mixture into the middle of each butterflied chicken breast.
7. Fold each chicken breast over filling to make a little pocket and secure with toothpicks.
8. Arrange the chicken breasts onto the prepared baking sheet.
9. Bake for approximately 18-20 minutes.
10. Serve warm.

NUTRITIONAL INFORMATION PER SERVING:

Calories: 223
Fat: 8.7g
Carbohydrates: 3.6g
Fiber: 0.9g
Sugar: 1.5g
Protein: 32.3g
Sodium: 97mg

 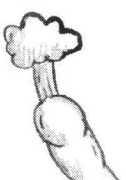   

BALSAMIC CHICKEN BREAST

Servings: 4
Preparation Time: 10 minutes
Cooking Time: 14 minutes

INGREDIENTS:

- ¼ cup balsamic vinegar
- 2 tablespoons olive oil
- 1½ teaspoons fresh lemon juice
- ½ teaspoon lemon-pepper seasoning
- 4 (6-ounce) boneless, skinless chicken breast halves, pounded slightly
- 6 cups fresh baby kale

INSTRUCTIONS:

1. In a glass baking dish, place the vinegar, oil, lemon juice and seasoning and mix well.
2. Add the chicken breasts and coat with the mixture generously.
3. Refrigerate to marinate for about 25-30 minutes.
4. Preheat the grill to medium heat.
5. Grease the grill grate.
6. Remove the chicken from bowl and discard the remaining marinade.
7. Place the chicken breasts onto the grill and cover with the lid.
8. Cook for about 5-7 minutes per side or until desired doneness.
9. Serve hot alongside the kale.

NUTRITIONAL INFORMATION PER SERVING:

Calories: 309
Fat: 11.3g
Carbohydrates: 11g
Fiber: 1.6g
Sugar: 0.2g
Protein: 39.2g
Sodium: 133mg

LEMONY CHICKEN THIGHS

Servings: 4
Preparation Time: 10 minutes
Cooking Time: 16 minutes

INGREDIENTS:

- 2 tablespoons olive oil, divided
- 1 tablespoon fresh lemon juice
- 1 tablespoon lemon zest, grated
- 2 teaspoons dried oregano
- 1 teaspoon dried thyme
- Salt and ground black pepper, as required
- 1½ pounds bone-in chicken thighs
- 6 cups fresh baby spinach

INSTRUCTIONS:

1. Preheat your oven to 420 degrees F.
2. Add 1 tablespoon of the oil, lemon juice, lemon zest, dried herbs, salt, and black pepper in a large mixing bowl and mix well.
3. Add the chicken thighs and coat with the mixture generously.
4. Refrigerate to marinate for at least 20 minutes.
5. In an oven-proof wok, heat the remaining oil over medium-high heat and sear the chicken thighs for about 2–3 minutes per side.
6. Immediately transfer the wok into the oven and bake for approximately 10 minutes.
7. Serve hot alongside the spinach.

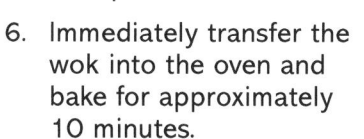

NUTRITIONAL INFORMATION PER SERVING:

Calories: 315
Fat: 22.3g
Carbohydrates: 2.7g
Fiber: 1.5g
Sugar: 0.4g
Protein: 30g
Sodium: 188mg

SPICY CHICKEN DRUMSTICKS

Servings: 5
Preparation Time: 10 minutes
Cooking Time: 40 minutes

INGREDIENTS:

- 2 tablespoons avocado oil
- 1 tablespoon fresh lime juice
- 1 teaspoon red chili powder
- 1 teaspoon garlic powder
- Salt, as required
- 5 (8-ounce) chicken drumsticks
- 8 cups fresh baby arugula

INSTRUCTIONS:

1. In a mixing bowl, mix avocado oil, lime juice, chili powder and garlic powder and mix well.
2. Add the chicken drumsticks and coat with the marinade generously.
3. Cover the bowl and

refrigerate to marinate for about 30-60 minutes.

4. Preheat your grill to medium-high heat.
5. Place the chicken drumsticks onto the grill and cook for about 30-40 minutes, flipping after every 5 minutes.
6. Serve hot alongside the arugula.

Nutritional Information per Serving:

Calories: 400
Fat: 13g
Carbohydrates: 2.2g
Fiber: 1g
Sugar: 0.9g
Protein: 64g
Sodium: 261mg

BAKED CHICKEN & BELL PEPPERS

Servings: 4
Preparation Time: 15 minutes
Cooking Time: 25 minutes

INGREDIENTS:

- 1 pound boneless, skinless chicken breasts, cut into thin strips
- ½ of green bell pepper, seeded and cut into strips
- ½ of red bell pepper, seeded and cut into strips
- 1 medium onion, sliced
- 2 tablespoons olive oil
- ½ teaspoon dried oregano
- 2 teaspoons chili powder
- 1½ teaspoons ground cumin
- 1 teaspoon garlic powder
- Salt, as required

INSTRUCTIONS:

1. Preheat your oven to 400 degrees F.
2. In a bowl, add all the ingredients and mix well.
3. Place the chicken mixture into a 9x13-inch baking dish and spread in an even layer.
4. Bake for approximately 20-25 minutes or until chicken is done completely.
5. Serve hot.

NUTRITIONAL INFORMATION PER SERVING:

Calories: 314
Fat: 16.4g
Carbohydrates: 7g
Fiber: 1.9g
Sugar: 3g
Protein: 34.1g
Sodium: 156mg

ORANGE CHICKEN

Servings: 6
Preparation Time: 10 minutes
Cooking Time: 20 minutes

INGREDIENTS:

- 3 garlic cloves, minced
- ½ cup fresh orange juice
- 1 tablespoon apple cider vinegar
- 2 tablespoons low-sodium soy sauce
- ¼ teaspoon ground ginger
- ¼ teaspoon ground cinnamon
- Freshly ground black pepper, as required
- 2 pounds skinless, bone-in chicken thighs
- 1/3 cup scallion, sliced

INSTRUCTIONS:

1. For marinate in a large bowl, mix together all ingredients except for chicken thighs and scallion.
2. Add the chicken thighs and coat with marinade generously.
3. Cover the bowl and refrigerate to marinate for about 4 hours.
4. Remove the chicken from bowl, reserving marinade.
5. Heat a lightly greased large non-stick wok over medium-high heat and cook the chicken thighs for about 5-6 minutes or till golden brown.
6. Flip the side and cook for about 4 minutes.
7. Stir in the reserved marinade and bring to a boil.
8. Reduce the heat to medium-low and cook, covered for about 6-8 minutes or until sauce becomes thick.
9. Stir in the scallion and remove from the heat.
10. Serve hot.

NUTRITIONAL INFORMATION PER SERVING:

Calories: 205
Fat: 5.5g
Carbohydrates: 3.6g
Fiber: 0.3g
Sugar: 2.2g
Protein: 34.4g
Sodium: 349mg

CHICKEN BREAST WITH ASPARAGUS

Servings: 5
Preparation Time: 15 minutes
Cooking Time: 16 minutes

INGREDIENTS:

For Chicken:

- ¼ cup extra-virgin olive oil
- ¼ cup fresh lemon juice
- 2 tablespoons maple syrup
- 1 garlic clove, minced
- Salt and ground black pepper, as required
- 5 (6-ounce) boneless, skinless chicken breasts

For Asparagus:

- 1½ pounds fresh asparagus
- 2 tablespoons extra-virgin olive oil

INSTRUCTIONS:

1. For marinade: in a large bowl, add oil, lemon juice, Erythritol, garlic, salt and black pepper and beat until well combined.
2. In a large resealable plastic bag, place the chicken and ¾ cup of marinade.
3. Seal the bag and shake to coat well.
4. Refrigerate overnight.
5. Cover the bowl of remaining marinade and refrigerate before serving.
6. Preheat the grill to medium heat. Grease the grill grate.
7. Remove the chicken from bag and discard the marinade.
8. Place the chicken onto grill grate and grill, covered for about 5-8 minutes per side.
9. Meanwhile, in a pan of boiling water, arrange a steamer basket.
10. Place the asparagus in steamer basket and steam, covered for about 5-7 minutes.
11. Drain the asparagus well and transfer into a bowl.
12. Add oil and toss to coat well.
13. Divide the chicken breasts and asparagus onto serving plates and serve.

NUTRITIONAL INFORMATION PER SERVING:

Calories: 319
Fat: 12.6g
Carbohydrates: 11g
Fiber: 2.9g
Sugar: 6g
Protein: 42.3g
Sodium: mg

CHICKEN WITH ZOODLES

Servings: 4
Preparation Time: 15 minutes
Cooking Time: 18 minutes

INGREDIENTS:

- 2 cups zucchini, spiralized with Blade
- Salt, as required
- 1½ pounds boneless, skinless chicken breasts
- Freshly ground black pepper, as required
- 1 tablespoon olive oil
- 1 cup low-fat plain Greek yogurt
- ¼ cup low-fat Parmesan cheese, shredded
- ½ cup low-sodium chicken broth
- ½ teaspoon Italian seasoning
- ½ teaspoon garlic powder
- 1 cup fresh spinach, chopped
- 3-6 slices sun-dried tomatoes
- 1 tablespoon garlic, chopped

INSTRUCTIONS:

1. Preheat your oven to 350 degrees F.
2. Line a large baking sheet with a parchment paper.
3. Place the zucchini noodles and salt onto the prepared baking sheet and toss to coat well.
4. Arrange the zucchini noodles in an even layer and Bake for approximately 15 minutes.
5. Meanwhile, season the chicken breasts with salt and black pepper.
6. In a large wok, heat the oil over medium-high heat and cook the chicken breasts for about 4-5 minutes per side or until cooked through.
7. With a slotted spoon, transfer the cooked chicken onto a plate and set aside.
8. In the same wok, add the yogurt, Parmesan cheese, broth, Italian seasoning and garlic powder and beat until well combined.
9. Place the wok over medium-high heat and cook for about 2-3 minutes or until it starts to thicken, stirring continuously.
10. Stir in the spinach, sun-dried tomatoes and garlic and cook for about 2-3 minutes.
11. Add the chicken breasts and cook for about 1-2 minutes.

    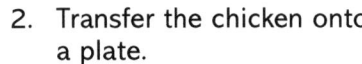

12. Divide the zucchini noodles onto serving plates and top each with chicken mixture.
13. Serve immediately.

NUTRITIONAL INFORMATION PER SERVING:

Calories: 285
Fat: 7.9g
Carbohydrates: 8.4g
Fiber: 1g
Sugar: 5g
Protein: 45.5g
Sodium: 308mg

CHICKEN WITH YELLOW SQUASH

Servings: 6
Preparation Time: 15 minutes
Cooking Time: 17 minutes

INGREDIENTS:

- 2 tablespoons olive oil, divided
- 1½ pounds skinless, boneless chicken breasts, cut into bite-sized pieces
- Salt and ground black pepper, as required
- 2 garlic cloves, minced
- 1½ pounds yellow squash, sliced
- 2 tablespoons fresh lemon juice
- 1 teaspoon fresh lemon zest, grated finely
- 2 tablespoons fresh parsley, minced

INSTRUCTIONS:

1. In a large wok, heat 1 tablespoon of oil over medium heat and stir fry chicken for about 6-8 minutes or until golden brown from all sides.
2. Transfer the chicken onto a plate.
3. In the same wok, heat remaining oil over medium heat and sauté garlic for about 1 minute.
4. Add the squash slices and cook for about 5-6 minutes,
5. Stir in the chicken and cook for about 2 minutes.
6. Stir in the lemon juice, zest and parsley and remove from heat.
7. Serve hot.

NUTRITIONAL INFORMATION PER SERVING:

Calories: 203
Fat: 9g
Carbohydrates: 4.4g
Fiber: 1.4g
Sugar: 2.1g
Protein: 26.8g
Sodium: 81mg

CHICKEN WITH BELL PEPPERS

Servings: 6
Preparation Time: 15 minutes
Cooking Time: 20 minutes

INGREDIENTS:

- 3 tablespoons olive oil, divided
- 1 yellow bell pepper, seeded and sliced
- 1 red bell pepper, seeded and sliced
- 1 green bell pepper, seeded and sliced
- 1 medium onion, sliced
- 1-pound boneless, skinless chicken breasts, sliced thinly 1 teaspoon dried oregano, crushed
- ¼ teaspoon garlic powder
- ¼ teaspoon ground cumin
- Salt and freshly ground black pepper, as required
- ¼ cup low-sodium chicken broth

INSTRUCTIONS:

1. In a wok, heat 1 tablespoon of oil over medium-high heat and cook the bell peppers and onion slices for about 4-5 minutes.
2. With a slotted spoon, transfer the peppers mixture onto a plate.
3. In the same wok, heat the remaining oil over medium-high heat and cook the chicken for about 8 minutes, stirring frequently.
4. Stir in the thyme, spices, salt, black pepper, and broth, and bring to a boil.
5. Add the peppers mixture and stir to combine.
6. Reduce the heat to medium and cook for about 3-5 minutes or until all the liquid is absorbed, stirring occasionally.
7. Serve immediately.

NUTRITIONAL INFORMATION PER SERVING:

Calories: 232
Fat: 12.8g
Carbohydrates: 6.5g
Fiber: 1.3g
Sugar: 3.8g
Protein: 22.8g
Sodium: 98mg

CHICKEN WITH MUSHROOMS

Servings: 4
Preparation Time: 15 minutes
Cooking Time: 20 minutes

INGREDIENTS:

- 2 tablespoons almond flour
- Salt and freshly ground black pepper, as required
- 4 (4-ounce) skinless, boneless chicken breasts
- 2 tablespoons olive oil
- 6 garlic cloves, chopped
- ¾ pound fresh mushrooms, sliced
- ¾ cup low-sodium chicken broth
- ¼ cup balsamic vinegar
- 1 bay leaf
- ¼ teaspoon dried thyme

INSTRUCTIONS:

1. In a bowl, mix together the flour, salt and black pepper.
2. Coat the chicken breasts with flour mixture evenly.
3. In a wok, heat the olive oil over medium-high heat and stir fry chicken for about 3 minutes.
4. Add the garlic and flip the chicken breasts.
5. Spread mushrooms over chicken and cook for about 3 minutes, shaking the wok frequently.
6. Add the broth, vinegar, bay leaf and thyme and stir to combine.
7. Reduce the heat to medium-low and simmer, covered for about 10 minutes, flipping chicken occasionally.
8. With a slotted spoon, transfer the chicken onto a warm serving platter and with a piece of foil, cover to keep warm.
9. Place the pan of sauce over medium-high heat and cook, uncovered for about 7 minutes.
10. Remove the pan from heat and discard the bay leaf.
11. Place mushroom sauce over chicken and serve hot.

NUTRITIONAL INFORMATION PER SERVING:

Calories: 247
Fat: 11.4g
Carbohydrates: 7.6g
Fiber: 1.1g
Sugar: 1.6g
Protein: 29.1g
Sodium: 99mg

CHICKEN WITH BROCCOLI & MUSHROOMS

Servings: 4
Preparation Time: 15 minutes
Cooking Time: 22 minutes

INGREDIENTS:

- 2 tablespoons olive oil, divided
- 4 (4-ounce) boneless, skinless chicken breasts, cut into small pieces
- Salt and freshly ground black pepper, as required
- 1 onion, chopped finely
- 1 teaspoon fresh ginger, grated
- 1 teaspoon garlic, minced
- 1 cup broccoli florets
- 1½ cups fresh mushrooms, sliced
- 8 ounces low-sodium chicken broth

INSTRUCTIONS:

1. In a large wok, heat 1 tablespoon of oil over medium-high heat and stir fry the chicken pieces, salt, and black pepper for about 4-5 minutes or until golden brown.
2. With a slotted spoon, transfer the chicken onto a plate.
3. In the same wok, heat the remaining oil over medium-high heat and sauté the onion, ginger, and garlic for about 4-5 minutes.
4. Add in mushrooms and cook for about 4-5 minutes, stirring frequently.
5. Add the broccoli and stir fry for about 3 minutes.
6. Add the cooked chicken and broth and stir fry for about 3-5 minutes
7. Add in the salt and black pepper and remove from the heat.
8. Serve hot.

NUTRITIONAL INFORMATION PER SERVING:

Calories: 211
Fat: 8.7g
Carbohydrates: 5.7g
Fiber: 1.5g
Sugar: 2g
Protein: 28.4g
Sodium: 1141mg

CHICKEN & VEGGIES STIR FRY

Servings: 6
Preparation Time: 15 minutes
Cooking Time: 15 minutes

INGREDIENTS:

- 2 tablespoons fresh lime juice
- 2 tablespoons fish sauce
- 1½ teaspoons arrowroot starch
- 4 teaspoons olive oil, divided
- 1-pound skinless, boneless chicken tenders, cubed
- 1 teaspoon fresh ginger, minced
- 2 garlic cloves, minced
- ¾ teaspoon red pepper flakes, crushed
- ¼ cup water
- 4 cups broccoli, cut into bite-sized pieces
- 3 cups red bell pepper, seeded and sliced
- ¼ cup pine nuts

INSTRUCTIONS:

1. In a bowl, add lime juice, fish sauce, and arrowroot starch and mix until well combined. Set aside.
2. In a large non-stick sauté pan, heat 2 teaspoons of oil over high heat and cook chicken for about 6-8 minutes, stirring frequently.
3. Transfer the chicken into a bowl and set aside.
4. In the same sauté pan, heat remaining oil over medium heat and sauté ginger, garlic and red pepper flakes for about 1 minute.
5. Add water, broccoli and bell pepper and stir fry for about 2-3 minutes.
6. Stir in chicken and lime juice mixture and cook for about 2-3 minutes.
7. Stir in pine nuts and immediately remove from heat.
8. Serve hot.

NUTRITIONAL INFORMATION PER SERVING:

- **Calories:** 207
  Fat: 10.7g
  Carbohydrates: 10g
  Fiber: 2.7g
  Sugar: 4.5g
  Protein: 20.4g
  Sodium: 513mg

CHICKEN & BROCCOLI BAKE

Servings: 6
Preparation Time: 15 minutes
Cooking Time: 24 minutes

INGREDIENTS:

- Olive oil cooking spray
- 6 (6-ounce) skinless, boneless chicken thighs
- 3 broccoli heads, cut into florets
- 4 garlic cloves, minced
- ¼ cup extra-virgin olive oil
- 1 teaspoon dried oregano, crushed
- 1 teaspoon dried rosemary, crushed
- Salt and freshly ground black pepper, as required

INSTRUCTIONS:

1. Preheat your oven to 375 degrees F.
2. Grease a large baking dish with cooking spray.
3. In a large bowl, add all the ingredients and toss to coat well.
4. In the bottom of the prepared baking dish, arrange the broccoli florets and top with chicken breasts in a single layer.
5. Bake for approximately 45 minutes.
6. Serve hot.

NUTRITIONAL INFORMATION PER SERVING:

Calories: 333
Fat: 15g
Carbohydrates: 9.4g
Fiber: 3.6g
Sugar: 2.2g
Protein: 41.7g
Sodium: 130mg

CHEESY CHICKEN & SPINACH

Servings: 4
Preparation Time: 15 minutes
Cooking Time: 20 minutes

INGREDIENTS:

- 2 tablespoons olive oil, divided
- 4 (4-ounce) boneless, skinless chicken thighs
- Salt and ground black pepper, as required
- 2 garlic cloves, minced
- 1 jalapeño pepper, chopped
- 10-ounce frozen spinach, thawed
- 1/3 cup low-fat Parmesan cheese, shredded

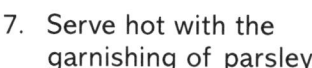

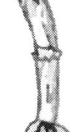

INSTRUCTIONS:

1. In a large wok, heat 1 tablespoon of the oil over medium-high heat and cook the chicken with salt and black pepper for about 5-6 minutes per side.
2. Transfer the chicken into a bowl.
3. In the same wok, heat remaining oil over medium-low heat and sauté the garlic for about 1 minute.
4. Add the spinach and cook for about 1 minute.
5. Add the cheese, salt and black pepper and stir to combine.
6. Spread the spinach mixture in the bottom of wok evenly.
7. Place chicken over spinach in a single layer.
8. Immediately adjust the heat to low and cook, covered for about 5 minutes.
9. Serve hot.

NUTRITIONAL INFORMATION PER SERVING:

Calories: 323
Fat: 17.5g
Carbohydrates: 3.5g
Fiber: 1.7g
Sugar: 0.4g
Protein: 37.5g
Sodium: 267mg

CHICKEN & CAULIFLOWER CURRY

Servings: 6
Preparation Time: 15 minutes
Cooking Time: 20 minutes

INGREDIENTS:

- ¼ cup olive oil
- 3 garlic cloves, minced
- 2 tablespoons curry powder
- 1½ pounds skinless, boneless chicken thighs, cut into bite-sized pieces
- Salt and ground black pepper, as required
- 1-pound cauliflower, cut into small pieces
- 1 green bell pepper, seeded and chopped
- 14 ounces unsweetened coconut milk
- ¼ cup fresh parsley, chopped

INSTRUCTIONS:

1. In a large wok, heat the oil over medium heat and sauté the garlic and curry powder for about 1 minute.
2. Add the chicken, salt and black pepper and cook for about 5-6 minutes, stirring frequently.
3. With a slotted spoon, transfer the chicken onto a plate.
4. In the wok, add the cauliflower and bell pepper and cook for about 2-3 minutes.
5. Add the coconut milk and simmer for about 5-7 minutes.
6. Stir in the cooked chicken, salt and black pepper and cook for about 2-3 minutes.
7. Serve hot with the garnishing of parsley.

NUTRITIONAL INFORMATION PER SERVING:

Calories: 348
Fat: 22g
Carbohydrates: 9g
Fiber: 3g
Sugar: 4.6g
Protein: 28.3g
Sodium: 114mg

CHICKEN & VEGGIES CASSEROLE

Servings: 4
Preparation Time: 15 minutes
Cooking Time: 25 minutes

INGREDIENTS:

- 1 tablespoon olive oil
- 1 small onion, chopped
- 1 pepperoni pepper, seeded and sliced thinly
- ½ of red bell pepper, seeded and sliced thinly
- 2 teaspoons garlic, minced
- 1 cup fresh spinach, trimmed and chopped
- ½ teaspoon dried oregano
- Salt and ground black pepper, as required
- 4 (5-ounce) skinless, boneless chicken breasts, butterflied and pounded

INSTRUCTIONS:

1. Preheat your oven to 350 degrees F.
2. Line a baking sheet with parchment paper.
3. In a saucepan, heat the olive oil over medium heat and sauté onion and both peppers for about 1 minute.

4. Add the garlic and spinach and cook for about 2-3 minutes or until just wilted.
5. Stir in oregano, salt and black pepper and remove the saucepan from heat.
6. Place the chicken mixture into the middle of each butterflied chicken breast.
7. Fold each chicken breast over filling to make a little pocket and secure with toothpicks.
8. Arrange the chicken breasts onto the prepared baking sheet.
9. Bake for approximately 18-20 minutes.
10. Serve hot.

NUTRITIONAL INFORMATION PER SERVING:

Calories: 223
Fat: 8.7g
Carbohydrates: 3.6g
Fiber: 0.9g
Sugar: 1.5g
Protein: 32.3g
Sodium: 97mg

CHICKEN & GREEN VEGGIES CURRY

Servings: 4
Preparation Time: 15 minutes
Cooking Time: 30 minutes

INGREDIENTS:

- 1-pound skinless, boneless chicken breasts, cubed
- 1 tablespoon olive oil
- 2 tablespoons green curry paste
- 1 cup unsweetened coconut milk
- 1 cup low-sodium chicken broth
- 1 cup asparagus spears, trimmed
- 1 cup green beans, trimmed
- Salt and ground black pepper, as required
- ¼ cup fresh cilantro leaves, chopped

INSTRUCTIONS:

1. In a wok, heat oil over medium heat and sauté the curry paste for about 1-2 minutes.
2. Add the chicken and cook for about 8-10 minutes.
3. Add coconut milk and broth and bring to a boil.
4. Reduce the heat low and cook for about 8-10 minutes.
5. Add asparagus, green beans, salt and black pepper and cook for about 4-5 minutes or until desired doneness.
6. Serve hot.

NUTRITIONAL INFORMATION PER SERVING:

Calories: 385
Fat: 26.7g
Carbohydrates: 9g
Fiber: 3g
Sugar: 3.2g
Protein: 29.5g
Sodium: 283mg

TURKEY & AVOCADO LETTUCE WRAPS

Servings: 2
Preparation Time: 15 minutes
Cooking Time: 13 minutes

INGREDIENTS:

- 4 ounces lean ground turkey
- ¼ cup white onion, minced
- 2 tablespoons sugar-free tomato sauce
- 1/8 teaspoon ground cumin
- Freshly ground black pepper, as required
- 2 teaspoons extra-virgin olive oil
- 1 cup tomato, chopped
- ½ cup avocado, peeled, pitted and chopped
- 1 tablespoon fresh cilantro, chopped
- 4 large butternut lettuce leaves

INSTRUCTIONS:

1. In a bowl, add the turkey, onion, tomato sauce, cumin and black pepper and mix until well combined.
2. In a large wok, heat the oil over medium heat and cook the turkey mixture for about 8-10 minutes.
3. Add the tomato and stir to combine.
4. Immediately reduce the heat to low and cook for about 2-3 minutes.
5. Remove from the heat and set aside to cool.
6. Arrange the lettuce leaves onto serving plates.
7. Place the turkey mixture over each lettuce leaf evenly and top with avocado pieces.
8. Garnish with cilantro and serve immediately.

NUTRITIONAL INFORMATION PER SERVING:

Calories: 253
Fat: 18.3g
Carbohydrates: 9.2g
Fiber: 2.9g
Sugar: 3.9g
Protein: 17.4g
Sodium: 149mg

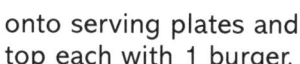

TURKEY BURGERS

Servings: 2
Preparation Time: 15 minutes
Cooking Time: 6 minutes

INGREDIENTS:

For Burgers:

- 8 ounces ground turkey
- Salt and ground black pepper, as required
- 1 ounce part-skim mozzarella cheese, cubed
- 1 tablespoon olive oil

For Serving:

- 4 cups fresh baby spinach
- 1 small cucumber, chopped

INSTRUCTIONS:

1. In a bowl, add the beef, salt and black pepper and mix until well combined.
2. Make 2 equal-sized patties from the mixture.
3. Place mozzarella cubes over each patty and with your finger, press inside.
4. In a wok, heat oil over medium heat and cook the patties for about 2-3 minutes per side.
5. Serve immediately alongside the spinach and cucumber.

NUTRITIONAL INFORMATION PER SERVING:

Calories: 263
Fat: 12.1g
Carbohydrates: 8.1g
Fiber: 2.1g
Sugar: 2.8g
Protein: 33.4g
Sodium: 271mg

TURKEY, APPLE & VEGGIES BURGERS

Servings: 4
Preparation Time: 20 minutes
Cooking Time: 12 minutes

INGREDIENTS:

For Burgers:

- 12 ounces lean ground turkey
- ½ of an apple, peeled, cored and grated
- ½ of red bell pepper, seeded and chopped finely
- ¼ cup red onion, minced
- 2 small garlic cloves, minced
- 1 tablespoon fresh ginger, minced
- 2½ tablespoons fresh cilantro, chopped
- 2 tablespoons curry paste
- 1 teaspoon ground cumin
- 1 teaspoon olive oil

For Serving:

- 6 cups fresh baby spinach

INSTRUCTIONS:

1. Preheat the grill to medium heat. Grease the grill grate.
2. For Burgers: in a large bowl, add all the ingredients except for oil and mix until well combined.
3. Make 4 equal-sized burgers from mixture.
4. Brush the burgers with olive oil evenly.
5. Place the burgers onto the grill and cook for about 5-6 minutes per side.
6. Divide the baby spinach onto serving plates and top each with 1 burger.
7. Serve immediately.

NUTRITIONAL INFORMATION PER SERVING:

Calories: 223
Fat: 12.1g
Carbohydrates: 11g
Fiber: 2.3g
Sugar: 4.2g
Protein: 19g
Sodium: 103mg

TURKEY STUFFED ZUCCHINI

Servings: 8
Preparation Time: 15 minutes
Cooking Time: 31 minutes

INGREDIENTS:

- 4 medium zucchinis
- 1-pound lean ground turkey breast
- ½ cup white onion, chopped
- ½ pound fresh mushrooms, sliced
- 1 large tomato, chopped
- 1 egg, beaten
- ¾ cup sugar-free spaghetti sauce
- ¼ cup seasoned whole wheat bread crumbs
- Freshly ground black pepper, as required
- 1 cup part-skim mozzarella cheese, shredded

INSTRUCTIONS:

1. Preheat your oven to 350 degrees F.
2. Cut each zucchini in half lengthwise.
3. With a sharp knife, cut a thin slice from the bottom of each zucchini to allow zucchini to sit flat.

4. With a small spoon, scoop out the pulp from each zucchini half, leaving ¼-inch shells.
5. Transfer the zucchini pulp into a large bowl and set aside.
6. Arrange the zucchini shells into an ungreased microwave-safe baking dish.
7. Cover the baking dish and microwave on High for about 3 minutes.
8. Drain the water from the microwave and set aside.
9. Heat a large non-stick wok over medium heat and cook the ground turkey and onion for about 6-8 minutes or until meat is no longer pink.
10. Drain the grease completely.
11. Remove from the heat.
12. In the bowl of zucchini pulp, add the cooked turkey, mushrooms, tomato, egg, spaghetti sauce, black pepper and ½ cup of the cheese and mix until well combined.
13. Place about ¼ cup of the turkey mixture into each zucchini shell and sprinkle with the remaining cheese.
14. Bake for about 20 minutes or until top becomes golden brown.
15. Serve hot.

NUTRITIONAL INFORMATION PER SERVING:

Calories: 142
Fat: 5.8g
Carbohydrates: 6.6g
Fiber: 2.1g
Sugar: 3.8g
Protein: 15.7g
Sodium: 197mg

TURKEY STUFFED ACORN SQUASH

Servings: 4
Preparation Time: 15 minutes
Cooking Time: 50 minutes

INGREDIENTS:

- 2 acorn squash, halved and seeded
- 1 pound lean ground turkey breast
- 1 cup red onion, chopped
- 1 cup celery stalk, chopped
- 1 cup fresh button mushrooms, sliced
- 8 ounces sugar-free tomato sauce
- 1 teaspoon dried oregano, crushed
- 1 teaspoon dried basil, crushed
- Freshly ground black pepper, as required
- 1 cup low-fat Cheddar cheese, shredded

INSTRUCTIONS:

1. Preheat your oven to 350 degrees F.
2. In the bottom of a microwave-safe glass baking dish, arrange the squash halves, cut side down.
3. Microwave on High for about 20 minutes or until almost tender.
4. Heat a large non-stick wok over medium heat and cook the ground turkey for about 4-5 minutes or until meat is no longer pink.
5. Drain the grease completely.
6. Add the onion and celery and cook for about 3-4 minutes.
7. Stir in the mushrooms and cook for about 2-3 minutes more.
8. Stir in the tomato sauce, dried herbs and black pepper and remove from the heat.
9. Spoon the turkey mixture into each squash half.
10. Cover the baking dish and bake for about 15 minutes.
11. Uncover the baking dish and sprinkle each squash half with Cheddar cheese.
12. Bake uncovered for about 3-5 minutes or until the cheese becomes bubbly.
13. Serve hot.

NUTRITIONAL INFORMATION PER SERVING:

Calories: 355
Fat: 18.2g
Carbohydrates: 15g
Fiber: 5g
Sugar: 9g
Protein: 34.6g
Sodium: 111mg

TURKEY & SPINACH MEATBALLS

Servings: 4
Preparation Time: 20 minutes
Cooking Time: 15 minutes

INGREDIENTS:

For Meatballs:

- 1-pound lean ground turkey
- 1 cup frozen chopped spinach, thawed and squeezed
- ½ cup feta cheese, crumbled
- ½ teaspoon dried oregano

 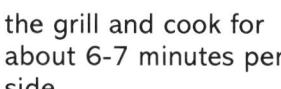

- Salt and ground black pepper, as required
- 2 tablespoons olive oil

For Salad:

- 4 cups lettuce, torn
- 2 large tomatoes, chopped
- 1 cup onion, sliced
- 2 tablespoons olive oil
- Salt and ground black pepper, as required

INSTRUCTIONS:

1. *For meatballs:* place all ingredients except for oil in a bowl and mix until well combined.
2. Make 12 equal-sized meatballs form the mixture.
3. Heat the olive oil in a large non-stick wok over medium heat and cook the meatballs for about 10-15 minutes or until done completely, flipping occasionally.
4. With a slotted spoon, transfer the meatballs onto a plate.
5. *Meanwhile, For Salad:* in a large salad bowl, add all ingredients and toss to coat well.
6. Divide meatballs and salad onto serving plates and serve.

NUTRITIONAL INFORMATION PER SERVING:

Calories: 309
Fat: 19.5g
Carbohydrates: 9g
Fiber: 2.3g
Sugar: 5g
Protein: 26.5g
Sodium: 349mg

TURKEY MEATBALLS KABOBS

Servings: 4
Preparation Time: 15 minutes
Cooking Time: 14 minutes

INGREDIENTS:

- 1 yellow onion, chopped roughly
- ½ cup lemongrass, chopped roughly
- 2 garlic cloves, chopped roughly
- 1½ pounds lean ground turkey
- 1 teaspoon sesame oil
- ½ tablespoons low-sodium soy sauce
- 1 tablespoon arrowroot starch
- 1/8 teaspoons powdered stevia
- Salt and ground black pepper, as required
- 6 cups fresh baby spinach

INSTRUCTIONS:

1. Preheat the grill to medium-high heat.
2. Grease the grill grate.
3. In a food processor, add the onion, lemongrass and garlic and pulse until chopped finely.
4. Transfer the onion mixture into a large bowl.
5. Add the remaining ingredients except for spinach and mix until well combined.
6. Make 12 equal-sized balls from meat mixture.
7. Thread the balls onto the presoaked wooden skewers.
8. Place the skewers onto the grill and cook for about 6-7 minutes per side.
9. Serve hot alongside the spinach.

NUTRITIONAL INFORMATION PER SERVING:

Calories: 292
Fat: 13.5g
Carbohydrates: 8g
Fiber: 1.7g
Sugar: 1.5g
Protein: 35.4g
Sodium: 316mg

TURKEY WITH PEAS

Servings: 6
Preparation Time: 15 minutes
Cooking Time: 40 minutes

INGREDIENTS:

- 2 tablespoons extra virgin olive oil
- 1-pound lean ground turkey
- 1 large white onion, chopped finely
- 2 garlic cloves, minced
- ½ tablespoon fresh ginger, minced
- 1 teaspoon ground coriander
- 1 teaspoon ground cumin
- ¼ teaspoon chili powder
- 2 medium tomatoes, seeded and chopped
- ½ cup low-sodium chicken broth
- Salt and freshly ground black pepper, as required
- 2 cups fresh peas, shelled
- 2 tablespoons fresh cilantro, chopped

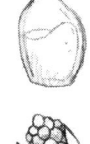

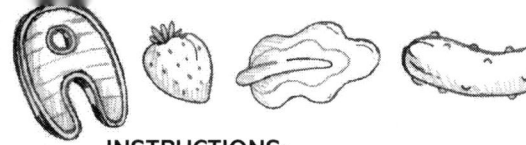
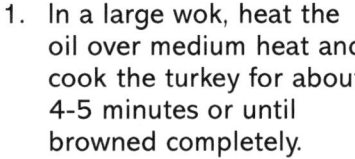

INSTRUCTIONS:

1. In a large wok, heat the oil over medium heat and cook the turkey for about 4-5 minutes or until browned completely.
2. With a slotted spoon, transfer the turkey into a large bowl.
3. In the same wok, add the onion and sauté for about 4-6 minutes.
4. Add the garlic, ginger, coriander, cumin and chili powder and sauté for about 1 minute.
5. Add the tomatoes and cook for about 2-3 minutes, crushing completely with the back of the spoon.
6. Stir in the cooked turkey, broth, salt and black pepper and bring to a boil.
7. Reduce the heat to medium-low and simmer, covered for about 8-10 minutes, stirring occasionally.
8. Stir in peas and cook for about 15-20 minutes.
9. Remove from the heat and serve hot with the garnishing of cilantro leaves.

NUTRITIONAL INFORMATION PER SERVING:

Calories: 211
Fat: 10.5g
Carbohydrates: 11g
Fiber: 3.7g
Sugar: 4.9g
Protein: 1.5g
Sodium: 98mg

TURKEY & VEGGIE CASSEROLE

Servings: 6
Preparation Time: 15 minutes
Cooking Time: 50 minutes

INGREDIENTS:

- 2 medium zucchinis, sliced
- 2 medium tomatoes, sliced
- ¾ pound ground turkey
- 1 large yellow onion, chopped
- 2 garlic cloves, minced
- 1 cup sugar-free tomato sauce
- ½ cup low-fat cheddar cheese, shredded
- 2 cups cottage cheese, shredded
- 1 egg yolk
- 1 tablespoon fresh rosemary, minced
- Salt and ground black pepper, as required

INSTRUCTIONS:

1. Preheat your oven to 500 degrees F.
2. Grease a large roasting pan
3. Arrange zucchini and tomato slices into the prepared roasting pan and spray with some cooking spray.
4. Roast for about 10-12 minutes.
5. Remove from oven and set aside.
6. Now, preheat your oven to 350 degrees F.
7. Meanwhile, heat a nonstick wok over medium-high heat and cook the turkey for about 4-5 minutes or until browned.
8. Add the onion and garlic and sauté for about 4-5 minutes.
9. Stir in tomato sauce and cook for about 2-3 minutes.
10. Remove from the heat and place the turkey mixture into a 13x9-inch shallow baking dish.
11. In a bowl, add the remaining ingredients and mix until well combined.
12. Place the roasted vegetables over turkey mixture, followed by the cheese mixture evenly.
13. Bake for approximately 35 minutes.
14. Remove from the oven and set aside for about 5-10 minutes.
15. Cut into equal-sized 8 wedges and serve.

NUTRITIONAL INFORMATION PER SERVING:

Calories: 258
Fat: 11.9g
Carbohydrates: 10g
Fiber: 2.5g
Sugar: 4.3g
Protein: 30.4g
Sodium: 676mg

TURKEY CHILI

Servings: 8
Preparation Time: 15 minutes
Cooking Time: 2¼ hours

INGREDIENTS:

- 2 tablespoons olive oil
- 1 small yellow onion, chopped
- 1 green bell pepper, seeded and chopped
- 4 garlic cloves, minced
- 1 jalapeño pepper, chopped

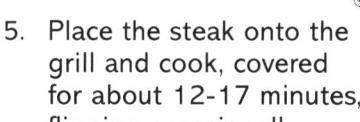

- 1 teaspoon dried thyme, crushed
- 2 tablespoons red chili powder
- 1 tablespoon ground cumin
- 2 pounds lean ground turkey
- 2 cups fresh tomatoes, chopped finely
- 2 ounces sugar-free tomato paste
- 2 cups homemade low-sodium chicken broth
- 1 cup water
- Salt and ground black pepper, as required

INSTRUCTIONS:

1. In a large Dutch oven, heat oil over medium heat and sauté the onion and bell pepper for about 5-7 minutes.
2. Add the garlic, jalapeño pepper, thyme and spices and sauté for about 1 minute.
3. Add the turkey and cook for about 4-5 minutes.
4. Stir in the tomatoes, tomato paste and cacao powder and cook for about 2 minutes.
5. Add in the broth and water and bring to a boil.
6. Now, reduce the heat to low and simmer, covered for about 2 hours.
7. Add in salt and black pepper and remove from the heat.
8. Serve hot.

NUTRITIONAL INFORMATION PER SERVING:

Calories: 234
Fat: 12.6g
Carbohydrates: 6.9g
Fiber: 2.1g
Sugar: 3.2g
Protein: 24.9g
Sodium: 328mg

RED MEAT RECIPES

STEAK & TOMATO SALAD

Servings: 5
Preparation Time: 15 minutes
Cooking Time: 15 minutes

INGREDIENTS:

For Steak:

- 2 tablespoons fresh oregano, chopped
- ½ tablespoon garlic, minced
- 1 tablespoon fresh lemon peel, grated
- ½ teaspoon red pepper flakes, crushed
- Salt and ground black pepper, as required
- 1 (1-pound) (1-inch thick) boneless beef top sirloin steak

For Salad:

- 6 cups fresh salad greens
- 2 cups cherry tomatoes, halved
- 2 tablespoons olive oil
- 2 tablespoons fresh lime juice
- Salt and ground black pepper, as required

INSTRUCTIONS:

1. Preheat the gas grill to medium heat.
2. Lightly grease the grill grate.
3. For steak: in a bowl, add the oregano, garlic, lemon peel, red pepper flakes, salt and black pepper and mix well.
4. Rub the steak with garlic mixture evenly.
5. Place the steak onto the grill and cook, covered for about 12-17 minutes, flipping occasionally.
6. Remove the steak from the grill and place onto a cutting board for about 10 minutes.
7. Meanwhile, **For Salad**: in a large serving bowl, place all ingredients and toss to coat well.
8. Cut the steak into bite-sized pieces.
9. Add the steak pieces into the bowl of salad and toss to coat well.
10. Serve immediately.

NUTRITIONAL INFORMATION PER SERVING:

Calories: 259
Fat: 11.8g
Carbohydrates: 9.4g
Fiber: 33.9g
Sugar: 2.6g
Protein: 29.4g
Sodium: 121mg

STEAK, EGG & VEGGIES SALAD

Servings: 4
Preparation Time: 20 minutes
Cooking Time: 9 minutes

INGREDIENTS:

For Steak:

- 2 tablespoons extra-virgin olive oil
- 1-pound flank steak, sliced thinly
- Salt and ground black pepper, as required

For Salad:

- 4 hard-boiled eggs, peeled and halved
- 1 cup radishes, cut into matchsticks
- 1 cup cucumber, cut into matchsticks
- 1 cup tomato, chopped
- ½ cup scallion greens, chopped

For Dressing:

- ¼ cup fresh orange juice
- 3 tablespoons extra-virgin olive oil
- 2 tablespoons low-sodium soy sauce
- 2 tablespoons white vinegar
- 1 tablespoon fresh lime juice
- 1 tablespoon maple syrup
- 1 teaspoon fresh lime zest, grated
- 1 garlic clove, minced

INSTRUCTIONS:

1. Heat oil in a large heavy-bottomed pan over medium-high heat and sear the beef slices with salt and black pepper for about 4-5 minutes or until cooked through.
2. Transfer the beef slices onto a plate and set aside.
3. For Dressing: in a bowl, add all ingredients and beat until well combined.
4. Divide beef slices, eggs, veggies and scallion into serving bowls and drizzle with dressing.
5. Serve immediately.

NUTRITIONAL INFORMATION PER SERVING:

Calories: 389
Fat: 22g
Carbohydrates: 10g
Fiber: 1.6g
Sugar: 7.6g
Protein: 38.8g
Sodium: 582mg

STEAK & KALE SALAD

Servings: 2
Preparation Time: 15 minutes
Cooking Time: 8 minutes

INGREDIENTS:

For Steak:

- 2 teaspoons olive oil
- 2 (4-ounce) strip steaks
- Salt and ground black pepper, as required

For Salad:

- ½ cup carrot, peeled and shredded
- ½ cup cucumber, peeled, seeded and sliced
- 3 cups fresh kale, tough ribs removed and chopped

For Dressing:

- 1 tablespoon extra-virgin olive oil
- 1 tablespoon fresh lemon juice
- Salt and ground black pepper, as required

INSTRUCTIONS:

1. For steak: in a large heavy-bottomed wok, heat the oil over high heat and cook the steaks with salt and black pepper for about 3-4 minutes per side.
2. Transfer the steaks onto a cutting board for about 5 minutes before slicing.
3. For Salad: place all ingredients in a salad bowl and mix.
4. For Dressing: place all ingredients in another bowl and beat until well combined.
5. Cut the steaks into desired sized slices against the grain.
6. Place the salad onto each serving plate.
7. Top each plate with steak slices.
8. Drizzle with dressing and serve.

NUTRITIONAL INFORMATION PER SERVING:

Calories: 273
Fat: 13.1g
Carbohydrates: 15.7g
Fiber: 2.3g
Sugar: 3.3g
Protein: 25.1g
Sodium: 509mg

STEAK & VEGGIE SALAD

Servings: 8
Preparation Time: 20 minutes
Cooking Time: 16 minutes

INGREDIENTS:

For Steak:

- 2 garlic cloves, crushed
- 1 teaspoon fresh ginger, grated
- 1 tablespoon honey
- 2 tablespoons olive oil
- Salt and ground black pepper, as required
- 1½ pounds flank steak, trimmed

For Dressing:

- 1 garlic clove, minced
- 4 tablespoons extra-virgin olive oil
- 3 tablespoons fresh lime juice
- ¼ teaspoon red pepper flakes, crushed
- Salt and freshly ground black pepper, as required

For Salad:

- 3 cup cucumber, sliced
- 3 cup cherry tomatoes, halved
- 1 cup red onion, sliced thinly
- 4 tablespoons fresh mint leaves
- 8 cup fresh spinach, torn

INSTRUCTIONS:

1. For steak: in a large sealable bag, mix together all ingredients except steak.
2. Add steak and coat with marinade generously.
3. Seal the bag and refrigerate to marinate for about 24 hours.
4. Remove from the refrigerator and set aside in room temperature for about 15 minutes.
5. Heat a lightly greased grill pan over medium-high heat and cook the steak for about 6-8 minutes per side.
6. Remove the steak from grill pan and place onto a cutting board for about 10 minutes before slicing.
7. **For Dressing**: in a small bowl, add all ingredients and beat well.
8. **For Salad**: in a large salad bowl, mix together all ingredients.
9. With a sharp knife, cut into desired slices.
10. Divide salad onto serving plates and top with steak slices.
11. Drizzle with dressing and serve immediately.

NUTRITIONAL INFORMATION PER SERVING:

Calories: 298
Fat: 17.9g
Carbohydrates: 9g
Fiber: 2.3g
Sugar: 5g
Protein: 25.7g
Sodium: 97mg

BEEF & BOK CHOY SOUP

Servings: 6
Preparation Time: 15 minutes
Cooking Time: 30 minutes

INGREDIENTS:

- 1 tablespoon olive oil
- 1-pound ground beef
- ½ pound fresh mushrooms, sliced
- 1 small yellow onion, chopped
- 1 garlic clove, minced
- 1-pound head bok choy, stalks and leaves separated and chopped
- 2 tablespoons low-sodium soy sauce
- 5 cups low-sodium chicken broth
- Freshly ground black pepper, as required

INSTRUCTIONS:

1. In a large pan, heat oil over medium-high heat and cook the beef for about 5 minutes.
2. Add the onion, mushrooms and garlic and cook for about 5 minutes.
3. Add the bok choy stalks and cook for about 4-5 minutes.
4. Add soy sauce and broth and bring to a boil.
5. Reduce the heat to low. Cover and cook for about 10 minutes.
6. Stir in the bok choy leaves and cook for about 5 minutes.
7. Stir in black pepper and serve hot.

NUTRITIONAL INFORMATION PER SERVING:

Calories: 191
Fat: 5.9g
Carbohydrates: 5.1g
Fiber: 1.4g
Sugar: 2.8g
Protein: 29g
Sodium: 900mg

BEEF & CABBAGE STEW

Servings: 8
Preparation Time: 15 minutes
Cooking Time: 1 hour 5o min.

INGREDIENTS:

- 2 pounds beef stew meat, trimmed and cubed into 1-inch size
- 1 1/3 cups hot low-sodium chicken broth
- 2 yellow onions, chopped
- 2 bay leaves
- 1 teaspoon Greek seasoning
- Salt and ground black pepper, as required
- 3 celery stalks, chopped
- 1 (8-ounce) package shredded cabbage
- 1 (6-ounce) can sugar-free tomato sauce
- 1 (8-ounce) can sugar-free whole plum tomatoes, chopped roughly with liquid

INSTRUCTIONS:

1. Heat a large nonstick pan over medium-high heat and cook the beef for about 4-5 minutes or until browned.
2. Drain excess grease from the pan.
3. Stir in the broth, onion, bay leaves, Greek seasoning, salt and black pepper and bring to a boil.
4. Reduce the heat to low and cook, covered for about 1¼ hours.
5. Stir in the celery and cabbage and cook, covered for about 30 minutes.
6. Stir in the tomato sauce and chopped plum tomatoes and cook, uncovered for about 15-20 minutes.
7. Stir in the salt and remove from heat.
8. Discard bay leaves and serve hot.

NUTRITIONAL INFORMATION PER SERVING:

Calories: 247
Fat: 7.5g
Carbohydrates: 7g
Fiber: 2.1g
Sugar: 3.9g
Protein: 36.5g
Sodium: 346mg

BEEF & CARROT STEW

Servings: 6
Preparation Time: 15 minutes
Cooking Time: 55 minutes

INGREDIENTS:

- 1½ pounds beef stew meat, trimmed and chopped
- Salt and ground black pepper, as required
- 1 tablespoon olive oil
- 1 cup homemade tomato puree
- 4 cups homemade low-sodium beef broth
- 3 carrots, peeled and sliced
- 2 garlic cloves, minced
- ½ tablespoons dried thyme
- 1 teaspoon dried parsley
- 1 teaspoon dried rosemary
- 1 tablespoon paprika
- 1 teaspoon onion powder
- 1 teaspoon garlic powder
- 3 tablespoons fresh parsley, chopped

INSTRUCTIONS:

1. In a large bowl, add the beef cubes, salt, and black pepper, and toss to coat well.
2. In a Dutch oven, heat oil over medium-high heat and cook the beef cubes for about 4–5 minutes or until browned.
3. Add in remaining ingredients except for parsley and stir to combine.
4. Adjust the heat to high and bring to a boil.
5. Now, adjust the heat to low and simmer, covered for about 40–50 minutes.
6. Stir in the salt and black pepper and remove from the heat.
7. Garnish with parsley and serve hot.

NUTRITIONAL INFORMATION PER SERVING:

Calories: 295
Fat: 10.5g
Carbohydrates: 8g
Fiber: 2.2g
Sugar: 4g
Protein: 39g
Sodium: 644mg

BAKED BEEF STEW

Servings: 8
Preparation Time: 15 minutes
Cooking Time: 2¼ hours

INGREDIENTS:

- 1 teaspoon ground coriander
- ¾ teaspoon ground cumin
- ½ teaspoon cayenne pepper
- 2 tablespoons coconut oil
- 3 pounds beef stew meat, cubed
- Salt and ground black pepper, as required
- ½ yellow onion, chopped
- 2 garlic cloves, minced
- 2 cups low-sodium chicken broth
- 1 (15-ounce) can sugar-free diced tomatoes
- 1 medium head cauliflower, cut into 1-inch florets

INSTRUCTIONS:

1. Preheat your oven to 300 degrees F.
2. In a small bowl, mix together spices. Set aside.
3. In a large ovenproof pan, heat the oil over medium heat and cook beef with salt and black pepper for about 10 minutes or until browned from all sides.

4. Transfer the beef into a bowl.
5. In the same pan, add the onion and sauté for about 3-4 minutes.
6. Add the garlic and spice mixture and sauté for about 1 minute.
7. Add the cooked beef, broth and tomatoes and bring to a gentle boil.
8. Immediately cover the pan and transfer into oven.
9. Bake for approximately 1½ hours.
10. Remove from the oven and stir in the cauliflower.
11. Bake, covered for about 30 minutes more or until cauliflower is done completely.
12. Serve hot.

NUTRITIONAL INFORMATION PER SERVING:

Calories: 372
Fat: 14.2g
Carbohydrates: 5.1g
Fiber: 1.7g
Sugar: 2.5g
Protein: 53.4g
Sodium: 162mg

BEEF LETTUCE WRAPS

Servings: 2
Preparation Time: 15 minutes
Cooking Time: 13 minutes

INGREDIENTS:

- 2 tablespoons white onion, chopped
- 5 ounces lean ground beef
- 2 tablespoons light thousand island dressing
- 1/8 teaspoon white vinegar
- 1/8 teaspoon onion powder
- 4 lettuce leaves
- 2 tablespoons low-fat cheddar cheese, shredded
- 1 small cucumber, julienned

INSTRUCTIONS:

1. Heat a small, lightly greased wok over medium-high heat and sauté the onion for about 2-3 minutes.
2. Add the beef and cook for about 8-10 minutes or until cooked through.
3. Remove from the heat and set aside.
4. In a bowl, add the dressing, vinegar and onion powder and mix well.
5. Arrange the lettuce leaves onto serving plates.
6. Place beef mixture over each lettuce leaf, followed by the cheese and cucumber.
7. Drizzle with sauce and serve.

NUTRITIONAL INFORMATION PER SERVING:

Calories: 203
Fat: 8.8g
Carbohydrates: 5.3g
Fiber: 0.5g
Sugar: 3.3g
Protein: 23.5g
Sodium: 418mg

SIMPLE BEEF BURGERS

Servings: 4
Preparation Time: 15 minutes
Cooking Time: 10 minutes

INGREDIENTS:

- 1 pound ground beef
- 1 large egg, lightly beaten
- ½ cup seasoned breadcrumbs
- Salt and ground black pepper, as required
- 1 tablespoon olive oil
- 6 cups fresh spinach, torn
- 1 large tomato, chopped

INSTRUCTIONS:

1. Preheat the grill to medium heat.
2. Grease the grill grate.
3. In a large bowl, add the beef, egg, breadcrumbs, salt and black pepper and mix until well combined.
4. Make 4 (½-inch thick) patties from the mixture.
5. With your thumb, press a shallow indentation in the center of each patty.
6. Brush both sides of each patty with oil.
7. Place the burgers onto the grill and cook, covered for about 4-5 minutes per side.
8. Serve alongside the spinach and tomato.

NUTRITIONAL INFORMATION PER SERVING:

Calories: 320
Fat: 13.8g
Carbohydrates: 11g
Fiber: 2g
Sugar: 1.5g
Protein: 39.2g
Sodium: 344mg

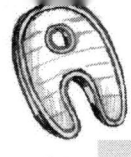

BEEF & SPINACH BURGERS

Servings: 4
Preparation Time: 15 minutes
Cooking Time: 12 minutes

INGREDIENTS:

For Burgers:

- 1-pound ground beef
- 1 cup fresh baby spinach leaves, chopped
- ½ of small yellow onion, chopped
- ¼ cup sun-dried tomatoes, chopped
- 1 egg, beaten
- ¼ cup feta cheese, crumbled
- Salt and ground black pepper, as required
- 2 tablespoons olive oil

For Serving:

- 3 cups fresh spinach, torn
- 3 cups lettuce, torn
- 2 tomatoes, sliced

INSTRUCTIONS:

1. *For Burgers:* in a large bowl, add all ingredients except for oil and mix until well combined.
2. Make 4 equal-sized patties from the mixture.
3. In a wok, heat the oil over medium-high heat and cook the patties for about 5-6 minutes per side or until desired doneness.
4. Divide the lettuce, spinach, and tomato slices and onto serving plates.
5. Top each with 1 burger and serve.

NUTRITIONAL INFORMATION PER SERVING:

Calories: 319
Fat: 20.2g
Carbohydrates: 6.4g
Fiber: 2g
Sugar: 3.3g
Protein: 27.6g
Sodium: 305mg

SPICY BEEF BURGERS

Servings: 4
Preparation Time: 20 minutes
Cooking Time: 10 minutes

INGREDIENTS:

For Burgers

- 1-pound lean ground beef
- ¼ cup fresh parsley, chopped
- ¼ cup fresh parsley, chopped
- ¼ cup fresh cilantro, chopped
- 1 tablespoon fresh ginger, chopped
- 1 teaspoon ground cumin
- 1 teaspoon ground coriander
- ½ teaspoon ground cinnamon
- Salt and ground black pepper, as required

For Salad:

- 6 cup fresh baby arugula
- 2 cups cherry tomatoes, quartered
- 1 tablespoon fresh lemon juice
- 1 tablespoon extra-virgin olive oil

INSTRUCTIONS:

1. In a bowl, add the beef, ¼ cup of parsley, cilantro, ginger, spices, salt and black pepper and mix until well combined.
2. Make 4 equal-sized patties from the mixture.
3. Heat a greased grill pan over medium-high heat and cook the patties for about 3 minutes per side or until desired doneness.
4. Meanwhile, in a bowl, add arugula, tomatoes, lemon juice and oil and toss to coat well.
5. Divide the salad onto serving plates and top each with 1 patty.
6. Serve immediately.

NUTRITIONAL INFORMATION PER SERVING:

Calories: 274
Fat: 11.2g
Carbohydrates: 6.4g
Fiber: 2.1g
Sugar: 3.2g
Protein: 36.3g
Sodium: 131mg

SPICED BEEF MEATBALLS

Servings: 4
Preparation Time: 15 minutes
Cooking Time: 20 minutes

INGREDIENTS:

- <u>1-pound ground beef</u>
- <u>1 tablespoon olive oil</u>
- <u>1 teaspoon dehydrated onion flakes, crushed</u>
- ½ teaspoon granulated garlic
- ½ teaspoon ground cumin
- ½ teaspoon red pepper flakes, crushed
- Salt, as required
- 6 cups fresh baby spinach
- 1 cup tomato, chopped

INSTRUCTIONS:

1. Preheat your oven to 400 degrees F.
2. Line a larger baking sheet with parchment paper.
3. In a mixing bowl, place all the ingredients and with your hands, mix until well combined.
4. Shape the mixture into desired and equal-sized balls.
5. Arrange meatballs into the prepared baking sheet in a single layer and Bake for approximately 15-20 minutes or until done completely.
6. Serve hot alongside spinach and tomato.

NUTRITIONAL INFORMATION PER SERVING:

Calories: 262
Fat: 10.9g
Carbohydrates: 3.9g
Fiber: 1.7g
Sugar: 1.5g
Protein: 36.2g
Sodium: 152mg

BEEF & VEGGIE MEATBALLS

Servings: 6
Preparation Time: 15 minutes
Cooking Time: 30 minutes

INGREDIENTS:

For Meatballs:

- ½ cup carrot, peeled and grated
- ½ cup zucchini, grated
- ½ cup yellow squash, grated
- Salt, as required
- 1-pound lean ground beef
- 1 egg, beaten
- ¼ of a small onion, chopped finely
- 1 garlic clove, minced
- 2 tablespoons mixed fresh herbs (parsley, basil, cilantro, chopped final

For Serving:

- 6 cups fresh baby spinach
- 3 large tomatoes, sliced

INSTRUCTIONS:

1. Preheat your oven to 400 degrees F.
2. Line a large baking sheet with parchment paper.
3. In a large colander, place the carrot, zucchini and yellow squash and sprinkle with 2 pinches of salt. Set aside for at least 10 minutes.
4. Transfer the veggies over a paper towel and squeeze out all the moisture
5. In a large mixing bowl, add squeezed vegetables, beef, egg, onion, garlic, herbs and salt and mix until well combined.
6. Shape the mixture into equal-sized balls.
7. Arrange the meatballs onto the prepared baking sheet in a single layer.
8. Bake for approximately 25-30 minutes or until done completely.
9. Divide the spinach and tomato slices onto serving plates.
10. Top each plate with meatballs and serve.

NUTRITIONAL INFORMATION PER SERVING:

Calories: 184
Fat: 5.8g
Carbohydrates: 6.9g
Fiber: 2.4g
Sugar: 1.5g
Protein: 25.9g
Sodium: 124mg

SPICY BEEF KOFTAS

Servings: 6
Preparation Time: 15 minutes
Cooking Time: 10 minutes

INGREDIENTS:

- 1-pound ground beef
- 2 tablespoons low-fat plain Greek yogurt
- 2 tablespoons yellow onion, grated
- 2 teaspoons garlic, minced
- 2 tablespoons fresh cilantro, minced
- 1 teaspoon ground coriander
- 1 teaspoon ground cumin
- 1 teaspoon ground turmeric
- Salt and ground black pepper, as required
- 1 tablespoon olive oil
- 8 cups fresh salad greens

INSTRUCTIONS:

1. In a large bowl, add all the ingredients except for greens and mix until well combined.
2. Make 12 equal-sized oblong patties from the mixture.
3. In a large non-stick wok, heat the oil over medium-high heat and cook the patties for about 10 minutes or until browned from both sides, flipping occasionally.

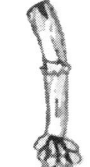

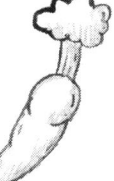

4. Serve the Koftas with salad greens

NUTRITIONAL INFORMATION PER SERVING:

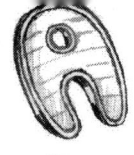

Calories: 193
Fat: 7.4g
Carbohydrates: 6.6g
Fiber: 2.6g
Sugar: 1.1g
Protein: 24.5g
Sodium: 111mg

BEEF KABOBS

Servings: 6
Preparation Time: 15 minutes
Cooking Time: 8 minutes

INGREDIENTS:

- 3 garlic cloves, minced
- 1 tablespoon fresh lemon zest, grated
- 2 teaspoons fresh rosemary, minced
- 2 teaspoons fresh parsley, minced
- 2 teaspoons fresh oregano, minced
- 2 teaspoons fresh thyme, minced
- 4 tablespoons olive oil
- 2 tablespoons fresh lemon juice
- Salt and ground black pepper, as required
- 2 pounds beef sirloin, cut into cubes
- 8 cups fresh baby greens

INSTRUCTIONS:

1. In a bowl, add all the ingredients except the beef and greens and mix well.
2. Add the beef and coat with the herb mixture generously.
3. Refrigerate to marinate for at least 20-30 minutes.
4. Preheat the grill to medium-high heat. Grease the grill grate.
5. Remove the beef cubes from the marinade and thread onto metal skewers.
6. Place the skewers onto the grill and cook for about 6-8 minutes, flipping after every 2 minutes.
7. Remove from the grill and place onto a platter for about 5 minutes before serving.
8. Serve alongside the greens.

NUTRITIONAL INFORMATION PER SERVING:

Calories: 240
Fat: 15g
Carbohydrates: 2.5g
Fiber: 1.1g
Sugar: 0.7g
Protein: 23.7g
Sodium: 84mg

GARLICKY BEEF TENDERLOIN

Servings: 19
Preparation Time: 10 minutes
Cooking Time: 50 minutes

INGREDIENTS:

- 1 (3-pound) center-cut beef tenderloin roast
- 4 garlic cloves, minced
- 1 tablespoon fresh rosemary, minced
- Salt and ground black pepper, as required
- 1 tablespoon olive oil
- 15 cups fresh spinach

INSTRUCTIONS:

1. Preheat your oven to 425 degrees F.
2. Grease a large shallow roasting pan.
3. Place the roast into the prepared roasting pan.
4. Rub the roast with garlic, rosemary, salt, and black pepper, and drizzle with oil.
5. Roast the beef for about 45-50 minutes.
6. Remove from oven and place the roast onto a cutting board for about 10 minutes.
7. With a knife, cut beef tenderloin into desired-sized slices and serve alongside the spinach.

NUTRITIONAL INFORMATION PER SERVING:

Calories: 283
Fat: 15.6g
Carbohydrates: 1.9g
Fiber: 1g
Sugar: 0.2g
Protein: 32.6g
Sodium: 123mg

SIMPLE STEAK

Servings: 4
Preparation Time: 10 minutes
Cooking Time: 10 minutes

INGREDIENTS:

- 1 tablespoon olive oil
- 4 (6-ounce) flank steaks
- Salt and ground black pepper, as required
- 6 cups fresh salad greens

INSTRUCTIONS:

1. In a wok, heat the oil over medium-high heat and cook steaks with salt and black pepper for about 3-5 minutes per side.
2. Transfer the steaks onto serving plates and serve alongside the greens.

ROSEMARY STEAK

Servings: 6
Preparation Time: 15 minutes
Cooking Time: 15 minutes

INGREDIENTS:

- 3 garlic cloves, minced
- 2 tablespoons fresh rosemary, chopped
- Salt and ground black pepper, as required
- 2 pounds flank steak, trimmed
- 8 cups fresh baby kale

INSTRUCTIONS:

1. Preheat the grill to medium-high heat.
2. Grease the grill grate.
3. In a large bowl, add all the ingredients except the steak and kale mix until well combined.
4. Add the steak and coat with the mixture generously.
5. Set aside for about 10 minutes.
6. Place the steak onto the grill and cook for about 12-15 minutes, flipping after every 3-4 minutes.
7. Remove from the grill and place the steak onto a cutting board for about 5 minutes.
8. Meanwhile, for sauce: in a bowl, add all the ingredients and mix well.
9. With a sharp knife, cut the steak into desired sized slices.
10. Serve the steak slices alongside the kale.

NUTRITIONAL INFORMATION PER SERVING:

Calories: 386
Fat: 17.9g
Carbohydrates: 5.9g
Fiber: 2.6g
Sugar: 0.7g
Protein: 48.6g
Sodium: 167mg

SPICED FLANK STEAK

Servings: 5
Preparation Time: 10 minutes
Cooking Time: 20 minutes

INGREDIENTS:

- ½ teaspoons dried thyme, crushed
- ½ teaspoons dried oregano, crushed
- 1 teaspoon red chili powder
- ½ teaspoons ground cumin
- ¼ teaspoons garlic powder
- Salt and ground black pepper, as required
- 1½ pounds flank steak, trimmed
- 6 cups salad greens

INSTRUCTIONS:

1. In a large bowl, add the dried herbs and spices and mix well.
2. Add the steaks and rub with mixture generously.
3. Set aside for about 15-20 minutes.
4. Preheat the grill to medium heat. Grease the grill grate.
5. Place the steak onto the grill over medium coals and cook for about 18–20 minutes, flipping once halfway through.
6. Remove the steak from grill and place onto a cutting board for about 10 minutes before slicing.
7. With a knife, cut steak into desired sized slices and serve alongside the greens.

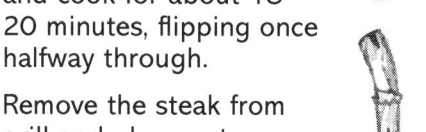

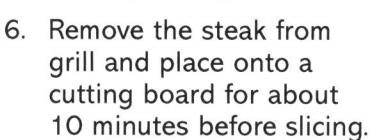

NUTRITIONAL INFORMATION PER SERVING:

Calories: 277
Fat: 11.5g
Carbohydrates: 2.4g
Fiber: 0.9g
Sugar: 0.1g
Protein: 38.6g
Sodium: 152mg

SIMPLE FLANK STEAK

Servings: 4
Preparation Time: 10 minutes
Cooking Time: 8 minutes

INGREDIENTS:

For Steak:

- 2 tablespoons extra-virgin olive oil
- 4 (6-ounce) flank steaks
- Salt and ground black pepper, as required

For Salad:

- 6 cups fresh baby arugula
- 3 tablespoons extra-virgin olive oil
- 2 tablespoons balsamic vinegar
- Salt and ground black pepper, as required

INSTRUCTIONS:

1. In a sauté pan, heat the oil over medium-high heat and cook the steaks with salt and black pepper for about 3-4 minutes per side.
2. *Meanwhile, For Salad:* in a salad bowl, place all ingredients and toss to coat well.
3. Divide the arugula onto serving plates and top each with 1 steak.
4. Serve immediately.

NUTRITIONAL INFORMATION PER SERVING:

Calories: 385
Fat: 24.7g
Carbohydrates: 1.2g
Fiber: 0.5g
Sugar: 0.7g
Protein: 38.4g
Sodium: 145mg

STEAK WITH GREEN BEANS

Servings: 2
Preparation Time: 15 minutes
Cooking Time: 10 minutes

INGREDIENTS:

For Steak:

- 2 (5-ounce) sirloin steaks, trimmed
- Salt and ground black pepper, as required
- 1 tablespoon extra-virgin olive oil
- 1 garlic clove, minced

For Green Beans:

- ½ pound fresh green beans
- ½ tablespoon olive oil
- ½ tablespoon fresh lemon juice

INSTRUCTIONS:

1. For steak: season the steaks with salt and black pepper evenly.
2. In a cast-iron sauté pan, heat the olive oil over high heat and sauté garlic for about 15-20 seconds.
3. Add the steaks and cook for about 3 minutes per side.
4. Flip the steaks and cook for about 3-4 minutes or until desired doneness, flipping once.
5. Meanwhile, for green beans: in a pan of boiling water, arrange a steamer basket.
6. Place the green beans in steamer basket and steam, covered for about 4-5 minutes.
7. Carefully transfer the beans into a bowl.
8. Add olive oil and lemon juice and toss to coat well.
9. Divide green beans onto serving plates.
10. Top each with 1 steak and serve.

NUTRITIONAL INFORMATION PER SERVING:

Calories: 388
Fat: 18.9g
Carbohydrates: 8.7g
Fiber: 3.9g
Sugar: 1.7g
Protein: 45.5g
Sodium: 176mg

VEGGIE & FETA STUFFED STEAK

Servings: 6
Preparation Time: 15 minutes
Cooking Time: 35 minutes

INGREDIENTS:

- 1 tablespoon dried oregano leaves
- 1/3 cup fresh lemon juice
- 2 tablespoons olive oil
- 1 (2-pound) beef flank steak, pounded into ½-inch thickness.
- 1/3 cup olive tapenade
- 1 cup frozen chopped spinach, thawed and squeezed
- ¼ cup feta cheese, crumbled
- 4 cups fresh cherry tomatoes
- Salt, as required

INSTRUCTIONS:

1. In a large baking dish, add the oregano, lemon juice and oil and mix well.
2. Add the steak and coat with the marinade generously.
3. Refrigerate to marinate for about 4 hours, flipping occasionally.
4. Preheat your oven to 425 degrees F.
5. Line a shallow baking dish with parchment paper.
6. Remove the steak from baking dish, reserving the remaining marinade in a bowl.
7. Cover the bowl of marinade and refrigerate.
8. Arrange the steak onto a cutting board.

9. Place the tapenade onto the steak evenly and top with the spinach, followed by the feta cheese.
10. Carefully roll the steak tightly to form a log.
11. With 6 kitchen string pieces, tie the log at 6 places.
12. Carefully cut the log between strings into 6 equal pieces, leaving the string in place.
13. In a bowl, add the reserved marinade, tomatoes and salt and toss to coat.
14. Arrange the log pieces onto the prepared baking dish, cut-side up.
15. Now, arrange the tomatoes around the log pieces evenly.
16. Bake for approximately 25-35 minutes.
17. Remove from the oven and set aside for about 5 minutes before serving.

NUTRITIONAL INFORMATION PER SERVING:

Calories: 395
Fat: 18.2g
Carbohydrates: 7g
Fiber: 2.2g
Sugar: 3.8g
Protein: 48.4g
Sodium: 387mg

BEEF & BROCCOLI BOWL

Serving: 1
Preparation Time: 15 minutes
Cooking Time: 12 minutes

INGREDIENTS:

- 4 ounces lean ground beef
- 1 cup broccoli, cut into bite-sized pieces
- 2 tablespoons low-sodium chicken broth
- ¼ cup tomatoes, chopped
- ¼ teaspoon onion powder
- ¼ teaspoon garlic powder
- Pinch of red pepper flakes
- Salt, as required
- 1 ounce low-fat cheddar cheese

INSTRUCTIONS:

1. Heat a lightly greased wok over medium heat and cook the beef for about 8-10 minutes or until browned completely.
2. Meanwhile, in a microwave-safe bowl, place the broccoli and broth.
3. With a plastic wrap, cover the bowl and microwave for about 4 minutes.
4. Remove from the microwave and set aside.
5. Drain the grease from wok.
6. Add the tomatoes, garlic powder, onion powder, red pepper flakes and salt and stir to combine well.
7. Add the broccoli and toss to coat well.
8. Remove from the heat and transfer the beef mixture into a serving bowl.
9. Top with cheddar cheese and serve.

NUTRITIONAL INFORMATION PER SERVING:

Calories: 322
Fat: 18g
Carbohydrates: 9g
Fiber: 3.1g
Sugar: 3.3g
Protein: 32.8g
Sodium: 459mg

BEEF TACO BOWL

Servings: 4
Preparation Time: 15 minutes
Cooking Time: 15 minutes

INGREDIENTS:

- 1 teaspoon red chili powder
- 1 teaspoon ground cumin
- Salt and freshly ground black pepper, as required
- 1-pound flank steak, trimmed
- 2 scallions
- 1 lime, cut in half
- 8 cups lettuce, torn
- 1 red bell pepper, seeded and sliced
- 1 cup tomato, chopped
- ½ cup fresh cilantro, chopped
- ¼ cup light sour cream

INSTRUCTIONS:

1. Preheat the grill to medium-high heat. Grease the grill grate.
2. In a small bowl, mix together the spices, salt and black pepper.
3. Rub the steak with spice mixture generously.
4. Place the steak onto the grill and cook for about 4-6 minutes per side or until desired doneness.
5. Remove from the grill and place the steak onto a cutting board for about 5

minutes.

6. Now, place the scallions onto the grill and cook for about 1 minute per side.
7. Place the lime halves onto the grill, cut-side down and cook for about 1 minute.
8. Remove the scallions and lime halves from the grill and place onto a plate.
9. Chop the scallions roughly.
10. With a sharp knife, cut the steak into thin slices.
11. In a bowl, place the beef slices and chopped scallions.
12. Squeeze the lime halves over steak mixture and toss to coat well.
13. Divide lettuce into serving bowls and top each with bell pepper, followed by tomato, cilantro and beef mixture.
14. Top each bowl with sour cream and serve.

NUTRITIONAL INFORMATION PER SERVING:

Calories: 288
Fat: 13g
Carbohydrates: 8.7g
Fiber: 2.4g
Sugar: 3.3g
Protein: 33.5g
Sodium: 129mg

VEGGIE STUFFED STEAK

Servings: 4
Preparation Time: 15 minutes
Cooking Time: 35 minutes

INGREDIENTS:

- 1 (1½-pound) flank steak
- Salt and freshly ground black pepper, as required
- 1 tablespoon olive oil
- 2 small garlic cloves, minced
- 6 ounces fresh spinach, chopped finely
- 1 medium green bell pepper, seeded and chopped
- 1 medium tomato, chopped finely

INSTRUCTIONS:

1. Preheat your oven to 425 degrees F.
2. Grease a large baking dish.
3. Place flank steak onto a flat surface.
4. Hold a sharp knife parallel to work surface, slice the steak horizontally, without cutting all the way through, that you can open like a book.
5. With a meat mallet, flatten the steak to an even thickness. Sprinkle the steak with salt and black pepper evenly.
6. In a wok, heat oil over medium heat and sauté garlic for about 1 minute.
7. Add spinach, with salt and black pepper and cook for about 2 minutes.
8. Stir in bell pepper and tomato and immediately remove from heat.
9. Transfer the spinach into a bowl and set aside to cool slightly.
10. Place the filling on the top of steak evenly.
11. Roll up the steak to seal the filling.
12. With cotton twine, tie the steak.
13. Place the steak roll into the prepared baking dish.
14. Roast for about 30-35 minutes.
15. Remove from oven and let it cool slightly.
16. With a sharp knife, cut the roll into desired sized slices and serve.

NUTRITIONAL INFORMATION PER SERVING:

Calories: 264
Fat: 11,9g
Carbohydrates: 5.3g
Fiber: 0.9g
Sugar: 1.5g
Protein: 32.8g
Sodium: 104mg

STEAK WITH BROCCOLI

Servings: 4
Preparation Time: 15 minutes
Cooking Time: 20 minutes

INGREDIENTS:

- 16 ounces sirloin steak, trimmed and cut into thin strips
- Salt and freshly ground black pepper, as required
- 2 tablespoons olive oil, divided
- 2 garlic cloves, minced
- 1 Serrano pepper, seeded and chopped finely
- 2 C. broccoli florets
- 2 tablespoons low-sodium soy sauce
- 2 tablespoons fresh lime juice

INSTRUCTIONS:

1. Season the steak slices with black pepper.
2. Heat 1 tablespoon of oil in a large wok over medium heat and cook the steak slices for about 6-8 minutes or until browned from all sides.
3. With a slotted spoon, transfer the steak slices onto a plate.
4. Heat the remaining oil in the same wok over medium heat and sauté the garlic and Serrano pepper for about 1 minute.
5. Add the broccoli and stir fry for about 2-3 minutes.
6. Stir in the cooked steak slices, soy sauce and lime juice and cook for about 3-4 minutes.
7. Serve hot.

NUTRITIONAL INFORMATION PER SERVING:

Calories: 214
Fat: 11.8g
Carbohydrates: 4.6g
Fiber: 2.5g
Sugar: 2.2g
Protein: 24.6g
Sodium: 80mg

BEEF WITH MUSHROOMS

Servings: 4
Preparation Time: 15 minutes
Cooking Time: 15 minutes

INGREDIENTS:

For Beef:

- 4 (6-ounce) beef tenderloin fillets
- Salt and freshly ground black pepper, as required
- 2 tablespoons olive oil, divided
- 1 teaspoon garlic, smashed
- 1 tablespoon fresh thyme, chopped

For Mushrooms:

- 2 tablespoons olive oil
- 1 pound fresh mushrooms, sliced
- 2 teaspoons garlic, smashed
- Salt and freshly ground black pepper, as required

INSTRUCTIONS:

1. For beef: season the beef fillets with salt and black pepper evenly and set aside.
2. In a cast-iron wok, heat the oil over medium heat and sauté the garlic and thyme for about 1 minute.
3. Add the fillets and cook for about 5-7 minutes per side.
4. Meanwhile, for mushrooms: in another cast-iron wok, heat the oil over medium heat and cook the mushrooms, garlic, salt, and black pepper for about 7-8 minutes, stirring frequently.
5. Divide the fillets onto serving plates.
6. Top with mushroom mixture and serve.

NUTRITIONAL INFORMATION PER SERVING:

Calories: 388
Fat: 17.9g
Carbohydrates: 4.9g
Fiber: 1.4g
Sugar: 2g
Protein: 50.9g
Sodium: 150mg

STEAK WITH CARROT & KALE

Servings: 4
Preparation Time: 15 minutes
Cooking Time: 12 minutes

INGREDIENTS:

- 2 tablespoons olive oil
- 4 garlic cloves, minced
- 1 pound beef sirloin steak, cut into bite-sized pieces
- Freshly ground black pepper, as required
- 1½ cups carrots, peeled and cut into matchsticks
- 1½ cups fresh kale, tough ribs removed and chopped
- 3 tablespoons low-sodium soy sauce

INSTRUCTIONS:

1. In a wok, heat the oil over medium heat and sauté the garlic for about 1 minute.
2. Add the beef and black pepper and stir to combine.
3. Increase the heat to medium-high and cook for about 3-4 minutes or until browned from all sides.
4. Add the carrot, kale and soy sauce and cook for about 4-5 minutes.
5. Stir in the black pepper and remove from the heat.
6. Serve hot.

NUTRITIONAL INFORMATION PER SERVING:

Calories: 311
Fat: 14.8g
Carbohydrates: 4.9g
Fiber: 1.4g
Sugar: 2g
Protein: 50.9g
Sodium: 700mg

GROUND BEEF WITH VEGGIES

Servings: 4
Preparation Time: 15 minutes
Cooking Time: 25 minutes

INGREDIENTS:

- 1 pound lean ground beef
- 2 tablespoons extra-virgin olive oil
- 2 garlic cloves, minced
- ½ of yellow onion, chopped
- 2 cups fresh mushrooms, sliced
- 1 cup fresh kale, tough ribs removed and chopped
- ¼ cup low-sodium beef broth
- 2 tablespoons balsamic vinegar
- 2 tablespoons fresh parsley, chopped

INSTRUCTIONS:

1. Heat a large non-stick wok over medium-high heat and cook the ground beef for about 8-10 minutes, breaking up the chunks with a wooden spoon.
2. With a slotted spoon, transfer the beef into a bowl.
3. In the same wok, add the onion and garlic for about 3 minutes.
4. Add the mushrooms and cook for about 5-minutes.
5. Add the cooked beef, kale, broth and vinegar and bring to a boil.
6. Reduce the heat to medium-low and simmer for about 3 minutes.
7. Stir in parsley and serve immediately.

NUTRITIONAL INFORMATION PER SERVING:

Calories: 299
Fat: 14.3g
Carbohydrates: 4.9g
Fiber: 1g
Sugar: 1.3g
Protein: 36.6g

BEEF CHILI

Servings: 8
Preparation Time: 15 minutes
Cooking Time: 1¾ hours

INGREDIENTS:

- 2 tablespoons olive oil
- 3 pounds ground beef
- 1 cup yellow onion, chopped finely
- ½ cup celery, chopped finely
- ½ cup green bell pepper, seeded and chopped finely
- ½ cup red bell pepper, seeded and chopped finely
- 1 (15-ounce) can crushed tomatoes with juice
- 1½ cups tomato juice
- 1½ teaspoons Worcestershire sauce
- ½ teaspoon dried oregano
- 3 tablespoons red chili powder
- 1 teaspoon ground cumin
- 1 teaspoon garlic powder
- 1 teaspoon salt
- ½ teaspoon ground black pepper

INSTRUCTIONS:

1. In a large pan, heat the oil over medium-high heat and cook the beef for about 8-10 minutes or until browned.
2. Drain the grease from pan, leaving about 2 tablespoons inside.
3. In the pan, add the onions, celery and bell peppers over medium-high heat and cook for about 5 minutes, stirring frequently.
4. Add the tomatoes, tomato juice, Worcestershire sauce, oregano and spices and stir to combine.
5. Reduce the heat to low and simmer, covered for about 1-1½ hours, stirring occasionally.
6. Serve hot.

NUTRITIONAL INFORMATION PER SERVING:

Calories: 326
Fat: 16.3g
Carbohydrates: 11g
Fiber: 3.6g
Sugar: 6g
Protein: 35.9g
Sodium: 690mg

BEEF STUFFED BELL PEPPERS

Servings: 5
Preparation Time: 20 minutes
Cooking Time: 40 minutes

INGREDIENTS:

- 5 large bell peppers, tops and seeds removed
- 1 tablespoon olive oil
- ½ of large onion, chopped
- ½ teaspoon dried oregano
- ½ teaspoon dried thyme
- Salt and ground black pepper, as required
- 1-pound ground beef
- 1 large zucchini, chopped
- 3 tablespoons homemade tomato paste

INSTRUCTIONS:

1. Preheat your oven to 350 degrees F.
2. Grease a small baking dish.
3. In a large pan of boiling water, place the bell peppers and cook for about 4-5 minutes.
4. Remove from the water and place onto a paper towel, cut side down.
5. Meanwhile, in a large nonstick wok, heat the olive oil over medium heat and sauté onion for about 3-4 minutes.
6. Add the ground beef, oregano, salt, and pepper and cook for about 8-10 minutes.
7. Add the zucchini and cook for about 2-3 minutes.
8. Remove from the heat and drain any juices from the beef mixture.
9. Add the tomato paste and stir to combine.
10. Arrange the bell peppers into the prepared baking dish, cut side upward.
11. Stuff the bell peppers with the beef mixture evenly.
12. Bake for approximately 15 minutes.
13. Serve warm.

NUTRITIONAL INFORMATION PER SERVING:

Calories: 255
Fat: 9g
Carbohydrates: 14g
Fiber: 3g
Sugar: 8g
Protein: 30.1g
Sodium: 110mg

GARLICKY PORK TENDERLOIN

Servings: 6
Preparation Time: 10 minutes
Cooking Time: 38 minutes

INGREDIENTS:

- 3 medium garlic cloves, minced
- 3 teaspoons dried rosemary, crushed
- ½ teaspoon cayenne pepper
- Salt and ground black pepper, as required
- 2 pounds pork tenderloin
- 10 cups fresh baby spinach

INSTRUCTIONS:

1. Preheat your oven to 400 degrees F.
2. Grease a roasting pan.
3. In a bowl, mix together all the ingredients except for pork and spinach.
4. Rub the pork with garlic mixture evenly.
5. Place the pork into the prepared roasting pan.
6. Roast for about 25 minutes or until desired doneness.
7. Remove the roasting pan from oven and place the pork tenderloin onto a cutting board for about 10-15 minutes.
8. With a sharp knife, cut the pork tenderloin into desired size slices and serve alongside spinach.

NUTRITIONAL INFORMATION PER SERVING:

Calories: 232
Fat: 5.6g
Carbohydrates: 2.8g
Fiber: 1.4g
Sugar: 0.3g
Protein: 41.2g
Sodium: 153mg

PORK STUFFED AVOCADO

Servings: 8
Preparation Time: 15 minutes
Cooking Time: 10 minutes

INGREDIENTS:

- 4 ripe avocados, halved and pitted
- 3 tablespoons fresh lime juice
- 1 tablespoon olive oil
- 1 medium onion, chopped
- 1 pound ground pork
- 1 packet taco seasoning
- Salt and ground black pepper, as required
- 2/3 cup low-fat Mexican cheese, shredded
- ½ cup lettuce, shredded
- ½ cup cherry tomatoes, quartered

INSTRUCTIONS:

1. Carefully remove about 2-3 tablespoons of flesh from each avocado half.
2. Chop the avocado flesh and reserve it.
3. Arrange the avocado halves onto a tray and drizzle each with lime juice.
4. In a medium wok, heat oil over medium heat and sauté the onion for about 5 minutes.
5. Add the ground pork,

taco seasoning, salt and black pepper and cook for about 8-10 minutes, breaking up the meat with a wooden spoon.

6. Remove from the heat and drain the grease from the wok.
7. Stuff each avocado half with pork and top with reserved avocado, cheese, lettuce and tomato.
8. Serve immediately.

NUTRITIONAL INFORMATION PER SERVING:

Calories: 356
Fat: 27.1g
Carbohydrates: 11g
Fiber: 7g
Sugar: 1.4g
Protein: 20g
Sodium: 120mg

PORK BURGERS

Servings: 4
Preparation Time: 15 minutes
Cooking Time: 6 minutes

INGREDIENTS:

For Patties:

- 1 pound lean ground pork
- ¼ cup fresh parsley, chopped
- ¼ cup fresh cilantro, chopped
- 1 tablespoon fresh ginger, chopped
- 1 teaspoon ground cumin
- 1 teaspoon ground coriander
- ½ teaspoon ground cinnamon
- Salt and ground black pepper, as required

For Salad:

- 6 cups fresh baby arugula
- 2 cups cherry tomatoes, quartered
- 1 tablespoon fresh lemon juice
- 1 tablespoon extra-virgin olive oil

INSTRUCTIONS:

1. In a bowl, add the pork, parsley, cilantro, ginger, spices, salt and black pepper and mix until well combined.
2. Make 4 equal-sized patties from the mixture.
3. Heat a greased grill pan over medium-high heat and cook the patties for about 3 minutes per side or until desired doneness.
4. Meanwhile, in a bowl, add arugula, tomatoes, lemon juice and oil and toss to coat well.
5. Divide the salad onto serving plates and top each with 1 patty.
6. Serve immediately.

NUTRITIONAL INFORMATION PER SERVING:

Calories: 294
Fat: 21.2g
Carbohydrates: 6.4g
Fiber: 2.1g
Sugar: 3.2g
Protein: 21.2g
Sodium: 200mg

PORK & VEGGIE BURGERS

Servings: 4
Preparation Time: 15 minutes
Cooking Time: 16 minutes

INGREDIENTS:

For Patties:

- 1 pound ground pork
- 1 carrot, peeled and chopped finely
- 1 medium raw beetroot, trimmed, peeled and chopped finely
- 1 small onion, chopped finely
- 2 Serrano peppers, seeded and chopped
- 1 tablespoon fresh cilantro, chopped finely
- Salt and ground black pepper, as required
- 3 tablespoons olive oil

For Serving:

- 1 large onion, sliced
- 2 large tomatoes, sliced
- 4 lettuce leaves

INSTRUCTIONS:

1. For patties: in a large bowl, add all ingredients except for oil and mix until well combined.
2. Make equal-sized 8 patties from mixture.
3. In a large non-stick sauté pan, heat the olive oil over medium heat and cook the patties in 2 batches for about 3-4 minutes per side or until golden brown.
4. Divide the onion, tomato and lettuce onto serving plates.

5. Top each plate with 2 patties and serve.

NUTRITIONAL INFORMATION PER SERVING:

Calories: 371
Fat: 27.8g
Carbohydrates: 11g
Fiber: 2.9g
Sugar: 6g
Protein: 21.1g
Sodium: mg

ROSEMARY PORK TENDERLOIN

Servings: 3
Preparation Time: 10 minutes
Cooking Time: 22 minutes

INGREDIENTS:

- 1 teaspoon fresh rosemary, minced
- 1 garlic clove, minced
- 1 tablespoon fresh lemon juice
- 1 tablespoon olive oil
- 1 teaspoon Dijon mustard
- 1 teaspoon powdered Erythritol
- Salt and ground black pepper, as required
- 1-pound pork tenderloin
- 5 cups fresh baby kale

INSTRUCTIONS:

1. Preheat your oven to 400 degrees F.
2. Grease a large rimmed baking sheet.
3. In a mixing bowl, place all ingredients except the pork tenderloin and cheese and beat until well combined.
4. Add pork tenderloin and coat with the mixture generously.
5. Arrange the pork tenderloin onto the prepared baking sheet.
6. Bake for approximately 20-22 minutes.
7. Remove baking sheet from the oven and place the pork tenderloin onto a cutting board for about 5 minutes.
8. With a sharp knife, cut the pork tenderloin into ¾-inch-thick slices and serve alongside the kale.

NUTRITIONAL INFORMATION PER SERVING:

Calories: 299
Fat: 10.6g
Carbohydrates: 8g
Fiber: 1.9g
Sugar: 0.1g
Protein: 42.3g
Sodium: 186mg

PORK WITH VEGGIES

Servings: 4
Preparation Time: 15 minutes
Cooking Time: 15 minutes

INGREDIENTS:

- 1-pound pork loin, cut into thin strips
- 2 tablespoons olive oil, divided
- 1 teaspoon garlic, minced
- 1 teaspoon fresh ginger, minced
- 2 tablespoons low-sodium soy sauce
- 1 tablespoon fresh lemon juice
- 1 tablespoon Erythritol
- 1 teaspoon arrowroot starch
- 10 ounces broccoli florets
- 1 carrot, peeled and sliced
- 1 large red bell pepper, seeded and cut into strips
- 2 scallions, cut into 2-inch pieces

INSTRUCTIONS:

1. In a bowl, mix well pork strips, ½ tablespoon of olive oil, garlic, and ginger.
2. For sauce; add the soy sauce, lemon juice, Erythritol, and arrowroot starch in a small bowl and mix well.
3. Heat the remaining olive oil in a large nonstick wok over high heat and sear the pork strips for about 3-4 minutes or until cooked through.
4. With a slotted spoon, transfer the pork into a bowl.
5. In the same wok, add the carrot and cook for about 2-3 minutes.
6. Add the broccoli, bell pepper, and scallion and cook, covered for about 1-2 minutes.
7. Stir the cooked pork and sauce, and cook for about 3-5 minutes or until desired doneness, stirring occasionally.
8. Remove from the heat and serve.

NUTRITIONAL INFORMATION PER SERVING:

Calories: 315
Fat: 19.4g
Carbohydrates: 8.3g
Fiber: 2.6g
Sugar: 3g
Protein: 27.4g
Sodium: 438mg

SEAFOOD RECIPES

SALMON & ARUGULA OMELET

Servings: 4
Preparation Time: 10 minutes
Cooking Time: 7 minutes

Ingredients:

- 6 eggs
- 2 tablespoons unsweetened almond milk
- Salt and ground black pepper, as required
- 2 tablespoons olive oil
- 4 ounces smoked salmon, cut into bite-sized chunks
- 2 cups fresh arugula, chopped finely
- 4 scallions, chopped finely

Instructions:

1. In a bowl, place the eggs, coconut milk, salt and black pepper and beat well. Set aside.
2. In a nonstick wok, heat the oil over medium heat.
3. Place the egg mixture evenly and cook for about 30 seconds without stirring.
4. Place the salmon, arugula and scallions on top of egg mixture evenly.
5. Reduce heat to low and cook, covered for about 4-5 minutes or until omelet is done completely.
6. Uncover the wok and cook for about 1 minute.
7. Carefully transfer the omelet onto a serving plate and serve.

Nutritional Information per Serving:

Calories: 210
Fat: 14.9g
Carbohydrates: 5.2g
Fiber: 0.9g
Sugar: 0.9g
Protein: 14.8g
Sodium: 682mg

TUNA OMELET

Servings: 2
Preparation Time: 10 minutes
Cooking Time: 5 minutes

Ingredients:

- 4 eggs
- ¼ cup unsweetened almond milk
- 1 tablespoon scallions, chopped
- 1 garlic clove, minced
- ½ of jalapeño pepper, minced
- Salt and ground black pepper, as required
- 1 (5-ounce) can water-packed tuna, drained and flaked
- 1 tablespoon olive oil
- 3 tablespoons green bell pepper, seeded and chopped
- 3 tablespoons tomato, chopped
- ¼ cup low-fat cheddar cheese, shredded

Instructions:

1. In a bowl, add the eggs, almond milk, scallions, garlic, jalapeño pepper, salt, and black pepper, and beat well.
2. Add the tuna and stir to combine.
3. In a large nonstick frying pan, heat oil over medium heat.
4. Place the egg mixture in an even layer and cook for about 1–2 minutes, without stirring.
5. Carefully lift the edges to run the uncooked portion flow underneath.
6. Spread the veggies over the egg mixture and sprinkle with the cheese.
7. Cover the frying pan and cook for about 30–60 seconds.
8. Remove the lid and fold the omelet in half.
9. Remove from the heat and cut the omelet into 2 portions.
10. Serve immediately.

Nutritional Information per Serving:

Calories: 340
Fat: 21.5g
Carbohydrates: 3.4g
Fiber: 0.8g
Sugar: 1.7g
Protein: 33.3g
Sodium: 348mg

SALMON & VEGGIE SALAD

Servings: 2
Preparation Time: 15 minutes

INGREDIENTS:

- 6 ounces cooked wild salmon, chopped
- 1 cup cucumber, sliced
- 1 cup red bell pepper, seeded and sliced
- ½ cup grape tomatoes, quartered
- 1 tablespoon scallion green, chopped
- 1 cup lettuce, torn
- 1 cup fresh spinach, torn
- 2 tablespoons olive oil
- 2 tablespoons fresh lemon juice

INSTRUCTIONS:

1. In a salad bowl, place all ingredients and gently toss to coat well.
2. Serve immediately.

NUTRITIONAL INFORMATION PER SERVING:

Calories: 279
Fat: 19.8g
Carbohydrates: 10g
Fiber: 2.3g
Sugar: 5g
Protein: 18.6g
Sodium: 59mg

TUNA SALAD

Servings: 4
Preparation Time: 15 minutes

INGREDIENTS:

For Dressing:

- 2 tablespoons fresh dill, minced
- 2 tablespoons olive oil
- 1 tablespoon fresh lime juice
- Salt and ground black pepper, as required

For Salad:

- 4 cups fresh spinach, torn
- 2 (6-ounce) cans water-packed tuna, drained and flaked
- 6 hard-boiled eggs, peeled and sliced
- 1 cup tomato, chopped
- 1 large cucumber, sliced

INSTRUCTIONS:

1. **For Dressing**: place dill, oil, lime juice, salt, and black pepper in a small bowl and beat until well combined.
2. Divide the spinach onto serving plates and top each with tuna, egg, cucumber, and tomato.
3. Drizzle with dressing and serve.

NUTRITIONAL INFORMATION PER SERVING:

Calories: 284
Fat: 14.6g
Carbohydrates: 7g
Fiber: 1.8g
Sugar: 3.1g
Protein: 32.1g
Sodium: 204mg

SHRIMP & GREENS SALAD

Servings: 6
Preparation Time: 15 minutes
Cooking Time: 6 minutes

INGREDIENTS:

- 3 tablespoons olive oil, divided
- 1 garlic clove, crushed and divided
- 2 tablespoons fresh rosemary, chopped
- 1-pound shrimp, peeled and deveined
- Salt and ground black pepper, as required
- 4 cups fresh arugula
- 2 cups lettuce, torn
- 2 tablespoons fresh lime juice

INSTRUCTIONS:

1. In a large wok, heat 1 tablespoon of oil over medium heat and sauté 1 garlic clove for about 1 minute.
2. Add the shrimp with salt and black pepper and cook for about 4-5 minutes.
3. Remove from the heat and set aside to cool.
4. Ina large bowl, add the shrimp, arugula, remaining oil, lime juice, salt and black pepper and gently toss to coat.
5. Serve immediately.

NUTRITIONAL INFORMATION PER SERVING:

Calories: 332
Fat: 21.7g
Carbohydrates: 11g
Fiber: 3.9g
Sugar: 2.9g
Protein: 24.3g
Sodium: 420mg

SHRIMP, APPLE & CARROT SALAD

Servings: 4
Preparation Time: 20 minutes
Cooking Time: 3 minutes

INGREDIENTS:

- 12 medium shrimp
- 1½ cups Granny Smith apple, cored and sliced thinly
- 1½ cups carrot, peeled and cut into matchsticks
- ½ cup fresh mint leaves, chopped
- 2 tablespoons balsamic vinegar
- ¼ cup extra-virgin olive oil
- 1 teaspoon lemongrass, chopped
- 1 teaspoon garlic, minced
- 2 sprigs fresh cilantro, leaves separated and chopped

INSTRUCTIONS:

1. In a large pan of the salted boiling water, add the shrimp and lemon and cook for about 3 minutes.
2. Remove from the heat and drain the shrimp well.
3. Set aside to cool.
4. After cooling, peel and devein the shrimps.
5. Transfer the shrimp into a large bowl.
6. Add the remaining all ingredients except cilantro and gently stir to combine.
7. Cover the bowl and refrigerate for about 1 hour.
8. Top with cilantro just before serving.

NUTRITIONAL INFORMATION PER SERVING:

Calories: 255
Fat: 14g
Carbohydrates: 18g
Fiber: 3.8g
Sugar: 10g
Protein: 16g
Sodium: 194mg

SHRIMP & GREEN BEANS SALAD

Servings: 5
Preparation Time: 20 minutes
Cooking Time: 8 minutes

INGREDIENTS:

For Shrimp:

- 2 tablespoons olive oil
- 2 tablespoons fresh key lime juice
- 4 large garlic cloves, peeled
- 2 sprigs fresh rosemary leaves
- ½ teaspoon garlic salt
- 20 large shrimp, peeled and deveined

For Salad:

- 1-pound fresh green beans, trimmed
- ¼ cup olive oil
- 1 onion, sliced
- Salt and ground black pepper, as required
- ½ cup garlic and herb feta cheese, crumbled

INSTRUCTIONS:

1. *For shrimp marinade:* in a blender, add all the ingredients except shrimp and pulse until smooth.
2. Transfer the marinade in a large bowl.
3. Add the shrimp and coat with marinade generously.
4. Cover the bowl and refrigerate to marinate for at least 30 minutes.
5. Preheat the broiler of oven.
6. Arrange the rack in top position of the oven.
7. Line a large baking sheet with a piece of foil.
8. Place the shrimp with marinade onto the prepared baking sheet.
9. Broil for about 3-4 minutes per side.
10. Transfer the shrimp mixture into a bowl and refrigerate until using.
11. *Meanwhile, For Salad:* in a pan of the salted boiling water, add the green beans and cook for about 3-4 minutes.
12. Drain the green beans well and rinse under cold running water.
13. Transfer the green beans into a large bowl.
14. Add the onion, shrimp, salt and black pepper and stir to combine.
15. Cover and refrigerate to chill for about 1 hour.
16. Stir in cheese just before serving.

NUTRITIONAL INFORMATION PER SERVING:

Calories: 332
Fat: 21.7g
Carbohydrates: 11g
Fiber: 3.9g
Sugar: 2.9g
Protein: 24.3g
Sodium: 420mg

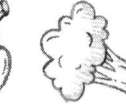

SHRIMP & OLIVES SALAD

Servings: 4
Preparation Time: 15 minutes
Cooking Time: 3 minutes

INGREDIENTS:

- 1 pound shrimp, peeled and deveined
- 1 lemon, quartered
- 2 tablespoons olive oil
- 2 teaspoons fresh lemon juice
- Salt and freshly ground black pepper, as required
- 2 tomatoes, sliced
- ¼ cup onion, sliced
- ¼ cup green olives
- ¼ cup fresh cilantro, chopped finely

INSTRUCTIONS:

1. In a pan of lightly salted boiling water, add the quartered lemon.
2. Then, add the shrimp and cook for about 2-3 minutes or until pink and opaque.
3. With a slotted spoon, transfer the shrimp into a bowl of ice water to stop the cooking process.
4. Drain the shrimp completely and then pat dry with paper towels.
5. In a small bowl, add the oil, lemon juice, salt, and black pepper, and beat until well combined.
6. Divide the shrimp, tomato, onion, olives, and cilantro onto serving plates.
7. Drizzle with oil mixture and serve.

NUTRITIONAL INFORMATION PER SERVING:

Calories: 219
Fat: 10g
Carbohydrates: 5.4g
Fiber: 1.2g
Sugar: 2g
Protein: 26.6g
Sodium: 393mg

SHRIMP & ARUGULA SALAD

Servings: 4
Preparation Time: 15 minutes
Cooking Time: 5 minutes

INGREDIENTS:

For Shrimp:

- 1-pound large shrimp, peeled and deveined
- ½ tablespoon fresh lemon juice

For Salad:

- 6 cups fresh arugula
- 2 tablespoons extra-virgin olive oil
- 1 tablespoon fresh lemon juice
- Salt and ground black pepper, as required

INSTRUCTIONS:

1. In a large pan of salted boiling water, add the shrimp and lemon juice and cook for about 2 minutes.
2. With a slotted spoon, remove the shrimp from pan and place into an ice bath.
3. Drain the shrimp well.
4. In a large bowl, add the shrimp, arugula, oil, lemon juice, salt and black pepper and gently toss to coat.
5. Serve immediately.

NUTRITIONAL INFORMATION PER SERVING:

Calories: 204
Fat: 9.2g
Carbohydrates: 2.9g
Fiber: 0.5g
Sugar: 0.7g
Protein: 26.7g
Sodium: 325mg

SHRIMP & VEGGIES SALAD

Servings: 6
Preparation Time: 20 minutes
Cooking Time: 5 minutes

INGREDIENTS:

For Dressing:

- 2 tablespoons natural almond butter
- 1 garlic clove, crushed
- 1 tablespoon fresh cilantro, chopped
- 2 tablespoons fresh lime juice
- 1 tablespoon maple syrup
- ½ teaspoon cayenne pepper
- ¼ teaspoon salt
- 1 tablespoon water
- 1/3 cup olive oil

For Salad:

- 1-pound shrimp, peeled and deveined
- Salt and ground black pepper, as required
- 1 teaspoon olive oil
- 1 cup carrot, peeled and julienned
- 1 cup red cabbage, shredded
- 1 cup green cabbage, shredded
- 1 cup cucumber, julienned
- 4 cups fresh baby arugula
- ¼ cup fresh basil, chopped
- ¼ cup fresh cilantro, chopped
- 4 cups lettuce, torn
- ¼ cup almonds, chopped

INSTRUCTIONS:

1. **For Dressing:** in a bowl, add all ingredients except oil and beat until well combined.
2. Slowly, add oil, beating continuously until smooth.
3. **For Salad:** in a bowl, add shrimp, salt, black pepper and oil and toss to coat well.
4. Heat a wok over medium-high heat and cook shrimp for about 2 minutes per side.
5. Remove from the heat and set aside to cool.
6. In a large serving bowl, add all the cooked shrimp, remaining salad ingredients and dressing and toss to coat well.
7. Serve immediately.

NUTRITIONAL INFORMATION PER SERVING:

Calories: 276
Fat: 17.7g
Carbohydrates: 10g
Fiber: 2.7g
Sugar: 5g
Protein: 20.3g
Sodium: 305mg

SCALLOP & TOMATO SALAD

Servings: 4
Preparation Time: 15 minutes
Cooking Time: 6 minutes

INGREDIENTS:

For Scallops:

- 1¼ pounds fresh sea scallops, side muscles removed
- Salt and freshly ground black pepper, as required
- 2 tablespoons olive oil
- 1 garlic clove, minced

For Salad

- 6 cup mixed baby greens
- ¼ cup yellow grape tomatoes, halved
- ¼ cup red grape tomatoes, halved
- 2 tablespoons olive oil
- 2 tablespoons fresh lemon juice
- Salt and freshly ground black pepper, as required

INSTRUCTIONS:

1. Sprinkle the scallops with salt and black pepper evenly.
2. In a large wok, heat the oil over medium-high heat and cook the scallops for about 2-3 minutes per side.
3. Meanwhile, **For Salad**: in a bowl, add all ingredients and toss to coat well.
4. Divide the salad onto serving plates.
5. Top each plate with scallops and serve.

NUTRITIONAL INFORMATION PER SERVING:

Calories: 254
Fat: 1.9g
Carbohydrates: 6.9g
Fiber: 1.1g
Sugar: 0.8g
Protein: 24.9g
Sodium: 359mg

FISH STEW

Servings: 10
Preparation Time: 15 minutes
Cooking Time: 50 minutes

INGREDIENTS:

- ¼ cup coconut oil
- ½ cup yellow onion, chopped
- 1 cup celery stalk, chopped
- ½ cup green bell pepper, seeded and chopped
- 1 garlic clove, minced
- 4 cups water
- 4 beef bouillon cubes
- 20 ounces okra, trimmed and chopped
- 2 (14-ounce) cans sugar-free diced tomatoes with liquid
- 2 bay leaves
- 1 teaspoon dried thyme, crushed
- 2 teaspoons red pepper flakes, crushed
- ¼ teaspoon hot pepper sauce
- Salt and ground black pepper, as required
- 32 ounces catfish fillets
- ½ cup fresh cilantro, chopped

INSTRUCTIONS:

1. In a large wok, melt the coconut oil over medium heat and sauté the onion, celery and bell pepper for about 4-5 minutes.
2. Meanwhile, in a large soup pan, mix together bouillon cubes and water and bring to a boil over medium heat.
3. Transfer the onion mixture and remaining ingredients except for catfish into the pan of boiling water and bring to a boil.
4. Reduce the heat to low and cook, covered for about 30 minutes.
5. Stir in catfish fillets and cook for about 10-15 minutes.
6. Stir in the cilantro and remove from the heat.
7. Serve hot.

NUTRITIONAL INFORMATION PER SERVING:

Calories: 261
Fat: 16.8g
Carbohydrates: 10g
Fiber: 3.3g
Sugar: 3.9g
Protein: 17.2g
Sodium: 373mg

SHRIMP STEW

Servings: 6
Preparation Time: 15 minutes
Cooking Time: 20 minutes

INGREDIENTS:

- ¼ cup olive oil
- ¼ cup yellow onion, chopped
- ¼ cup green bell pepper, seeded and chopped
- 1 garlic clove, minced
- 1½ pounds raw shrimp, peeled and deveined
- 1 (14-ounce) can diced tomatoes with chilies
- 1 cup unsweetened coconut milk
- 2 tablespoons Sriracha
- 2 tablespoons fresh lime juice
- Salt and ground black pepper, as required
- ¼ cup fresh cilantro, chopped

INSTRUCTIONS:

1. Heat oil in a pan over medium heat and sauté the onion for about 4 - 5 minutes.
2. Add the bell pepper and garlic and sauté for about 4-5 minutes.
3. Add the shrimp and tomatoes and cook for about 3-4 minutes.
4. Stir in the coconut milk and Sriracha and cook for about 4-5 minutes.
5. Stir in the lime juice, salt, and black pepper, and remove from the heat.
6. Garnish with cilantro and serve hot.

NUTRITIONAL INFORMATION PER SERVING:

Calories: 236
Fat: 11.1g
Carbohydrates: 6.7g
Fiber: 1.2g
Sugar: 2.2g
Protein: 26.6g
Sodium: 343mg

SALMON LETTUCE WRAPS

Servings: 2
Preparation Time: 10 minutes

INGREDIENTS:

- ¼ cup part-skim mozzarella cheese, cubed
- ¼ cup tomato, chopped
- 2 tablespoons fresh dill, chopped
- 1 teaspoon fresh lemon juice
- Salt, as required
- 4 lettuce leaves
- 1/3 pound cooked salmon, chopped

INSTRUCTIONS:

1. In a small bowl, combine mozzarella, tomato, dill, lemon juice, and salt until well combined.
2. Arrange the lettuce leaves onto serving plates.
3. Divide the salmon and tomato mixture over each lettuce leaf and serve immediately.

NUTRITIONAL INFORMATION PER SERVING:

Calories: 124
Fat: 5.5g
Carbohydrates: 3.1g
Fiber: 0.8g
Sugar: 0.7g
Protein: 16.6g
Sodium: 141mg

SPICY SALMON

Servings: 4
Preparation Time: 105 minutes
Cooking Time: 8 minutes

INGREDIENTS:

- 4 tablespoons extra-virgin olive oil, divided
- 2 tablespoons fresh lemon juice
- 1 teaspoon ground turmeric
- 1 teaspoon ground cumin
- Salt and ground black pepper, as required
- 4 (4-ounce) boneless, skinless salmon fillets
- 6 cups fresh arugula

INSTRUCTIONS:

1. In a bowl, mix together 2 tablespoons of oil, lemon juice, turmeric, cumin, salt and black pepper.
2. Add the salmon fillets and coat with the oil mixture generously. Set aside.
3. In a non-stick wok, heat the remaining oil over medium heat.
4. Place salmon fillets, skin-side down and cook for about 3-5 minutes.
5. Change the side and cook for about 2-3 minutes more.
6. Divide the salmon onto serving plates and serve immediately alongside the arugula.

NUTRITIONAL INFORMATION PER SERVING:

Calories:	283
Fat:	21.4g
Carbohydrates:	1.9g
Fiber:	0.7g
Sugar:	0.8g
Protein:	23g
Sodium: 99mg	

LEMONY SALMON

Servings: 4
Preparation Time: 10 minutes
Cooking Time: 14 minutes

INGREDIENTS:

- 2 garlic cloves, minced
- 1 tablespoon fresh lemon zest, grated
- 2 tablespoons olive oil
- 2 tablespoons fresh lemon juice
- Salt and ground black pepper, as required
- 4 (6-ounce) boneless, skinless salmon fillets
- 6 cups fresh spinach

INSTRUCTIONS:

1. Preheat the grill to medium-high heat.
2. Grease the grill grate.
3. In a bowl, place all ingredients except for salmon and spinach and mix well.
4. Add the salmon fillets and coat with garlic mixture generously.
5. Grill the salmon fillets for about 6-7 minutes per side.
6. Serve immediately alongside the spinach.

NUTRITIONAL INFORMATION PER SERVING:

Calories: 300
Fat: 17.8g
Carbohydrates: 2.6g
Fiber: 1.1g
Sugar: 0.5g
Protein: 34.5g
Sodium: 151mg

ZESTY SALMON

Servings: 4
Preparation Time: 10 minutes
Cooking Time: 10 minutes

INGREDIENTS:

- 1 tablespoon butter, melted
- 1 tablespoon fresh lemon juice
- 1 teaspoon Worcestershire sauce
- 1 teaspoon lemon zest, grated finely.
- 4 (6-ounce) salmon fillets
- Salt and ground black pepper, as required

INSTRUCTIONS:

1. In a baking dish, place butter, lemon juice, Worcestershire sauce, and lemon zest, and mix well.
2. Coat the fillets with mixture and then arrange skin side-up in the baking dish.
3. Set aside for about 15 minutes.
4. Preheat the broiler of oven.
5. Arrange the oven rack about 6-inch from the heating element.
6. Line a broiler pan with a piece of foil.
7. Remove the salmon fillets from baking dish and

season with salt and black pepper.

8. Arrange the salmon fillets onto the prepared broiler pan, skin side down.
9. Broil for about 8-10 minutes.
10. Serve hot.

NUTRITIONAL INFORMATION PER SERVING:

Calories: 260
Fat: 13.6g
Carbohydrates: 1.5g
Fiber: 0.5g
Sugar: 1g
Protein: 33.8g
Sodium: 157mg

STUFFED SALMON

Servings: 4
Preparation Time: 15 minutes
Cooking Time: 16 minutes

INGREDIENTS:

For Salmon:

- 4 (6-ounce) skinless salmon fillets
- Salt and ground black pepper, as required
- 2 tablespoons fresh lemon juice
- 2 tablespoons olive oil, divided
- 1 tablespoon unsalted butter
- **For Filling**:
- 4 ounces low-fat cream cheese, softened
- ¼ cup low-fat Parmesan cheese, grated finely
- 4 ounces frozen spinach, thawed and squeezed
- 2 teaspoons garlic, minced
- Salt and ground black pepper, as required

INSTRUCTIONS:

1. Season each salmon fillet with salt and black pepper and then drizzle with lemon juice and 1 tablespoon of oil.
2. Arrange the salmon fillets onto a smooth surface.
3. With a sharp knife, cut a pocket into each salmon fillet about ¾ of the way through, being careful not to cut all the way.
4. For filling: in a bowl, add the cream cheese, Parmesan cheese, spinach, garlic, salt and black pepper and mix well.
5. Place about 1-2 tablespoons of spinach mixture into each salmon pocket and spread evenly.
6. In a wok, heat the remaining oil and butter over medium-high heat and cook the salmon fillets for about 6-8 minutes per side.
7. Remove the salmon fillets from heat and transfer onto the serving plates.
8. Serve immediately.

NUTRITIONAL INFORMATION PER SERVING:

Calories: 400
Fat: 28.8g
Carbohydrates: 2.5g
Fiber: 0.7g
Sugar: 0.4g
Protein: 37.4g
Sodium: 317mg

SALMON WITH ASPARAGUS

Servings: 6
Preparation Time: 10 minutes
Cooking Time: 20 minutes

INGREDIENTS:

- 6 (4-ounce) salmon fillets
- 2 tablespoons extra-virgin olive oil
- 3 tablespoons fresh parsley, minced
- ¼ teaspoon ginger powder
- Salt and freshly ground black pepper, as required
- 1½ pounds fresh asparagus

INSTRUCTIONS:

1. Preheat your oven to 400 degrees.
2. Grease a large baking dish.
3. In a bowl, place all ingredients and mix well.
4. Arrange the salmon fillets into the prepared baking dish in a single layer.
5. Bake for approximately 15-20 minutes or until desired doneness of salmon.
6. Meanwhile, in a pan of boiling water, add asparagus and cook for about 4-5 minutes.
7. Drain the asparagus well.
8. Divide the asparagus onto serving plates evenly.
9. Top each plate with 1 salmon fillet and serve.

NUTRITIONAL INFORMATION PER SERVING:

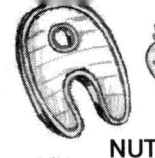

Calories: 214
Fat: 11.8g
Carbohydrates: 4.6g
Fiber: 2.5g
Sugar: 2.2g
Protein: 24.6g
Sodium: 80mg

SALMON PARCEL

Servings: 6
Preparation Time: 15 minutes
Cooking Time: 20 minutes

INGREDIENTS:

- 6 (4-ounce) salmon fillets
- Salt and freshly ground black pepper, as required
- 1 yellow bell pepper, seeded and cubed
- 1 red bell pepper, seeded and cubed
- 4 plum tomatoes, cubed
- 1 small onion, sliced thinly
- ½ cup fresh parsley, chopped
- ¼ cup extra-virgin olive oil
- 2 tablespoons fresh lemon juice

INSTRUCTIONS:

1. Preheat your oven to 400 degrees F.
2. Arrange 6 pieces of foil onto a smooth surface.
3. Place 1 salmon fillet on each piece of foil and sprinkle with salt and black pepper.
4. In a bowl, mix together bell peppers, tomato and onion.
5. Place veggie mixture over each fillet evenly and top with parsley and capers evenly.
6. Drizzle with oil and lemon juice.
7. Fold each piece of foil around salmon mixture to seal it.
8. Arrange the foil packets onto a large baking sheet in a single layer.
9. Bake for approximately 25 minutes.
10. Remove from the oven and place the foil packets onto serving plates.
11. Carefully unwrap each foil packet and serve.

NUTRITIONAL INFORMATION PER SERVING:

Calories: 261
Fat: 15.8g
Carbohydrates: 8g
Fiber: 1.9g
Sugar: 5g
Protein: 23.7g
Sodium: 93mg

SALMON WITH CAULIFLOWER MASH

Servings: 4
Preparation Time: 15 minutes
Cooking Time: 20 minutes

INGREDIENTS:

For Cauliflower Mash:

- 1-pound cauliflower, cut into florets
- 1 tablespoon extra-virgin olive oil
- 3 garlic cloves, minced
- 1 teaspoon fresh thyme leaves
- Salt and freshly ground black pepper, as required

For Salmon:

- 1 (1-inch) piece fresh ginger, grated finely
- 1 tablespoon honey
- 1 tablespoon fresh lemon juice
- 1 tablespoon Dijon mustard
- 2 tablespoons olive oil
- 4 (6-ounce) salmon fillets
- 2 tablespoons fresh parsley, chopped

INSTRUCTIONS:

1. For mash: in a large saucepan of water, arrange a steamer basket and bring to a boil.
2. Place the cauliflower florets in the steamer basket and steam, covered for about 10 minutes.
3. Drain the cauliflower and set aside.
4. In a small frying pan, heat the oil over medium heat and sauté the garlic for about 2 minutes.
5. Remove the frying pan from heat and transfer the garlic oil in a large food processor.
6. Add the cauliflower, thyme, salt and black pepper and pulse until smooth.
7. Transfer the cauliflower mash into a bowl and set aside.
8. Meanwhile, in a bowl, mix together ginger, honey, lemon juice and Dijon mustard. Set aside.
9. In a large non-stick wok, heat olive oil over medium-high heat and cook the salmon fillets for about 3-4 minutes per side.

10. Stir in honey mixture and immediately remove from heat.
11. Divide warm cauliflower mash onto serving plates.
12. Top each plate with 1 salmon fillet and serve.

NUTRITIONAL INFORMATION PER SERVING:

Calories: 308
Fat: 14.4g
Carbohydrates: 11g
Fiber: 3.2g
Sugar: 6g
Protein: 35.7g
Sodium: 195mg

SALMON WITH SALSA

Servings: 4
Preparation Time: 15 minutes
Cooking Time: 8 minutes

INGREDIENTS:

For Salsa:

- 2 large ripe avocados, peeled, pitted and cut into small chunks
- 1 small tomato, chopped
- 2 tablespoons red onion, chopped finely
- ¼ cup fresh cilantro, chopped finely
- 1 tablespoon jalapeño pepper, seeded and minced finely
- 1 garlic clove, minced finely
- 3 tablespoons fresh lime juice
- Salt and ground black pepper, as required

For Salmon:

- 4 (5-ounce) (1-inch thick) salmon fillets
- Sea salt and ground black pepper, as required
- 3 tablespoons olive oil
- 1 tablespoon fresh rosemary leaves, chopped
- 1 tablespoon fresh lemon juice

INSTRUCTIONS:

1. For salsa: add all ingredients in a bowl and gently stir to combine.
2. With a plastic wrap, cover the bowl and refrigerate before serving.
3. For salmon: season each salmon fillet with salt and black pepper generously.
4. In a large wok, heat the oil over medium-high heat.
5. Place the salmon fillets, skins side up and cook for about 4 minutes.
6. Carefully change the side of each salmon fillet and cook for about 4 minutes more.
7. Stir in the rosemary and lemon juice and remove from the heat.
8. Divide the salsa onto serving plates evenly.
9. To each plate with 1 salmon fillet and serve.

NUTRITIONAL INFORMATION PER SERVING:

Calories: 450
Fat: 30g
Carbohydrates: 12g
Fiber: 9g
Sugar: 4g
Protein: 31.3g
Sodium: 100mg

WALNUT CRUSTED SALMON

Servings: 2
Preparation Time: 15 minutes
Cooking Time: 20 minutes

INGREDIENTS:

- ½ cup walnuts
- 1 tablespoon fresh dill, chopped
- 2 tablespoons fresh lemon rind, grated
- Salt and ground black pepper, as required
- 1 tablespoon coconut oil, melted
- 3-4 tablespoons Dijon mustard
- 4 (3-ounce) salmon fillets
- 4 teaspoons fresh lemon juice
- 3 cups fresh baby spinach

INSTRUCTIONS:

1. Preheat your oven to 350 degrees F.
2. Line a large baking sheet with parchment paper.
3. Place the walnuts in a food processor and pulse until chopped roughly.
4. Add the dill, lemon rind, garlic salt, black pepper, and butter, and pulse until a crumbly mixture forms.
5. Place the salmon fillets onto the prepared baking sheet in a single layer, skin-side down.
6. Coat the top of each salmon fillet with Dijon mustard.
7. Place the walnut mixture over each fillet and gently press into the surface of salmon.

8. Bake for approximately 15–20 minutes.
9. Remove the salmon fillets from oven and transfer onto the serving plates.
10. Drizzle with the lemon juice and serve alongside the spinach.

NUTRITIONAL INFORMATION PER SERVING:

Calories: 366
Fat: 23.2g
Carbohydrates: 6.2g
Fiber: 2.9g
Sugar: 1.1g
Protein: 36.9g
Sodium: 460mg

GARLICKY TILAPIA

Servings: 4
Preparation Time: 10 minutes
Cooking Time: 5 minutes

INGREDIENTS:

- 2 tablespoons olive oil
- 4 (5-ounce) tilapia fillets
- 3 garlic cloves, minced
- 1 tablespoon fresh ginger, minced
- 2-3 tablespoons low-sodium chicken broth
- Salt and ground black pepper, as required
- 6 cups fresh baby spinach

INSTRUCTIONS:

1. In a large sauté pan, heat the oil over medium heat and cook the tilapia fillets for about 3 minutes.
2. Flip the side and stir in the garlic and ginger.
3. Cook for about 1-2 minutes.
4. Add the broth and cook for about 2-3 more minutes.
5. Stir in salt and black pepper and remove from heat.
6. Serve hot alongside the spinach.

NUTRITIONAL INFORMATION PER SERVING:

Calories: 196
Fat: 8.6g
Carbohydrates: 3.4g
Fiber: 1.2g
Sugar: 0.3g
Protein: 2g
Sodium: 127mg

TILAPIA PICCATA

Servings: 4
Preparation Time: 15 minutes
Cooking Time: 8 minutes

INGREDIENTS:

- 3 tablespoons fresh lemon juice
- 2 tablespoons olive oil
- 2 garlic cloves, minced
- ½ teaspoon lemon zest, grated
- 2 teaspoons capers, drained
- 2 tablespoons fresh basil, minced
- 4 (6-ounce) tilapia fillets
- Salt and ground black pepper, as required
- 6 cups fresh baby kale

INSTRUCTIONS:

1. Preheat the broiler of the oven.
2. Arrange an oven rack about 4-inch from the heating element.
3. Grease a broiler pan.
4. In a small bowl, add the lemon juice, oil, garlic and lemon zest and beat until well combined.
5. Add the capers and basil and stir to combine.
6. Reserve 2 tablespoons of mixture in a small bowl.
7. Coat the fish fillets with remaining capers mixture and sprinkle with salt and black pepper.
8. Place the tilapia fillets onto the broiler pan and broil for about 3-4 minutes side.
9. Remove from the oven and place the fish fillets onto serving plates.
10. Drizzle with reserved capers mixture and serve alongside the kale.

NUTRITIONAL INFORMATION PER SERVING:

Calories: 240
Fat: 9.1g
Carbohydrates: 7g
Fiber: 1.7g
Sugar: 0.3g
Protein: 34.2g
Sodium: 170mg

COD IN DILL SAUCE

Servings: 2
Preparation Time: 10 minutes
Cooking Time: 13 minutes

INGREDIENTS:

- 2 (6-ounce) cod fillets
- 1 teaspoon onion powder
- Salt and ground black pepper, as required
- 3 tablespoons butter, divided
- 2 garlic cloves, minced
- 1-2 lemon slices
- 2 teaspoons fresh dill weed
- 3 cups fresh spinach, torn

INSTRUCTIONS:

1. Season each cod fillet evenly with onion powder, salt and black pepper.
2. In a medium wok, heat 1 tablespoon of oil over high heat and cook the cod fillets for about 4-5 minutes per side.
3. Transfer the cod fillets onto a plate.
4. Meanwhile, in a frying pan, heat the remaining oil over low heat and sauté the garlic and lemon slices for about 40-60 seconds.
5. Stir in the cooked cod fillets and dill and cook, covered for about 1-2 minutes.
6. Remove the cod fillets from heat and transfer onto the serving plates.
7. Top with the pan sauce and serve immediately alongside the spinach.

NUTRITIONAL INFORMATION PER SERVING:

Calories: 311
Fat: 19.1g
Carbohydrates: 4.2g
Fiber: 1.3g
Sugar: 0.7g
Protein: 32.4g
Sodium: 345mg

COD & VEGGIES BAKE

Servings: 4
Preparation Time: 15 minutes
Cooking Time: 20 minutes

INGREDIENTS:

- 1 teaspoon olive oil
- ½ cup onion, minced
- 1 cup zucchini, chopped
- 1 garlic clove, minced
- 2 tablespoons fresh basil, chopped
- 2 cups fresh tomatoes, chopped
- Salt and ground black pepper, as required
- 4 (6-ounce) cod steaks
- 1/3 cup feta cheese, crumbled

INSTRUCTIONS:

1. Preheat your oven to 450 degrees F.
2. Grease a large shallow baking dish.
3. In a wok, heat oil over medium heat and sauté the onion, zucchini and garlic for about 4-5 minutes.
4. Stir in the basil, tomatoes, salt and black pepper and immediately remove from heat.
5. Place the cod steaks into prepared baking dish in a single layer and top with tomato mixture evenly.
6. Sprinkle with the cheese evenly.
7. Bake for approximately 15 minutes or until desired doneness.
8. Serve hot.

NUTRITIONAL INFORMATION PER SERVING:

Calories: 208
Fat: 5.6g
Carbohydrates: 6.6g
Fiber: 1.7g
Sugar: 4g
Protein: 33.5g
Sodium: 293mg

COD & VEGGIE PIZZA

Servings: 3
Preparation Time: 20 minutes
Cooking Time: 1 hour

INGREDIENTS:

For Base:

- Olive oil cooking spray
- ¼ cup oat flour
- 2 teaspoons dried rosemary, crushed
- Freshly ground black pepper, as required
- 4 egg whites
- 2½ teaspoons olive oil
- ½ cup low-fat Parmesan cheese, grated freshly
- 2 cups zucchini, grated and squeezed

For Topping:

- 1 cup tomato paste
- 1 teaspoon fresh rosemary, minced
- 1 teaspoon fresh basil, minced
- Freshly ground black pepper, as required
- 4 cups fresh mushrooms, chopped
- 1 tomato, chopped
- 3 ounces boneless cod fillet, chopped
- 1½ cups onion, sliced into rings
- 1 red bell pepper, seeded and chopped

- 1 green bell pepper, seeded and chopped
- 1/3 cup low-fat mozzarella, shredded

INSTRUCTIONS:

1. Preheat your oven to 400 degrees F.
2. Grease a pie dish with cooking spray.
3. For base: in a large bowl, add all the ingredients and mix until well combined.
4. Transfer the mixture into the prepared pie dish and press to smooth the surface.
5. Bake for approximately 40 minutes.
6. Remove from the oven and set aside to cool for at least 15 minutes.
7. Carefully turn out the crust onto a baking sheet.
8. For topping: in s bowl, add tomato paste, herbs and black pepper.
9. Spread tomato sauce mixture over crust evenly.
10. Arrange the vegetables over tomato sauce, followed by the cheese.
11. Bake for about 20 minutes or until cheese is melted.
1. Serve hot.

NUTRITIONAL INFORMATION PER SERVING:

Calories: 340
Fat: 10g
Carbohydrates: 20g
Fiber: 8.7g
Sugar: 10g
Protein: 30.88g
Sodium: 462mg

GARLICKY HADDOCK

Servings: 2
Preparation Time: 10 minutes
Cooking Time: 11 minutes

INGREDIENTS:

- 2 tablespoons olive oil, divided
- 4 garlic cloves, minced and divided
- 1 teaspoon fresh ginger, grated finely
- 2 (4-ounce) haddock fillets
- Salt and freshly ground black pepper, as required
- 3 C. fresh baby spinach

INSTRUCTIONS:

1. In a wok, heat 1 tablespoon of oil over medium heat and sauté 2 garlic cloves and ginger for about 1 minute.
2. Add the haddock fillets, salt and black pepper and cook for about 3-5 minutes per side or until desired doneness.
3. Meanwhile, in another wok, heat remaining oil over medium heat and heat and sauté remaining garlic for about 1 minute.
4. Add the spinach, salt and black pepper and cook for about 4-5 minutes.
5. Divide the spinach onto serving plates and top each with 1 haddock fillet.
6. Serve immediately.

NUTRITIONAL INFORMATION PER SERVING:

Calories: 340
Fat: 10g
Carbohydrates: 20g
Fiber: 8.7g
Sugar: 10g
Protein: 30.88g
Sodium: 462mg

HADDOCK IN PARSLEY SAUCE

Servings: 2
Preparation Time: 10 minutes
Cooking Time: 9 minutes

INGREDIENTS:

- 2 (5-ounce) haddock fillets
- Salt and ground black pepper, as required
- 2 tablespoons olive oil
- 1 tablespoon fresh parsley, chopped
- 1 tablespoon fresh lime juice
- 3 cups fresh arugula

INSTRUCTIONS:

1. In a large wok, heat the oil over medium-high heat.
2. Place the haddock fillets, skins side up and cook for about 4 minutes.
3. Carefully change the side of each fillet and cook for about 4 minutes more.
4. Stir in the parsley and lime juice and remove from the heat.
5. Serve hot alongside the arugula.

NUTRITIONAL INFORMATION PER SERVING:

Calories: 288
Fat: 15.5g
Carbohydrates: 1.3g
Fiber: 0.5g
Sugar: 0.6g
Protein: 35.2g
Sodium: 210mg

HALIBUT WITH ZUCCHINI

Servings: 4
Preparation Time: 15 minutes
Cooking Time: 20 minutes

INGREDIENTS:

- 1 teaspoon olive oil
- ½ cup yellow onion, minced
- 1 cup zucchini, chopped
- 2 garlic cloves, minced
- 2 tablespoons fresh basil, chopped
- 2 cups fresh tomatoes, chopped
- Salt and freshly ground black pepper, as required
- 4 (6-ounce) halibut steaks
- 1/3 cup feta cheese, crumbled

INSTRUCTIONS:

1. Preheat your oven to 450 degrees F.
2. Grease a large shallow baking dish.
3. In a wok, heat the oil over medium heat and sauté the onion, zucchini and garlic for about 4-5 minutes.
4. Stir in the basil, tomatoes and black pepper and immediately remove from heat.
5. Place the halibut steaks into the prepared baking dish in a single layer.
6. Top with the tomato mixture evenly and sprinkle with cheese evenly.
7. Bake for approximately 15 minutes or until desired doneness.
8. Serve hot.

NUTRITIONAL INFORMATION PER SERVING:

Calories: 261
Fat: 8.1g
Carbohydrates: 6.8g
Fiber: 1.8g
Sugar: 4g
Protein: 39g
Sodium: 276mg

ROASTED MACKEREL

Servings: 2
Preparation Time: 10 minutes
Cooking Time: 20 minutes

INGREDIENTS:

- 2 (7-ounce) mackerel fillets
- 1 tablespoon olive oil
- Salt and ground black pepper, as required
- 3 cups fresh baby greens

INSTRUCTIONS:

1. Preheat your oven to 350 degrees F.
2. Arrange a rack in the middle of oven.
3. Lightly grease a baking dish.
4. Brush the fish fillets with melted butter and then season with salt and black pepper.
5. Arrange the fish fillets into the prepared baking dish in a single layer.
6. Bake for approximately 20 minutes.
7. Serve hot alongside the greens.

NUTRITIONAL INFORMATION PER SERVING:

Calories: 400
Fat: 30g
Carbohydrates: 1g
Fiber: 0.5g
Sugar: 0.5g
Protein: 25.9g
Sodium: 685mg

HERBED SEA BASS

Servings: 2
Preparation Time: 10 minutes
Cooking Time: 20 minutes

INGREDIENTS:

- 2 (1¼-pound) whole sea bass, gutted, gilled, scaled and fins removed
- Salt and ground black pepper, as required
- 6 fresh bay leaves
- 2 fresh thyme sprigs
- 2 fresh parsley sprigs
- 2 fresh rosemary sprigs
- 2 tablespoons butter, melted
- 2 tablespoons fresh lemon juice
- 3 cups fresh arugula

INSTRUCTIONS:

1. Season the cavity and outer side of each fish with salt and black pepper evenly.
2. With a plastic wrap, cover each fish and refrigerate for 1 hour.
3. Preheat your oven to 450 degrees F.
4. Lightly grease a baking dish.
5. Arrange 2 bay leaves in the bottom of the prepared baking dish.
6. Divide herb sprigs and remaining bay leaves inside the cavity of each fish.
7. Arrange both fish over bay leave in the baking dish and drizzle with butter.
8. Roast for about 15-20 minutes or until fish is cooked through.
9. Remove the baking dish from oven and place the fish onto a platter.

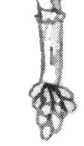

10. Drizzle the fish with lemon juice and serve alongside the arugula.

NUTRITIONAL INFORMATION PER SERVING:

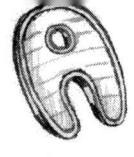

Calories: 331
Fat: 12.2g
Carbohydrates: 0.7g
Fiber: 0.3g
Sugar: 0.5g
Protein: 53g
Sodium: 234mg

LEMONY TROUT

Servings: 4
Preparation Time: 15 minutes
Cooking Time: 25 minutes

INGREDIENTS:

- 2 (1½-pound) wild-caught trout, gutted and cleaned
- Salt and ground black pepper, as required
- 1 lemon, sliced
- 2 tablespoons fresh dill, minced
- 2 tablespoons butter, melted
- 2 tablespoons fresh lemon juice

INSTRUCTIONS:

1. Preheat your oven to 475 degrees F.
2. Arrange a wire rack onto a foil-lined baking sheet.
3. Sprinkle the trout with salt and black pepper from inside and outside generously.
4. Fill the cavity of each fish with lemon slices and dill.
5. Place the trout onto the prepared baking sheet and drizzle with the melted butter and lemon juice.
6. Bake for approximately 25 minutes.
7. Remove the baking sheet from oven and transfer the trout onto a serving platter.
8. Serve hot.

NUTRITIONAL INFORMATION PER SERVING:

Calories: 480
Fat: 22.2g
Carbohydrates: 1g
Fiber: 2.4g
Sugar: 0.2g
Protein: 70.2g
Sodium: 204mg

TUNA BURGERS

Servings: 2
Preparation Time: 15 minutes
Cooking Time: 6 minutes

INGREDIENTS:

- 1 (15-ounce) can water-packed tuna, drained
- ½ celery stalk, chopped
- 2 tablespoons fresh parsley, chopped
- 1 teaspoon fresh dill, chopped
- 2 tablespoon walnuts, chopped
- 2 tablespoons mayonnaise
- 1 egg, beaten
- 1 tablespoon butter
- 3 cups lettuce

INSTRUCTIONS:

1. *For Burgers:* add all ingredients except the butter and lettuce in a bowl and mix until well combined.
2. Make 2 equal-sized patties from mixture.
3. In a frying pan, melt butter over medium heat and cook the patties for about 2-3 minutes.
4. Carefully flip the side and cook for about 2-3 minutes.
5. Divide the lettuce onto serving plates.
6. Top each plate with 1 burger and serve.

NUTRITIONAL INFORMATION PER SERVING:

Calories: 400
Fat: 18g
Carbohydrates: 7g
Fiber: 1.3g
Sugar: 2g
Protein: 59.7g
Sodium: 294mg

TUNA STUFFED AVOCADO

Servings: 2
Preparation Time: 15 minutes

INGREDIENTS:

- 1 large avocado, halved and pitted
- 1 tablespoon onion, chopped finely
- 2 tablespoons fresh lemon juice
- 5 ounces cooked tuna, chopped
- Salt and ground black pepper, as required

INSTRUCTIONS:

1. With a spoon, scoop out the flesh from the middle of each avocado half and transfer into a bowl.
2. Add the onion and lemon juice and mash until well combined.
3. Add tuna, salt and black pepper and stir to combine.
4. Divide the tuna mixture in both avocado halves evenly and serve immediately.

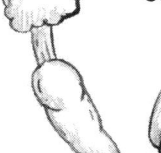

NUTRITIONAL INFORMATION PER SERVING:

Calories: 311
Fat: 22.4g
Carbohydrates: 8.1g
Fiber: 5g
Sugar: 1g
Protein: 20.6g
Sodium: 121mg

FISH & SPINACH CURRY

Servings: 4
Preparation Time: 15 minutes
Cooking Time: 15 minutes

INGREDIENTS:

- 1 tablespoon coconut oil
- 1 small yellow onion, chopped
- 2 garlic cloves, minced
- 1 teaspoon fresh ginger, minced
- 1 large tomato, peeled and chopped
- 1 tablespoon curry powder
- ¼ cup water
- 1¼ cups unsweetened coconut milk
- 1-pound skinless grouper fillets, cubed into 2-inch size
- ¾ pound fresh spinach, chopped
- Salt, as required
- 2 tablespoons fresh parsley, chopped

INSTRUCTIONS:

1. In a large wok, melt the coconut oil over medium heat and sauté the onion, garlic and ginger for about 5 minutes.
2. Add the tomatoes and curry powder and cook for about 2-3 minutes, crushing with the back of spoon.
3. Add the water and coconut milk and bring to a gentle boil.
4. Stir in grouper pieces and spinach and cook for about 4-5 minutes.
5. Stir in the salt and parsley and serve hot.

NUTRITIONAL INFORMATION PER SERVING:

Calories: 229
Fat: 7g
Carbohydrates: 8g
Fiber: 3.7g
Sugar: 2.4g
Protein: 31.6g
Sodium: 172mg

CRAB CAKES

Servings: 4
Preparation Time: 15 minutes
Cooking Time: 28 minutes

INGREDIENTS:

For Crab Cakes:

- 2 tablespoons olive oil, divided
- ½ cup onion, chopped finely
- 3 tablespoons blanched almond flour
- ¼ cup egg whites
- 2 tablespoons mayonnaise
- 1 tablespoon dried parsley, crushed
- 1 teaspoon yellow mustard
- 1 teaspoon Worcestershire sauce
- 1 tablespoon Old Bay seasoning
- Salt and ground black pepper, as required
- 1-pound lump crabmeat, drained

For Salad:

- 5 cups fresh baby arugula
- 2 tomatoes, chopped
- 2 tablespoons olive oil
- Salt and ground black pepper, as required

INSTRUCTIONS:

1. *For crab cakes:* Heat 2 teaspoons of olive oil in a wok over medium heat and sauté onion for about 8-10 minutes.
2. Remove the frying pan from heat and set aside to cool slightly.
3. Place cooked onion and remaining ingredients except for crabmeat in a mixing bowl and mix until well combined.
4. Add the crabmeat and gently stir to combine.
5. Make 8 equal-sized patties from mixture.
6. Arrange the patties onto a foil-lined tray and refrigerate for about 30 minutes.
7. In a large frying pan, heat the remaining oil over medium-low heat and cook patties in 2 batches for about 3-4 minutes per side or until desired doneness.
8. *For Salad:* In a bowl, add all ingredients, and toss to coat well.
9. Divide salad onto serving plates and to each with 2 patties.
10. Serve immediately.

NUTRITIONAL INFORMATION PER SERVING:

Calories: 314
Fat: 31.4g
Carbohydrates: 7.9g
Fiber: 2.1g
Sugar: 3.3g
Protein: 19.6g
Sodium: 999mg

SHRIMP LETTUCE WRAPS

Servings: 4
Preparation Time: 15 minutes
Cooking Time: 25 minutes

INGREDIENTS:

- 1 teaspoon extra-virgin olive oil
- 1 garlic clove, minced
- 1½ pounds shrimp, peeled, deveined and chopped
- Salt, as required
- 8 large lettuce leaves
- 1 tablespoon fresh chives, minced

INSTRUCTIONS:

1. In a large sauté pan, heat the olive oil over medium heat and sauté garlic for about 1 minute.
2. Add the shrimp and cook for about 3-4 minutes.
3. Remove from heat and set aside to cool slightly.
4. Arrange lettuce leaves onto serving plates.
5. Divide the shrimp over the leaves evenly.
6. Garnish with chives and serve immediately.

NUTRITIONAL INFORMATION PER SERVING:

Calories: 215
Fat: 4.4g
Carbohydrates: 3.2g
Fiber: 0.1g
Sugar: 6g
Protein: 38.9g
Sodium: 455mg

SHRIMP KABOBS

Servings: 3
Preparation Time: 15 minutes
Cooking Time: 8 minutes

INGREDIENTS:

- ¼ cup olive oil
- 2 tablespoons fresh lime juice
- ½ chipotle pepper in adobo sauce, seeded and minced
- 1 garlic cloves, minced
- 1½ teaspoons powdered Erythritol
- ½ teaspoon red chili powder
- ½ teaspoon paprika
- ¼ teaspoon ground cumin
- Salt and ground black pepper, as required
- 1 pound medium raw shrimp, peeled and deveined
- 5 cups fresh salad greens

INSTRUCTIONS:

1. In a bowl, add all the ingredients except the shrimp and greens and mix well.
2. Add the shrimp and coat with the herb mixture generously.
3. Refrigerate to marinate for at least 30 minutes.
4. Preheat the grill to medium-high heat.
5. Grease the grill grate.
6. Thread the shrimp onto the re soaked wooden skewers.
7. Place the skewers onto the grill and cook for about 3-4 minutes per side.
8. Remove from the grill and place onto a platter for about 5 minutes before serving.

NUTRITIONAL INFORMATION PER SERVING:

Calories: 323
Fat: 19.1g
Carbohydrates: 7g
Fiber: 3.3g
Sugar: 0.8g
Protein: 34g
Sodium: 434mg

SHRIMP WITH ZUCCHINI NOODLES

Servings: 4
Preparation Time: 20 minutes
Cooking Time: 8 minutes

INGREDIENTS:

- 2 tablespoons olive oil
- 1 garlic clove, minced
- ¼ teaspoon red pepper flakes, crushed
- 1-pound shrimp, peeled and deveined
- Salt and ground black pepper, as required
- 1/3 cup low-sodium chicken broth
- 2 medium zucchinis, spiralized with blade C
- 1 cup cherry tomatoes, quartered

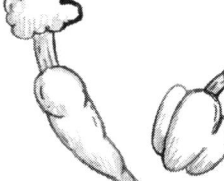

INSTRUCTIONS:

1. In a large non-stick wok, heat the olive oil over medium heat and sauté garlic and red pepper flakes for about 1 minute.
2. Add the shrimp, salt and black pepper and cook for about 1 minute per side.
3. Add the broth and zucchini noodles and cook for about 3-4 minutes.
4. Stir in the tomato quarters and remove from the heat.
5. Serve hot.

NUTRITIONAL INFORMATION PER SERVING:

Calories: 221
Fat: 9.2g
Carbohydrates: 7.2g
Fiber: 1.7g
Sugar: 2.9g
Protein: 27.7g
Sodium: 295mg

SHRIMP WITH SPINACH

Servings: 4
Preparation Time: 15 minutes
Cooking Time: 9 minutes

INGREDIENTS:

- 3 tablespoons extra-virgin olive oil
- 1-pound medium shrimp, peeled and deveined
- 1 medium onion, chopped
- 2 garlic cloves, chopped finely
- 1 fresh red chili, sliced
- 1-pound fresh spinach, chopped
- ¼ cup low-sodium chicken broth

INSTRUCTIONS:

1. In a large non-stick wok, heat 1 tablespoon of the oil over medium-high heat and cook the shrimp for about 2 minutes per side.
2. With a slotted spoon, transfer the shrimp onto a plate.
3. In the same wok, heat the remaining 2 tablespoons of oil over medium heat and sauté the garlic and red chili for about 1 minute.
4. Add the spinach and broth and cook for about 2-3 minutes, stirring occasionally.
5. Stir in the cooked shrimp and cook for about 1 minute.
6. Serve hot.

NUTRITIONAL INFORMATION PER SERVING:

Calories: 265
Fat: 12.9g
Carbohydrates: 9g
Fiber: 3g
Sugar: 1.7g
Protein: 29.6g
Sodium: 372mg

SHRIMP WITH BROCCOLI & CARROT

Servings: 5
Preparation Time: 15 minutes
Cooking Time: 8 minutes

INGREDIENTS:

For Sauce:

- 1 tablespoon fresh ginger, grated
- 2 garlic cloves, minced
- 3 tablespoons low-sodium soy sauce
- 1 tablespoon balsamic vinegar
- 1 teaspoon Erythritol
- ¼ teaspoon red pepper flakes, crushed

For Shrimp Mixture:

- 3 tablespoons olive oil
- 1½ pounds medium shrimp, peeled and deveined
- 12 ounces broccoli florets
- 8 ounces, carrot, peeled and sliced

INSTRUCTIONS:

1. For sauce: in a bowl, place all the ingredients and beat until well combined. Set aside.
2. In a large wok, heat oil over medium-high heat and cook the shrimp for about 2 minutes, stirring occasionally.
3. Add the broccoli and carrot and cook for about 3-4 minutes, stirring frequently.
4. Stir in the sauce mixture and cook for about 1-2 minutes.
5. Serve immediately.

NUTRITIONAL INFORMATION PER SERVING:

Calories: 251
Fat: 9.1g
Carbohydrates: 6.4g
Fiber: 2g
Sugar: 1.8g
Protein: 38.2g
Sodium: 927mg

SHRIMP, SPINACH & TOMATO CASSEROLE

Servings: 6
Preparation Time: 15 minutes
Cooking Time: 25 minutes

INGREDIENTS:

- 2 tablespoons extra-virgin olive oil
- 1 tablespoon garlic, minced
- 1½ pounds large shrimp, peeled and deveined
- ¾ teaspoon dried oregano, crushed
- ½ teaspoon red pepper flakes, crushed
- ¼ cup fresh spinach, chopped finely
- ¾ cup low-sodium chicken broth
- 1 tablespoon fresh lemon juice
- 2 cups tomatoes, chopped
- 4 ounces feta cheese, crumbled

INSTRUCTIONS:

1. Preheat your oven to 350 degrees F.
2. In a large wok, heat the oil over medium-high heat and sauté the garlic for about 1 minute.
3. Add the shrimp, oregano and red pepper flakes and cook for about 4-5 minutes.
4. Stir in the spinach and salt and immediately remove from the heat.
5. Transfer the shrimp mixture into a casserole dish and spread in an even layer.
6. In the same wok, add the broth and lemon juice over medium heat and simmer for about 3-5 minutes or until reduces to half.
7. Stir in the tomatoes and cook for about 2-3 minutes.
8. Remove from the heat and place the tomato mixture over shrimp mixture evenly.
9. Top with feta cheese evenly.
10. Bake for approximately 15-20 minutes or until top becomes golden brown.
11. Serve hot.

NUTRITIONAL INFORMATION PER SERVING:

Calories: 198
Fat: 8.9g
Carbohydrates: 6g
Fiber: 0.9g
Sugar: 2.5g
Protein: 24.9g
Sodium: 366mg

PRAWNS WITH BELL PEPPER

Servings: 4
Preparation Time: 20 minutes
Cooking Time: 8 minutes

INGREDIENTS:

- 2 tablespoons olive oil
- 4 garlic cloves, minced
- 1 fresh red chili, sliced
- 1-pound prawns, peeled and deveined
- ½ cup green bell pepper, seeded and julienned
- ½ cup yellow bell pepper, seeded and julienned
- ½ cup red bell pepper, seeded and julienned
- ½ cup orange bell pepper, seeded and julienned
- ½ cup white onion, sliced thinly
- ¼ cup low-sodium chicken broth
- Salt and ground black pepper, as required

INSTRUCTIONS:

1. In a large non-stick wok, heat olive oil over medium heat and sauté the garlic and red chili for about 2 minutes.
2. Add the prawn, bell peppers, onion and black pepper and stir fry for about 5 minutes.
3. Stir in the broth and cook for about 1 minute.
4. Serve hot.

NUTRITIONAL INFORMATION PER SERVING:

Calories: 220
Fat: 9.1g
Carbohydrates: 7.6g
Fiber: 1.1g
Sugar: 3.6g
Protein: 26.7g
Sodium: 322mg

PRAWNS WITH BROCCOLI

Servings: 4
Preparation Time: 20 minutes
Cooking Time: 10 minutes

INGREDIENTS:

- 2 tablespoons olive oil, divided
- 1-pound large prawns, peeled and deveined
- ½ of onion, chopped
- 3 garlic cloves, minced
- 3 cups broccoli floret

- 2 tablespoons low-sodium soy sauce
- Freshly ground black pepper, as required
- 2 tablespoons fresh parsley, chopped

INSTRUCTIONS:

1. In a large non-stick wok, heat 1 tablespoon of olive oil over medium heat and stir fry the prawns for about 1 minute per side.
2. With a slotted spoon, transfer the prawns onto a plate.
3. In the same wok, heat the remaining oil over medium heat and sauté the onion and garlic for about 2-3 minutes.
4. Add the broccoli, soy sauce and black pepper and stir fry for about 2-3 minutes.
5. Stir in the cooked prawns and stir fry for about 1-2 minutes.
6. Serve hot.

NUTRITIONAL INFORMATION PER SERVING:

Calories: 230
Fat: 9.2g
Carbohydrates: 8.9g
Fiber: 2.2g
Sugar: 2.3g
Protein: 28.6g
Sodium: 741mg

PRAWNS WITH ASPARAGUS

Servings: 4
Preparation Time: 15 minutes
Cooking Time: 13 minutes

INGREDIENTS:

- 3 tablespoons extra-virgin olive oil
- 1-pound prawns, peeled and deveined
- 1-pound asparagus, trimmed
- Salt and ground black pepper, as required
- 1 teaspoon garlic, minced
- 1 teaspoon fresh ginger, minced
- 1 tablespoon low-sodium soy sauce
- 2 tablespoons lemon juice

INSTRUCTIONS:

1. In a wok, heat 2 tablespoons of oil over medium-high heat and cook the prawns with salt and black pepper for about 3-4 minutes.
2. With a slotted spoon, transfer the prawns into a bowl. Set aside.
3. In the same wok, heat remaining 1 tablespoon of oil over medium-high heat and cook the asparagus, ginger, garlic, salt and black pepper and for about 6-8 minutes, stirring frequently.
4. Stir in the prawns and soy sauce and cook for about 1 minute.
5. Stir in the lemon juice and remove from the heat.
6. Serve hot.

NUTRITIONAL INFORMATION PER SERVING:

Calories: 226
Fat: 12.1g
Carbohydrates: 5.4g
Fiber: 2.5g
Sugar: 2.6g
Protein: 27.2g
Sodium: 491mg

PRAWNS WITH KALE

Servings: 4
Preparation Time: 15 minutes
Cooking Time: 20 minutes

INGREDIENTS:

- 1-pound prawns, peeled and deveined
- Salt, as required
- 3 tablespoons extra-virgin olive oil, divided
- 1 red onion, chopped finely
- 1 fresh red chili, sliced
- 1-pound fresh kale, tough ribs removed and chopped
- 3 tablespoons low-sodium soy sauce
- 3 tablespoons fresh orange juice
- 1 tablespoon orange zest, grated finely
- ½ teaspoon red pepper flakes, crushed
- Ground black pepper, as required

INSTRUCTIONS:

1. Season the prawns with a little salt.
2. In a large non-stick sauté pan, heat 2 tablespoons of olive oil over high heat and stir-fry the prawns for about 2-3 minutes.
3. With a slotted spoon, transfer the prawns onto a plate.

4. In the same sauté pan, heat the remaining oil over medium heat and sauté the onion for about 4-5 minutes.
5. Add the kale and stir-fry for about 2-3 minutes.
6. With a lid, cover the pan and cook for about 2 minutes.
7. Add the soy sauce, orange juice, zest, red pepper flakes and black pepper and stir to combine well.
8. Stir in the cooked prawns and cook for about 2-3 minutes.
9. Serve hot.

NUTRITIONAL INFORMATION PER SERVING:

Calories: 277
Fat: 12.6g
Carbohydrates: 16g
Fiber: 3.3g
Sugar: 2.9g
Protein: 29.2g
Sodium: 961mg

SCALLOPS WITH BROCCOLI

Servings: 2
Preparation Time: 15 minutes
Cooking Time: 9 minutes

INGREDIENTS:

- 2 tablespoons olive oil
- 1 cup broccoli, cut into small pieces
- 1 garlic clove, crushed
- ½ pound scallops
- 1 teaspoon fresh lemon juice
- Salt, as required

INSTRUCTIONS:

1. In a large wok, heat the oil over medium heat and cook the broccoli and garlic for about 3-4 minutes, stirring occasionally.
2. Add in the scallops and cook for about 3-4 minutes, flipping occasionally.
3. Stir in the lemon juice and remove from the heat.
4. Serve hot.

NUTRITIONAL INFORMATION PER SERVING:

Calories: 238
Fat: 15g
Carbohydrates: 6.3g
Fiber: 1.2g
Sugar: 0.8g
Protein: 20.4g
Sodium: 276mg

SCALLOPS WITH ASPARAGUS

Servings: 5
Preparation Time: 15 minutes
Cooking Time: 10 minutes

INGREDIENTS:

- 2 tablespoons olive oil
- ¼ cup yellow onion, chopped
- 2 garlic cloves, minced
- 2 tablespoons fresh rosemary, minced
- 1-pound fresh asparagus, trimmed and cut into 1-inch pieces
- 2 teaspoons fresh lemon zest, grated
- 1½ pounds baby scallops
- Salt and ground black pepper, as required
- 2 tablespoons fresh lemon juice

INSTRUCTIONS:

1. In a large wok, heat the oil over medium-high heat and sauté the onion for about 2 minutes.
2. Add the garlic and rosemary and sauté for about 1 minute.
3. Add the asparagus and lemon zest and cook for about 1-2 minutes.
4. Add the scallops and stir to combine.
5. Immediately reduce the heat to medium and cook, covered for about 4-5 minutes, stirring occasionally.
6. Stir in lemon juice, salt and black pepper and remove from the heat.
7. Serve hot.

NUTRITIONAL INFORMATION PER SERVING:

Calories: 196
Fat: 7g
Carbohydrates: 8.8g
Fiber: 2.7g
Sugar: 2.1g
Protein: 25.1g
Sodium: 254mg

SCALLOPS WITH SPINACH

Servings: 5
Preparation Time: 15 minutes
Cooking Time: 21 minutes

INGREDIENTS:

- 1 tablespoon olive oil
- 1½ pounds jumbo sea scallops
- Salt and ground black pepper, as required
- 1 cup onion, chopped
- 6 garlic cloves, minced
- 14 ounces fresh baby spinach

INSTRUCTIONS:

1. In a large non-stick wok, heat the oil over medium-high heat and cook the scallops with salt and black pepper for about 5 minutes, turning once after 2½ minutes.
2. Transfer the scallops into another bowl and cover them with a piece of foil to keep warm.
3. In the same wok, add onion and garlic over medium heat and sauté the onion and garlic for about 3 minutes.
4. Add the spinach and cook for about 2-3 minutes.
5. Season with salt and black pepper and remove from the heat.
6. Divide the spinach onto serving plates.
7. Top with scallops and serve immediately.

NUTRITIONAL INFORMATION PER SERVING:

Calories: 177
Fat: 4.4g
Carbohydrates: 9g
Fiber: 2.3g
Sugar: 1.4g
Protein: 25.6g
Sodium: 312mg

SHRIMP & SCALLOPS WITH VEGGIES

Servings: 5
Preparation Time: 20 minutes
Cooking Time: 11 minutes

INGREDIENTS:

- 3 tablespoons olive oil, divided
- 1-pound fresh asparagus, cut into 2-inch pieces
- 2 red bell peppers, seeded and chopped
- ¾ pound medium raw shrimp, peeled and deveined
- ¾ pound raw scallops
- 1 tablespoon dried parsley
- ½ teaspoon garlic, minced
- Salt and freshly ground black pepper, as required

INSTRUCTIONS:

1. In a large wok, heat 1 tablespoon of oil over medium heat and stir-fry the asparagus and bell peppers for about 4-5 minutes.
2. With a slotted spoon, transfer the vegetables onto a plate.
3. In the same wok, heat the remaining oil over medium heat and stir-fry shrimp and scallops for about 2 minutes.
4. Stir in the parsley, garlic, salt, and black pepper, and cook for about 1 minute.
5. Add in the cooked vegetables and cook for about 2-3 minutes.
6. Serve hot.

NUTRITIONAL INFORMATION PER SERVING:

Calories: 230
Fat: 8.8g
Carbohydrates: 8.5g
Fiber: 2.8g
Sugar: 2.9g
Protein: 29.4g
Sodium: 359mg

VEGETARIAN RECIPES

AVOCADO TOAST

Servings: 4
Preparation Time: 15 minutes
Cooking Time: 4 minutes

INGREDIENTS:

- 1 large avocado, peeled, pitted and chopped roughly
- ¼ teaspoon fresh lemon juice
- Salt and ground black pepper, as required
- 4 whole-wheat bread slices
- 4 hard-boiled eggs, peeled and sliced

INSTRUCTIONS:

1. In a bowl, add the avocado and with a fork, mash roughly.
2. Add the lemon juice, salt and black pepper and stir to combine well and Set aside.
3. Heat a nonstick frying pan on medium-high heat and toast the slice for about 2 minutes per side.
4. Repeat with the remaining slices.
5. Spread the avocado mixture over each slice evenly.
6. Top each with egg slices and serve immediately.

NUTRITIONAL INFORMATION PER SERVING:

Calories: 206
Fat: 13.9g
Carbohydrates: 14g
Fiber: 4.5g
Sugar: 1.4g
Protein: 9.6g
Sodium: 224mg

BAKED EGGS

Servings: 6
Preparation Time: 10 minutes
Cooking Time: 9 minutes

INGREDIENTS:

- 2 cups fresh spinach, chopped finely
- 12 large eggs
- ½ cup heavy cream
- ¾ cup low-fat parmesan cheese, shredded
- Salt and ground black pepper, as required

INSTRUCTIONS:

1. Preheat your oven to 425 degrees F.
2. Grease a 12 cups muffin tin.
3. Divide spinach in each muffin cup.
4. Crack an egg over spinach into each cup and drizzle with heavy cream.
5. Sprinkle with salt and black pepper, followed by Parmesan cheese.
6. Bake for approximately 7-9 minutes or until desired doneness of eggs.
7. Serve immediately.

NUTRITIONAL INFORMATION PER SERVING:

Calories: 213
Fat: 16.2g
Carbohydrates: 1.6g
Fiber: 0.2g
Sugar: 0.8g
Protein: 15.6g
Sodium: 370mg

EGGS IN BELL PEPPER RINGS

Servings: 2
Preparation Time: 10 minutes
Cooking Time: 6 minutes

INGREDIENTS:

- 1 bell pepper, seeded and cut into 4 (¼-inch) rings
- 4 eggs
- Salt and ground black pepper, as required
- 1 tablespoon fresh parsley, chopped
- 1 tablespoon fresh chives, chopped

INSTRUCTIONS:

1. Heat a lightly greased nonstick wok over medium heat
2. Place 4 bell pepper rings in the wok and cook for about 2 minutes.
3. Carefully flip the rings.
4. Crack an egg in the middle of each bell pepper ring and sprinkle with salt and black pepper.
5. Cook for about 2-4 minutes or until desired doneness of eggs.
6. Carefully transfer the bell pepper rings ono serving plates and serve with the garnishing of parsley and chives.

NUTRITIONAL INFORMATION PER SERVING:

Calories: 139
Fat: 8.9g
Carbohydrates: 3.6g
Fiber: 1.1g
Sugar: 2.2g
Protein: 11.7g
Sodium: 327mg

EGGS IN AVOCADO HALVES

Servings: 2
Preparation Time: 10 minutes
Cooking Time: 15 minutes

INGREDIENTS:

- 1 avocado, halved and pitted
- 2 eggs
- Salt and ground black pepper, as required
- ¼ cup cherry tomatoes, halved
- 2 cups fresh baby spinach

INSTRUCTIONS:

1. Preheat your oven to 425 degrees F.
2. Carefully remove about 2 tablespoons of flesh from each avocado half.
3. Place avocado halves into a small baking dish.
4. Carefully crack an egg in each avocado half and sprinkle with salt and black pepper.
5. Bake for approximately 15 minutes or until desired doneness of the eggs.
6. Arrange 1 avocado half onto each serving plate and serve alongside the cherry tomatoes and spinach.

NUTRITIONAL INFORMATION PER SERVING:

Calories: 247
Fat: 21.1g
Carbohydrates: 9.6g
Fiber: 6.6g
Sugar: 1.5g
Protein: 8.2g
Sodium: 169mg

BROCCOLI WAFFLES

Servings: 2
Preparation Time: 10 minutes
Cooking Time: 8 minutes

INGREDIENTS:

- 1/3 cup broccoli, chopped finely
- ¼ cup low-fat cheddar cheese, shredded
- 1 egg
- ½ teaspoon garlic powder
- ½ teaspoon dried onion, minced
- Salt and ground black pepper, as required

INSTRUCTIONS:

1. Preheat a mini waffle iron and then grease it.
2. In a medium bowl, place all ingredients and mix until well combined.
3. Place ½ of the mixture into preheated waffle iron and cook for about 3-4 minutes or until golden brown.
4. Repeat with the remaining mixture.
5. Serve warm.

NUTRITIONAL INFORMATION PER SERVING:

Calories: 96
Fat: 6.9g
Carbohydrates: 2g
Fiber: 0.5g
Sugar: 0.7g
Protein: 6.8g
Sodium: 97mg

CHEESY SPINACH WAFFLES

Servings: 4
Preparation Time: 10 minutes
Cooking Time: 20 minutes

INGREDIENTS:

- 1 large egg, beaten
- 1 cup ricotta cheese, crumbled
- ½ cup part-skim mozzarella cheese, shredded
- ¼ cup low-fat Parmesan cheese, grated
- 4 ounces frozen spinach, thawed and squeezed dry
- 1 garlic clove, minced
- Salt and ground black pepper, as required

INSTRUCTIONS:

1. Preheat a mini waffle iron and then grease it.
2. In a bowl, add all the ingredients and beat until well combined.
3. Place ¼ of the mixture into preheated waffle iron and cook for about 4-5 minutes or until golden brown.
4. Repeat with the remaining mixture.
5. Serve warm.

NUTRITIONAL INFORMATION PER SERVING:

Calories: 138
Fat: 8.1g
Carbohydrates: 4.8g
Fiber: 0.6g
Sugar: 0.4g
Protein: 11.7g
Sodium: 273mg

KALE SCRAMBLE

Servings: 2
Preparation Time: 10 minutes
Cooking Time: 6 minutes

INGREDIENTS:

- 4 eggs
- 1/8 teaspoon ground turmeric
- 1/8 teaspoon red pepper flakes, crushed
- Salt and ground black pepper, as required
- 1 tablespoon water
- 2 teaspoons olive oil
- 1 cup fresh kale, tough ribs removed and chopped

INSTRUCTIONS:

1. In a bowl, add the eggs, turmeric, red pepper flakes, salt, black pepper and water and with a whisk, beat until foamy.
2. In a wok, heat the oil over medium heat
3. Add the egg mixture and stir to combine.
4. Immediately reduce the heat to medium-low and cook for about 1-2 minutes, stirring frequently.
5. Stir in the kale and cook for about 3-4 minutes, stirring frequently.
6. Remove from the heat and serve immediately.

NUTRITIONAL INFORMATION PER SERVING:

Calories: 183
Fat: 13.4g
Carbohydrates: 4.3g
Fiber: 0.5g
Sugar: 0.7g
Protein: 12.1g
Sodium: 216mg

TOMATO & EGG SCRAMBLE

Servings: 2
Preparation Time: 10 minutes
Cooking Time: 5 minutes

INGREDIENTS:

- 4 eggs
- ¼ teaspoon red pepper flakes, crushed
- Salt and ground black pepper, as required
- ¼ cup fresh basil, chopped
- ½ cup tomatoes, chopped
- 1 tablespoon olive oil

INSTRUCTIONS:

1. In a large bowl, add eggs, red pepper flakes, salt and black pepper and beat well.
2. Add the basil and tomatoes and stir to combine.
3. In a large non-stick wok, heat the oil over medium-high heat.
4. Add the egg mixture and cook for about 3-5 minutes, stirring continuously.
5. Serve immediately.

NUTRITIONAL INFORMATION PER SERVING:

Calories: 195
Fat: 15.9g
Carbohydrates: 2.6g
Fiber: 0.7g
Sugar: 1.9g
Protein: 11.6g
Sodium: 203mg

TOFU & SPINACH SCRAMBLE

Servings: 2
Preparation Time: 10 minutes
Cooking Time: 8 minutes

INGREDIENTS:

- 1 tablespoon olive oil
- 1 garlic clove, minced
- ¼ pound medium-firm tofu, drained, pressed and crumbled
- 1/3 cup low-sodium vegetable broth
- 2¾ cups fresh baby spinach
- 2 teaspoons low-sodium soy sauce
- 1 teaspoon ground turmeric
- 1 teaspoon fresh lemon juice

INSTRUCTIONS:

1. In a frying pan, heat the olive oil over medium-high heat and sauté the garlic for about 1 minute
2. Add the tofu and cook for about 2-3 minutes, slowly adding the broth.
3. Add the spinach, soy sauce and turmeric and stir fry for about 3-4 minutes or until all the liquid is absorbed
4. Stir in the lemon juice and remove from the heat.
5. Serve immediately.

NUTRITIONAL INFORMATION PER SERVING:

Calories: 134
Fat: 10.1g
Carbohydrates: 5.8g
Fiber: 2.7g
Sugar: 1.3g
Protein: 8.5g
Sodium: 497mg

TOFU & VEGGIE SCRAMBLE

Servings: 2
Preparation Time: 15 minutes
Cooking Time: 15 minutes

INGREDIENTS:

- ½ tablespoon olive oil
- 1 small onion, chopped finely
- 1 small red bell pepper, seeded and chopped finely
- 1 cup cherry tomatoes, chopped finely
- 1½ cups firm tofu, crumbled and chopped
- Pinch of cayenne pepper
- Pinch of ground turmeric
- Sea salt, as required

INSTRUCTIONS:

1. In a wok, heat oil over medium heat and sauté the onion and bell pepper for about 4-5 minutes.
2. Add the tomatoes and cook for about 1-2 minutes.
3. Add the tofu, turmeric, cayenne pepper and salt and cook for about 6-8 minutes.
4. Serve hot.

NUTRITIONAL INFORMATION PER SERVING:

Calories: 201
Fat: 11.7g
Carbohydrates: 11g
Fiber: 4.2g
Sugar: 5.9g
Protein: 17g
Sodium: 147mg

APPLE OMELET

Servings: 1
Preparation Time: 10 minutes
Cooking Time: 9 minutes

INGREDIENTS:

- 2 teaspoons olive oil, divided
- ½ of large green apple, cored and sliced thinly
- ¼ teaspoon ground cinnamon
- 1/8 teaspoon ground nutmeg
- 2 large eggs
- 1/8 teaspoon vanilla extract
- Pinch of salt

INSTRUCTIONS:

1. In a nonstick frying pan, heat 1 teaspoon of oil over medium-low heat
2. Add apple slices and sprinkle with nutmeg and cinnamon.
3. Cook for about 4-5 minutes, turning once halfway through.
4. Meanwhile, in a bowl, add eggs, vanilla extract and salt and beat until fluffy.
5. Add the remaining oil in the pan and let it heat completely.
6. Place the egg mixture over apple slices evenly and cook for about 3-4 minutes or until desired doneness.
7. Carefully turn the pan over a serving plate and immediately fold the omelet
8. Serve hot.

NUTRITIONAL INFORMATION PER SERVING:

Calories: 258
Fat: 19.5g
Carbohydrates: 9g
Fiber: 1.2g
Sugar: 7g
Protein: 12.8g
Sodium: 295mg

MUSHROOM & TOMATO OMELET

Servings: 2
Preparation Time: 15 minutes
Cooking Time: 36 minutes

INGREDIENTS:

- 2 poblano peppers
- Olive oil cooking spray
- 1 small tomato
- ½ teaspoon dried oregano
- ½ teaspoon chicken bouillon seasoning
- 4 eggs, separated
- 2 tablespoons sour cream
- ½ cup fresh white mushrooms, sliced
- 2/3 cup part-skim mozzarella cheese, shredded and divided

INSTRUCTIONS:

1. Preheat your oven to broiler.
2. Line a baking sheet with a piece of foil.
3. Spray the poblano peppers with cooking spray lightly.
4. Arrange the peppers onto the prepared baking sheet in a single layer and broil for about 5-10 minutes per side or until skin becomes dark ad blistered.
5. Remove from the oven and set aside to cool.

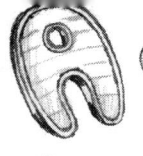

6. After cooking, remove the stems, skin and seeds from peppers and then cut each into thin strips.

7. Meanwhile, for sauce: with a knife, make 2 small slits in a crisscross pattern on the top of tomato.

8. In a microwave-safe plate, place the tomato and microwave on High for about 2-3 minutes.

9. In a blender, add the tomato, oregano and chicken bouillon seasoning and pulse until smooth.

10. Transfer the sauce into a bowl and set aside.

11. In a bowl, add the egg yolks and sour cream and beat until well combined.

12. In a clean glass bowl, add egg whites and with an electric mixer, beat until soft peaks form

13. Gently gold the egg yolk mixture into whipped egg whites

14. Heat a lightly greased wok over medium-low heat and cook half of the egg mixture cook for about 3-5 minutes or until bottom is set

15. Place half of the mushrooms and pepper strips over one half of omelet and sprinkle with half of the cheese

16. Cover the wok and cook for about 2-3 minutes

17. Uncover the wok and fold in the omelet

18. Transfer the omelet onto a plate

19. Repeat with the remaining egg mixture, mushrooms, pepper strips and cheese.

20. Top each omelet with sauce and serve.

NUTRITIONAL INFORMATION PER SERVING:

Calories: 209
Fat: 13.2g
Carbohydrates: 8.4g
Fiber: 1.6g
Sugar: 4.5g
Protein: 16g
Sodium: 193mg

VEGGIE OMELET

Servings: 4
Preparation Time: 10 minutes
Cooking Time: 25 minutes

INGREDIENTS:

- 6 large eggs
- ½ cup unsweetened almond milk
- Salt and ground black pepper, as required
- ½ of onion, chopped
- ¼ cup bell pepper, seeded and chopped
- ¼ cup fresh mushrooms, sliced
- 1 tablespoon chives, minced

INSTRUCTIONS:

1. Preheat your oven to 350 degrees F.
2. Lightly grease a pie dish.
3. In a bowl, add eggs, almond milk, salt and black pepper and beat until well combined.
4. In a separate bowl, mix together onion, bell pepper and mushrooms.
5. Place the egg mixture into the prepared pie dish evenly and top with vegetable mixture.
6. Sprinkle with chives evenly.
7. Bake for approximately 20-25 minutes.

8. Remove the pie dish from oven and set aside for about 5 minutes.

9. Cut into 4 portions and serve immediately.

NUTRITIONAL INFORMATION PER SERVING:

Calories: 121
Fat: 8g
Carbohydrates: 2.8g
Fiber: 0.6g
Sugar: 0.1g
Protein: 10.1g
Sodium: 167mg

VEGGIES QUICHE

Servings: 4
Preparation Time: 15 minutes
Cooking Time: 25 minutes

INGREDIENTS:

- 6 large eggs
- Salt and ground black pepper, as required
- ½ cup unsweetened almond milk
- ½ of onion, chopped
- ¼ cup fresh mushrooms, cut into slices
- ¼ cup red bell pepper, seeded and diced
- 1 tablespoon fresh chives, minced

INSTRUCTIONS:

1. Preheat your oven to 350 degrees F.
2. Lightly grease a pie dish.
3. In a bowl, add the eggs, salt, black pepper and coconut oil and beat until well combined.
4. In another bowl, mix together the onion, bell pepper and mushrooms.
5. Transfer the egg mixture

into the prepared pie dish evenly.
6. Top with the vegetable mixture evenly.
7. Sprinkle with chives evenly.
8. Bake for approximately 20-25 minutes.
9. Remove the pie dish from oven and set aside for about 5 minutes.
10. Cut into equal-sized wedges and serve.

NUTRITIONAL INFORMATION PER SERVING:

Calories: 121
Fat: 8g
Carbohydrates: 2.9g
Fiber: 0.6g
Sugar: 1.6g
Protein: 10g
Sodium: 187mg

ZUCCHINI & CARROT QUICHE

Servings: 3
Preparation Time: 10 minutes
Cooking Time: 40 minutes

INGREDIENTS:

- 5 eggs
- Salt and ground black pepper, as required
- 1 carrot, peeled and grated
- 1 small zucchini, shredded

INSTRUCTIONS:

1. Preheat your oven to 350 degrees F.
2. Lightly grease a small baking dish.
3. In a large bowl, add eggs, salt and black pepper and beat well
4. Add the carrot and zucchini and stir to combine

5. Transfer the mixture into the prepared baking dish evenly
6. Bake for approximately 40 minutes.
7. Remove the baking dish from oven and set aside for about 5 minutes.
8. Cut into equal-sized wedges and serve.

Nutritional Information per Serving:

Calories: 119
Fat: 7.4g
Carbohydrates: 3.9g
Fiber: 0.9g
Sugar: 2.2g
Protein: 9.9g
Sodium: 171mg

GREEN VEGGIES QUICHE

Servings: 4
Preparation Time: 15 minutes
Cooking Time: 20 minutes

INGREDIENTS:

- 6 eggs
- ½ cup unsweetened almond milk
- Salt and ground black pepper, as required
- 2 cups fresh baby spinach, chopped
- ½ cup green bell pepper, seeded and chopped
- 1 scallion, chopped
- ¼ cup fresh cilantro, chopped
- 1 tablespoon fresh chives, minced
- 3 tablespoons part-skim mozzarella cheese, grated

INSTRUCTIONS:

1. Preheat your oven to 400 degrees F.
2. Lightly grease a pie dish
3. In a large bowl, add the eggs, almond milk, salt and black pepper and beat until well combined. Set aside.
4. In another bowl, add the vegetables and herbs and mix well.
5. In the bottom of the prepared pie dish, place the veggie mixture evenly and top with the egg mixture.
6. Bake for approximately 20 minutes or until a wooden skewer inserted in the center comes out clean.
7. Remove from the oven and immediately sprinkle with the Parmesan cheese.
8. Set aside for about 5 minutes before slicing.
9. Cut into desired sized wedges and serve.

NUTRITIONAL INFORMATION PER SERVING:

Calories: 176
Fat: 4.1g
Carbohydrates: 5g
Fiber: 0.9g
Sugar: 4g
Protein: 15.4g
Sodium: 296mg

KALE & MUSHROOM FRITTATA

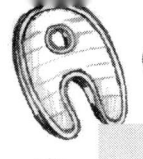

Servings: 5
Preparation Time: 15 minutes
Cooking Time: 30 minutes

INGREDIENTS:

- 8 eggs
- ½ cup unsweetened almond milk
- Salt and ground black pepper, as required
- 1 tablespoon extra-virgin olive oil
- 1 onion, chopped
- 1 garlic clove, minced
- 1 cup fresh mushrooms, chopped
- 1½ cups fresh kale, tough ribs removed and chopped

INSTRUCTIONS:

1. Preheat your oven to 350 degrees F.
2. In a large bowl, place the eggs, almond milk, salt and black pepper and beat well. Set aside.
3. In a large ovenproof wok, heat the oil over medium heat and sauté the onion and garlic for about 3-4 minutes.
4. Add the mushrooms, kale, salt and black pepper and cook for about 8-10 minutes.
5. Stir in the mushrooms and cook for about 3-4 minutes.
6. Add the kale and cook for about 5 minutes.
7. Place the egg mixture on top evenly and cook for about 4 minutes, without stirring.
8. Transfer the wok in the oven and Bake for approximately 12-15 minutes or until desired doneness.
9. Remove from the oven and place the frittata side for about 3-5 minutes before serving.
10. Cut into desired sized wedges and serve.

NUTRITIONAL INFORMATION PER SERVING:

Calories: 151
Fat: 10.2g
Carbohydrates: 5.6g
Fiber: 1g
Sugar: 1.7g
Protein: 10.3g
Sodium: 158mg

KALE & BELL PEPPER FRITTATA

Servings: 3
Preparation Time: 10 minutes
Cooking Time: 17 minutes

INGREDIENTS:

- 6 eggs
- Salt, as required
- 1 tablespoon olive oil
- ½ teaspoon ground turmeric
- 1 small red bell pepper, seeded and chopped
- 1 cup fresh kale, trimmed and chopped
- ¼ cup fresh chives, chopped

INSTRUCTIONS:

1. In a bowl, add the eggs and salt and beat well. Set aside.
2. In a cast-iron wok, heat the oil over medium-low heat and sprinkle with turmeric.
3. Immediately stir in the bell pepper and kale and sauté for about 2 minutes.
4. Place the beaten eggs over bell pepper mixture evenly and immediately reduce the heat to low.
5. Cover the wok and cook for about 10-15 minutes.
6. Remove from the heat and set aside for about 5 minutes.
7. Cut into equal-sized wedges and serve.

NUTRITIONAL INFORMATION PER SERVING:

Calories: 192
Fat: 13.6g
Carbohydrates: 6.4g
Fiber: 1g
Sugar: 2.8g
Protein: 12.3g
Sodium: 185mg

BELL PEPPER FRITTATA

Servings: 6
Preparation Time: 15 minutes
Cooking Time: 10 minutes

INGREDIENTS:

- 8 eggs
- 1 tablespoon fresh cilantro, chopped
- 1 tablespoon fresh basil, chopped
- ¼ teaspoon red pepper flakes, crushed
- Salt and ground black pepper, as required

- 2 tablespoons olive oil
- 1 bunch scallions, chopped
- 1 cup bell pepper, seeded and sliced thinly
- ½ cup goat cheese, crumbled

INSTRUCTIONS:

1. Preheat the broiler of oven.
2. Arrange a rack in upper third of the oven.
3. In a bowl, add the eggs, fresh herbs, red pepper flakes, salt and black pepper and beat well.
4. In an ovenproof wok, heat the oil over medium heat and sauté the scallion and bell pepper for about 1 minute.
5. Add the egg mixture over bell pepper mixture evenly and lift the edges to let the egg mixture flow underneath and cook for about 2-3 minutes.
6. Place the cheese on top in the form of dots.
7. Now, transfer the wok under broiler and broil for about 2-3 minutes.
8. Remove from the oven and set aside for about 5 minutes before serving.
9. Cut the frittata into desired sized slices and serve.

NUTRITIONAL INFORMATION PER SERVING:

Calories: 193
Fat: 15.2g
Carbohydrates: 3.2g
Fiber: 0.5g
Sugar: 1.6g
Protein: 11.7g
Sodium: 284mg

BROCCOLI FRITTATA

Servings: 6
Preparation Time: 15 minutes
Cooking Time: 13 minutes

INGREDIENTS:

- 8 eggs
- 1 tablespoon fresh cilantro, chopped
- 1 tablespoon fresh basil, chopped
- ¼ teaspoon red pepper flakes, crushed
- Salt and ground black pepper, as required
- 2 tablespoons olive oil
- 1 bunch scallions, chopped
- 1 cup broccoli, chopped finely
- ½ cup goat cheese, crumbled

INSTRUCTIONS:

1. Preheat the broiler of oven.
2. Arrange a rack in upper third of oven.
3. In a bowl, add eggs, fresh herbs, red pepper flakes, salt and black pepper and beat well.
4. In an ovenproof wok, heat the oil over medium heat and sauté scallion and broccoli for about 1-2 minutes.
5. Add the egg mixture over the broccoli mixture evenly and lift the edges to let the egg mixture flow underneath.
6. Cook for about 2-3 minutes.
7. Place the cheese on top in the form of dots.
8. Now, transfer the wok under broiler and broil for about 2-3 minutes.

9. Remove the wok from oven and set aside for about 5 minutes.
10. Cut the frittata into desired size slices and serve.

NUTRITIONAL INFORMATION PER SERVING:

Calories: 192
Fat: 15.3g
Carbohydrates: 2.8g
Fiber: 0.6g
Sugar: 0.9g
Protein: 12g
Sodium: 316mg

ZUCCHINI FRITTATA

Servings: 6
Preparation Time: 15 minutes
Cooking Time: 20 minutes

INGREDIENTS:

- 2 tablespoons unsweetened almond milk
- 8 eggs
- Freshly ground black pepper, as required
- 1 tablespoon olive oil
- 1 garlic clove, minced
- 2 medium zucchinis, cut into ¼-inch thick round slices
- ½ cup goat cheese, crumbled

INSTRUCTIONS:

1. Preheat your oven to 350 degrees F.
2. In a bowl, add the almond milk, eggs and black pepper and black pepper and beat well.
3. In an ovenproof wok, heat the oil over medium heat and sauté the garlic for about 1 minute.
4. Stir in the zucchini and cook for about 5 minutes.

5. Add the egg mixture and stir for about 1 minute.
6. Sprinkle the cheese on top evenly.
7. Immediately transfer the wok into the oven.
8. Bake for approximately 12 minutes or until eggs become set.
9. Remove from oven and set aside to cool for about 5 minutes.
10. Cut into desired sized wedges and serve.

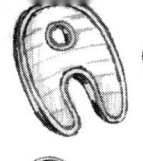

NUTRITIONAL INFORMATION PER SERVING:

Calories: 149
Fat: 11g
Carbohydrates: 3.4g
Fiber: 0.8g
Sugar: 2.1g
Protein: 10g
Sodium: 274mg

EGGS WITH SPINACH

Servings: 2
Preparation Time: 10 minutes
Cooking Time: 22 minutes

INGREDIENTS:

- 6 cups fresh baby spinach
- 2-3 tablespoons water
- 4 eggs
- Salt and ground black pepper, as required
- 2-3 tablespoons feta cheese, crumbled

INSTRUCTIONS:
1. Preheat your oven to 400 degrees F.
2. Lightly grease 2 small baking dishes.
3. In a large frying pan, add spinach and water over medium heat and cook for about 3-4 minutes.
4. Remove the frying pan from heat and drain the excess water completely.
5. Divide the spinach into prepared baking dishes evenly.
6. Carefully crack 2 eggs in each baking dish over spinach.
7. Sprinkle with salt and black pepper and top with feta cheese evenly.
8. Arrange the baking dishes onto a large cookie sheet.
9. Bake for approximately 15-18 minutes.
10. Serve warm.

NUTRITIONAL INFORMATION PER SERVING:

Calories: 171
Fat: 11.1g
Carbohydrates: 4.3g
Fiber: 2g
Sugar: 1.4g
Protein: 15g
Sodium: 377mg

EGGS WITH KALE & TOMATOES

Servings: 4
Preparation Time: 15 minutes
Cooking Time: 25 minutes

INGREDIENTS:

- 2 tablespoons olive oil
- 1 yellow onion, chopped
- 2 garlic cloves, minced
- 1 cup tomatoes, chopped
- ½ pound fresh kale, tough ribs removed and chopped
- 1 teaspoon ground cumin
- ¼ teaspoon red pepper flakes, crushed
- Salt and ground black pepper, as required
- 4 eggs
- 2 tablespoons fresh parsley, chopped

INSTRUCTIONS:
1. In a large nonstick wok, heat the olive oil over medium heat and sauté the onion for about 4-5 minutes.
2. Add in the garlic and sauté for about 1 minute.
3. Add the tomatoes, spices, salt and black pepper and cook for about 2-3 minutes, stirring frequently.
4. Add in the kale and cook for about 4-5 minutes.
5. Carefully crack eggs on top of kale mixture.
6. With the lid, cover the wok and cook for about 10 minutes or until desired doneness of eggs.
7. Serve hot with the garnishing of parsley.

NUTRITIONAL INFORMATION PER SERVING:

Calories: 175
Fat: 11.7g
Carbohydrates: 11g
Fiber: 2.2g
Sugar: 2.8g
Protein: 8.2g
Sodium: 130mg

EGGS WITH VEGGIES

Servings: 4
Preparation Time: 10 minutes
Cooking Time: 15 minutes

INGREDIENTS:

- 2 tablespoons olive oil, divided
- ¾ pound zucchini, quartered and sliced thinly
- 1 red bell pepper, seeded and chopped
- 1 medium onion, chopped
- 1 teaspoon fresh rosemary, chopped finely
- Salt and ground black pepper, as required
- 4 large eggs

INSTRUCTIONS:

1. In a large wok, heat 1 tablespoon of oil over medium-high heat and sauté the zucchini, bell pepper and onion for about 5-8 minutes.
2. Add the rosemary, salt and black pepper and stir to combine.
3. With a wooden spoon, make a large well in the center of wok by moving the veggie mixture towards the sides.
4. Reduce the heat to medium and pour the remaining oil in the well.
5. Carefully crack the eggs in the well and sprinkle the eggs with salt and black pepper.
6. Cook for about 1-2 minutes.
7. Cover the wok and cook for about 1-2 minutes more.
8. For serving, carefully scoop the veggie mixture onto 4 serving plates.
9. Top each serving with an egg and serve.

NUTRITIONAL INFORMATION PER SERVING:

Calories: 171
Fat: 11.1g
Carbohydrates: 4.3g
Fiber: 2g
Sugar: 1.4g
Protein: 15g
Sodium: 377mg

TOFU & MUSHROOM MUFFINS

Servings: 6
Preparation Time: 15 minutes
Cooking Time: 30 minutes

INGREDIENTS:

- 2 teaspoons olive oil, divided
- 1½ cups fresh mushrooms, chopped
- 1 scallion, chopped
- 1 teaspoon garlic, minced
- 1 teaspoon fresh rosemary, minced
- Freshly ground black pepper, as required
- 1 (12.3-ounce) package lite firm silken tofu, drained
- ¼ cup unsweetened almond milk
- 2 tablespoons nutritional yeast
- 1 tablespoon arrowroot starch
- ¼ teaspoon ground turmeric

INSTRUCTIONS:

1. Preheat your oven to 375 degrees F.
2. Grease a 12 cups muffin tin.
3. In a nonstick wok, heat 1 teaspoon of oil over medium heat and sauté scallion and garlic for about 1 minute.
4. Add mushrooms and sauté for about 5-7 minutes.
5. Stir in the rosemary and black pepper and remove from the heat.
6. Set aside to cool slightly.
7. In a food processor, add tofu and remaining ingredients and pulse until smooth.
8. Transfer the tofu mixture into a large bowl
9. Fold in mushroom mixture.
10. Transfer the mixture into prepared muffin cups evenly.
11. Bake for approximately 20-22 minutes or until a toothpick inserted in the center comes out clean.
12. Remove the muffin pan from the oven and place onto a wire rack to cool for about 10 minutes.
13. Carefully invert the muffins onto the wire rack and serve warm.

NUTRITIONAL INFORMATION PER SERVING:

Calories: 70
Fat: 3.6g
Carbohydrates: 4.3g
Fiber: 9.8g
Sugar: 1.3g
Protein: 55.7g
Sodium: 32mg

FRUIT SALAD

Servings: 4
Preparation Time: 15 minutes

INGREDIENTS:

For Salad

- 4 cups fresh baby arugula
- 1 cup fresh strawberries, hulled and sliced
- 2 oranges, peeled and segmented

For Dressing

- 2 tablespoons fresh lemon juice
- 2-3 drops liquid stevia
- 2 teaspoons extra-virgin olive oil
- Salt and ground black pepper, as required

INSTRUCTIONS:

1. *For Salad:* in a salad bowl, place all ingredients and mix.
2. *For Dressing:* place all ingredients in another bowl and beat until well combined.
3. Place dressing on top of salad and toss to coat well.
4. Serve immediately.

NUTRITIONAL INFORMATION PER SERVING:

Calories: 82
Fat: 2.7g
Carbohydrates: 13g
Fiber: 3g
Sugar: 10g
Protein: 1.7g
Sodium: 63mg

STRAWBERRY, ORANGE & ROCKET SALAD

Servings: 4
Preparation Time: 15 minutes

INGREDIENTS:

For Salad:

- 6 cups fresh rocket
- 1½ cups fresh strawberries, hulled and sliced
- 2 oranges, peeled and segmented

For Dressing:

- 2 tablespoons fresh lemon juice
- 1 tablespoon raw honey
- 2 teaspoons extra-virgin olive oil
- 1 teaspoon Dijon mustard
- Salt and ground black pepper, as required

INSTRUCTIONS:

1. *For Salad:* in a salad bowl, place all ingredients and mix.
1. *For Dressing:* place all ingredients in another bowl and beat until well combined.
1. Place dressing on top of salad and toss to coat well.
1. Serve immediately.

NUTRITIONAL INFORMATION PER SERVING:

Calories: 107
Fat: 2.9g
Carbohydrates: 17g
Fiber: 3.9g
Sugar: 16g
Protein: 2.1g
Sodium: 63mg

STRAWBERRY & ASPARAGUS SALAD

Servings: 8
Preparation Time: 15 minutes
Cooking Time: 5 minutes

INGREDIENTS:

- 2 pounds fresh asparagus, trimmed and sliced
- 3 cups fresh strawberries, hulled and sliced
- ¼ cup extra-virgin olive oil
- ¼ cup balsamic vinegar
- 2 tablespoons maple syrup
- Salt and ground black pepper, as required

INSTRUCTIONS:

1. In a pan of water, add the asparagus over medium-high heat and bring to a boil.
2. Boil the asparagus for about 2-3 minutes or until al dente.
3. Drain the asparagus and immediately transfer into a bowl of ice water to cool completely.
4. Drain the asparagus and pat dry with paper towels.
5. In a large bowl, add the asparagus and strawberries and mix.
6. In a small bowl, add the olive oil, vinegar, honey, salt and black pepper and beat until well blended.
7. Place the dressing over the asparagus strawberry mixture and gently toss to coat.
8. Refrigerate for about 1 hour before serving.

NUTRITIONAL INFORMATION PER SERVING:

Calories: 109
Fat: 6.6g
Carbohydrates: 12g
Fiber: 3.5g
Sugar: 7.8g
Protein: 2.9g
Sodium: 23mg

BLUEBERRIES & SPINACH SALAD

Servings: 4
Preparation Time: 15 minutes

INGREDIENTS:

For Salad:

- 6 cups fresh baby spinach
- 1½ cups fresh blueberries
- ¼ cup onion, sliced
- ¼ cup almond, sliced
- ¼ cup feta cheese, crumbled

For Dressing:

- 1/3 cup olive oil
- 2 tablespoons fresh lemon juice
- ¼ teaspoon liquid stevia
- 1/8 teaspoon garlic powder
- Salt, as required

INSTRUCTIONS:

1. *For Salad:* in a bowl, add the spinach, berries, onion and almonds and mix.
2. *For Dressing:* in another small bowl, add all the ingredients and beat until well blended.
3. Place the dressing over salad and gently toss to coat well.
4. Serve immediately.

NUTRITIONAL INFORMATION PER SERVING:

Calories: 250
Fat: 22.2g
Carbohydrates: 12g
Fiber: 3.2g
Sugar: 6.7g
Protein: 4.5g
Sodium: 181mg

MIXED BERRIES SALAD

Servings: 4
Preparation Time: 15 minutes

INGREDIENTS:

- 1 cup fresh strawberries, hulled and sliced
- ½ cups fresh blackberries
- ½ cup fresh blueberries
- ½ cup fresh raspberries
- 6 cup fresh arugula
- 2 tablespoons extra-virgin olive oil
- Salt and ground black pepper, as required

INSTRUCTIONS:

1. In a salad bowl, place all the ingredients and toss to coat well.
2. Serve immediately.

NUTRITIONAL INFORMATION PER SERVING:

Calories: 105
Fat: 20.2g
Carbohydrates: 12g
Fiber: 3.2g
Sugar: 6.7g
Protein: 4.5g
Sodium: mg

KALE & CITRUS FRUIT SALAD

Servings: 2
Preparation Time: 15 minutes

INGREDIENTS:

For Salad:

- 3 cups fresh kale, tough ribs removed and torn
- 1 orange, peeled and segmented
- 1 grapefruit, peeled and segmented
- 2 tablespoons unsweetened dried cranberries
- ¼ teaspoon white sesame seeds

For Dressing:

- 2 tablespoons extra-virgin olive oil
- 2 tablespoons fresh orange juice
- 1 teaspoon Dijon mustard
- ½ teaspoon raw honey
- Salt and ground black pepper, as required

INSTRUCTIONS:

1. *For Salad:* in a salad bowl, place all ingredients and mix.
1. *For Dressing:* place all ingredients in another bowl and beat until well combined.
1. Place dressing on top of salad and toss to coat well.
1. Serve immediately.

NUTRITIONAL INFORMATION PER SERVING:

Calories: 256
Fat: 14.5g
Carbohydrates: 25g
Fiber: 4.8g
Sugar: 16g
Protein: 4.6g
Sodium: 150mg

KALE, APPLE & CRANBERRY SALAD

Servings: 4
Preparation Time: 15 minutes

INGREDIENTS:

- 6 cups fresh baby kale
- 3 large apples, cored and sliced
- ¼ cup unsweetened dried cranberries
- ¼ cup almonds, sliced
- 2 tablespoons extra-virgin olive oil
- 1 tablespoon raw honey
- Salt and ground black pepper, as required

INSTRUCTIONS:

1. In a salad bowl, place all the ingredients and toss to coat well.
2. Serve immediately.

NUTRITIONAL INFORMATION PER SERVING:

Calories: 153
Fat: 10.3g
Carbohydrates: 40g
Fiber: 6.6g
Sugar: 20g
Protein: 4.7g
Sodium: 109mg

ROCKET, BEAT & ORANGE SALAD

Servings: 4
Preparation Time: 15 minutes

INGREDIENTS:

- 3 large oranges, peeled, seeded and sectioned
- 2 beets, trimmed, peeled and sliced
- 6 cups fresh rocket
- ¼ cup walnuts, chopped
- 3 tablespoons olive oil
- Pinch of salt

INSTRUCTIONS:

1. In a salad bowl, place all ingredients and gently toss to coat.
2. Serve immediately.

NUTRITIONAL INFORMATION PER SERVING:

Calories: 233
Fat: 15.6g
Carbohydrates: 23.1g
Fiber: 5.3g
Sugar: 17.6g
Protein: 4.8g
Sodium: 86mg

CUCUMBER & TOMATO SALAD

Servings: 6
Preparation Time: 15 minutes

INGREDIENTS:

For Salad:

- 3 large English cucumbers, sliced thinly
- 2 cups tomatoes, chopped
- 6 cup lettuce, torn

For Dressing:

- 4 tablespoons olive oil
- 2 tablespoons balsamic vinegar
- 1 tablespoon fresh lemon juice
- Salt and ground black pepper, as required

INSTRUCTIONS:

1. *For Salad:* in a large bowl, add the cucumbers, onion and dill and mix.
2. *For Dressing:* in a small bowl, add all the ingredients and beat until well combined.
3. Place the dressing over the salad and toss to coat well.
4. Serve immediately.

NUTRITIONAL INFORMATION PER SERVING:

Calories: 86
Fat: 7.3g
Carbohydrates: 5.1g
Fiber: 9.8g
Sugar: 2.8g
Protein: 1.1g
Sodium: 27mg

MIXED VEGGIE SALAD

Servings: 6
Preparation Time: 20 minutes

INGREDIENTS:

For Dressing:

- 1 small avocado, peeled, pitted and chopped
- ¼ cup low-fat plain Greek yogurt
- 1 small yellow onion, chopped
- 1 garlic clove, chopped
- 2 tablespoons fresh parsley
- 2 tablespoons fresh lemon juice

For Salad:

- 6 cups fresh spinach, shredded
- 2 medium zucchini, cut into thin slices
- ½ cup celery, sliced
- ½ cup red bell pepper, seeded and sliced thinly
- ½ cup yellow onion, sliced thinly
- ½ cup cucumber, sliced thinly

- ½ cup cherry tomatoes, halved
- ¼ cup Kalamata olives, pitted
- ½ cup feta cheese, crumbled

INSTRUCTIONS:

1. *For Dressing:* in a food processor, add all the ingredients and pulse until smooth.
2. *For Salad:* in a salad bowl, add all the ingredients and mix well.
3. Pour the dressing over salad and gently, toss to coat well.
4. Serve immediately.

NUTRITIONAL INFORMATION PER SERVING:

Calories: 152
Fat: 10.3g
Carbohydrates: 12g
Fiber: 4.8g
Sugar: 4.8g
Protein: 5.4g
Sodium: 238mg

EGGS & VEGGIE SALAD

Servings: 8
Preparation Time: 15 minutes

INGREDIENTS:

For Salad:

- 2 large English cucumbers, sliced thinly sliced
- 2 cups tomatoes, chopped
- 8 hard-boiled eggs, peeled and sliced
- 8 cups fresh baby spinach

For Dressing:

- 4 tablespoons olive oil
- 2 tablespoons balsamic vinegar
- 1 tablespoon fresh lemon juice
- Salt and ground black pepper, as required

INSTRUCTIONS:

1. *For Salad:* in a salad bowl, add the cucumbers, onion and dill and mix.
2. *For Dressing:* in a small bowl, add all the ingredients and beat until well blended.
3. Place the dressing over the salad and toss to coat well.
4. Serve immediately.

NUTRITIONAL INFORMATION PER SERVING:

Calories: 150
Fat: 11.7g
Carbohydrates: 6g
Fiber: 1.6g
Sugar: 3g
Protein: 7.3g
Sodium: 109mg

TOFU & VEGGIE SALAD

Servings: 8
Preparation Time: 20 minutes

INGREDIENTS:

For Dressing:

- ¼ cup balsamic vinegar
- ¼ cup low-sodium soy sauce
- 2 tablespoons water
- 1 teaspoon sesame oil, toasted
- 1 teaspoon Sriracha
- 3-4 drops liquid stevia

For Salad:

- 1½ pounds baked firm tofu, cubed
- 2 large zucchinis, sliced thinly
- 2 large yellow bell peppers, seeded and sliced thinly
- 3 cups cherry tomatoes, halved
- 2 cups radishes, sliced thinly
- 2 cups purple cabbage, shredded
- 10 cups fresh baby spinach

INSTRUCTIONS:

1. *For Dressing:* in a bowl, add all the ingredients and beat until well combined.
2. Divide the chickpeas, tofu and vegetables into serving bowls.
3. Drizzle with dressing and serve immediately.

NUTRITIONAL INFORMATION PER SERVING:

Calories: 122
Fat: 4.7g
Carbohydrates: 13.1g
Fiber: 4.6g
Sugar: 7g
Protein: 10.8g
Sodium: 511mg

KALE & CARROT SOUP

Servings: 5
Preparation Time: 15 minutes
Cooking Time: 40 minutes

INGREDIENTS:

- 2 tablespoons extra-virgin olive oil
- 4 medium carrots, chopped
- 2 celery stalks, chopped
- 1 large red onion, chopped finely
- 2 garlic cloves, crushed
- ½ pound curly kale, tough ribs removed and chopped finely
- 4½ cups homemade low-sodium vegetable broth
- Salt and ground black pepper, as required

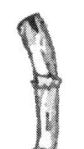

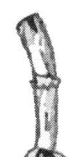

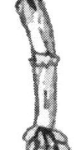

INSTRUCTIONS:

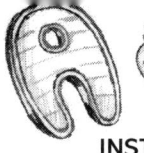

1. Heat the oil in a large soup pan over medium heat and cook the carrot, celery, onion and garlic for about 8-10 minutes, stirring frequently.
2. Add the kale and cook for about 5 minutes, stirring twice.
3. Add the broth and bring to a boil.
4. Cook, partially covered for about 20 minutes.
5. Stir in salt and black pepper and remove from the heat.
6. With an immersion blender, blend the soup until smooth.
7. Serve hot.

NUTRITIONAL INFORMATION PER SERVING:

Calories: 140
Fat: 6.9g
Carbohydrates: 13g
Fiber: 2.7g
Sugar: 4.4g
Protein: 6.6g
Sodium: 778mg

CHEESY MUSHROOM SOUP

Servings: 4
Preparation Time: 15 minutes
Cooking Time: 15 minutes

INGREDIENTS:

- 2 tablespoons olive oil
- 4 ounces fresh baby Portobello mushroom, sliced
- 4 ounces fresh white button mushrooms, sliced
- ½ cup yellow onion, chopped
- ½ teaspoon salt
- 1 teaspoon garlic, chopped
- 3 cups low-sodium vegetable broth
- 1 cup low-fat cheddar cheese

INSTRUCTIONS:

1. In a medium pan, heat the oil over medium heat and cook the mushrooms and onion with salt for about 5-7 minutes, stirring frequently.
2. Add the garlic, and sauté for about 1-2 minutes.
3. Stir in the broth and remove from the heat.
4. With a stick blender, blend the soup until mushrooms are chopped very finely.
5. In the pan, add the cheddar cheese and stir to combine.
6. Place the pan over medium heat and cook for about 3-5 minutes.
7. Remove from the heat and serve immediately.

NUTRITIONAL INFORMATION PER SERVING:

Calories: 204
Fat: 16.5g
Carbohydrates: 4.6g
Fiber: 0.9g
Sugar: 1.7g
Protein: 10.5g
Sodium: 523mg

SPINACH & MUSHROOM STEW

Servings: 4
Preparation Time: 15 minutes
Cooking Time: 30 minutes

INGREDIENTS:

- 2 tablespoons olive oil
- 2 onions, chopped
- 3 garlic cloves, minced
- ½ pound fresh button mushrooms, chopped
- ¼ pound fresh shiitake mushrooms, chopped
- ¼ pound fresh spinach, chopped
- Sea salt and freshly ground black pepper, as required
- ¼ cup low-sodium vegetable broth
- ½ cup coconut milk
- 2 tablespoons fresh parsley, chopped

INSTRUCTIONS:

1. In a large wok, heat oil over medium heat and sauté the onion and garlic for 4-5 minutes.
2. Add the mushrooms, salt, and black pepper and cook for 4-5 minutes.
3. Add the spinach, broth and coconut milk and bring to a gentle boil.
4. Simmer for 4-5 minutes or until desired doneness.
5. Stir in the parsley and remove from heat.
6. Serve hot.

NUTRITIONAL INFORMATION PER SERVING:

Calories: 181
Fat: 14.6g
Carbohydrates: 11.5g
Fiber: 3.4g
Sugar: 5g
Protein: 5.1g
Sodium: 90mg

VEGGIE STEW

Servings: 4
Preparation Time: 20 minutes
Cooking Time: 35 minutes

INGREDIENTS:

- 2 tablespoons olive oil
- 1 yellow onion, chopped
- 2 teaspoons fresh ginger, grated
- 1 teaspoon ground turmeric
- 1 teaspoon ground cumin
- Salt and ground black pepper, as required
- 1-2 cups water, divided
- 1 cup cabbage, shredded
- 1 cup broccoli, chopped
- 2 large carrots, peeled and sliced

INSTRUCTIONS:

1. In a large soup pan, heat the oil over medium heat and sauté onion for about 5 minutes.
2. Stir in the ginger and spices and sauté for about 1 minute.
3. Add 1 cup of water and bring to a boil.
4. Reduce the heat to medium-low and cook for about 10 minutes.
5. Add the vegetables and enough water that covers the half of vegetable mixture and stir to combine.
6. Increase the heat to medium-high and bring to a boil.
7. Reduce the heat to medium-low and cook, covered for about 10-15 minutes, stirring occasionally.
8. Serve hot.

NUTRITIONAL INFORMATION PER SERVING:

Calories: 105
Fat: 7.4g
Carbohydrates: 9g
Fiber: 2.8g
Sugar: 4g
Protein: 1.7g
Sodium: 77mg

TOFU & MUSHROOM SOUP

Servings: 3
Preparation Time: 15 minutes
Cooking Time: 25 minutes

INGREDIENTS:

- 3 tablespoons vegetable oil, divided
- 1 shallot, minced
- 1 ounce fresh ginger, minced
- 2 garlic cloves, minced
- 5½ ounces coconut milk
- 1 Roma tomato, chopped
- 1 lemongrass stalk, halved crosswise
- 6 ounces fresh mushrooms, sliced
- 14 ounces extra-firm tofu, pressed, drained and cut into ½-inch cubes
- Ground black pepper, as required
- 1 scallion, sliced
- 1 tablespoon fresh cilantro, chopped

INSTRUCTIONS:

1. In a pan, heat 2 tablespoons of oil over medium-high heat and sauté the shallot, ginger, garlic and a pinch of salt for about 1-2 minutes.
2. Add coconut milk and remaining water and bring to a boil.
3. Add the tomato and lemongrass and stir to combine.
4. Adjust the heat to low and simmer for about 8-10 minutes.
5. Meanwhile, in a large non-stick wok, heat the remaining oil over medium-high heat and cook the mushrooms, tofu, pinch of salt and black pepper for about 5-8 minutes, stirring occasionally.
6. Remove the lemongrass stalk from pan of soup and discard it.
7. Divide the cooked mushrooms and tofu into serving bowls evenly.
8. Top with hot soup and serve with the garnishing of scallion and cilantro.

NUTRITIONAL INFORMATION PER SERVING:

Calories: 344
Fat: 28.7g
Carbohydrates: 8.7g
Fiber: 1.5g
Sugar: 3.6g
Protein: 16.1g
Sodium: 33mg

TOFU & BELL PEPPER STEW

Servings: 6
Preparation Time: 15 minutes
Cooking Time: 15 minutes

INGREDIENTS:

- 2 tablespoons garlic
- 1 jalapeño pepper, seeded and chopped
- 1 (16-ounce) jar roasted red peppers, rinsed, drained and chopped
- 2 cups homemade low-sodium vegetable broth
- 2 cups filtered water
- 1 medium green bell pepper, seeded and sliced thinly
- 1 medium red bell pepper, seeded and sliced thinly
- 1 (16-ounce) package extra-firm tofu, drained and cubed
- 1 (10-ounce) package frozen baby spinach, thawed

INSTRUCTIONS:

1. Add the garlic, jalapeño pepper and roasted red peppers in a food processor and pulse until smooth.
2. In a large pan, add the puree, broth and water over medium-high heat and cook until boiling.
3. Add the bell peppers and tofu and stir to combine.
4. Reduce the heat to medium and cook for about 5 minutes.
5. Stir in the spinach and cook for about 5 minutes.
6. Serve hot.

NUTRITIONAL INFORMATION PER SERVING:

Calories: 132
Fat: 5g
Carbohydrates: 14g
Fiber: 3.1g
Sugar: 6.7g
Protein: 11.5g
Sodium: 75mg

CARROT SOUP WITH TEMPEH

Servings: 6
Preparation Time: 15 minutes
Cooking Time: 45 minutes

INGREDIENTS:

- ¼ cup olive oil, divided
- 1 large yellow onion, chopped
- Salt, as required
- 2 pounds carrots, peeled and cut into ½-inch rounds
- 2 tablespoons fresh dill, chopped
- 4½ cups low-sodium vegetable broth
- 12 ounces tempeh, cut into ½-inch cubes
- ¼ cup tomato paste
- 1 teaspoon fresh lemon juice

INSTRUCTIONS:

1. In a large soup pan, heat 2 tablespoons of the oil over medium heat and cook the onion with salt for about 6-8 minutes, stirring frequently.
2. Add the carrots and stir to combine.
3. Lower the heat to low and cook, covered for about 5 minutes, stirring frequently.
4. Add in the broth and bring to a boil over high heat.
5. Lower the heat to a low and simmer, covered for about 30 minutes.
6. Meanwhile, in a wok, heat the remaining oil over medium-high heat and cook the tempeh for about 3-5 minutes.
7. Stir in the dill and cook for about 1 minute.
8. Remove from the heat.
9. Remove the pan of soup from heat and stir in tomato paste and lemon juice.
10. With an immersion blender, blend the soup until smooth and creamy.
11. Serve the soup hot with the topping of tempeh.

NUTRITIONAL INFORMATION PER SERVING:

Calories:	294
Fat:	15.7g
Carbohydrates:	20g
Fiber:	4.9g
Sugar:	10g
Protein:	16.4g

Sodium: 273mg

VEGETARIAN BURGERS

Servings: 4
Preparation Time: 15 minutes
Cooking Time: 16 minutes

INGREDIENTS:

- 1-pound firm tofu, drained, pressed, and crumbled
- ¾ cup rolled oats
- ¼ cup flaxseeds
- 2 cups frozen spinach, thawed
- 1 medium onion, chopped finely
- 4 garlic cloves, minced
- 1 teaspoon ground cumin
- 1 teaspoon red pepper flakes, crushed

- Sea salt and freshly ground black pepper, as required
- 2 tablespoons olive oil
- 6 cups fresh salad greens

INSTRUCTIONS:

1. In a large bowl, add all the ingredients except oil and salad greens and mix until well combined.
2. Set aside for about 10 minutes.
3. Make desired size patties from mixture.
4. In a nonstick frying pan, heat the oil over medium heat and cook the patties for 6-8 minutes per side.
5. Serve these patties alongside the salad greens.

NUTRITIONAL INFORMATION PER SERVING:

Calories: 214
Fat: 11.8g
Carbohydrates: 4.6g
Fiber: 2.5g
Sugar: 2.2g
Protein: 24.6g
Sodium: 80mg

CAULIFLOWER WITH PEAS

Servings: 4
Preparation Time: 15 minutes
Cooking Time: 15 minutes

INGREDIENTS:

- 2 medium tomatoes, chopped
- ¼ cup water
- 2 tablespoons olive oil
- 3 garlic cloves, minced
- ½ tablespoon fresh ginger, minced
- 1 teaspoon ground cumin
- 2 teaspoons ground coriander
- 1 teaspoon cayenne pepper
- ¼ teaspoon ground turmeric
- 2 cups cauliflower, chopped
- 1 cup fresh green peas, shelled
- Salt and ground black pepper, as required
- ½ cup warm water

INSTRUCTIONS:

1. In a blender, add tomato and ¼ cup of water and pulse until smooth puree forms. Set aside.
2. In a large wok, heat the oil over medium heat and sauté the garlic, ginger, green chilies and spices for about 1 minute.
3. Add the cauliflower, peas and tomato puree and cook, stirring for about 3-4 minutes.
4. Add the warm water and bring to a boil.
5. Reduce the heat to medium-low and cook, covered for about 8-10 minutes or until vegetables are done completely.
6. Serve hot.

NUTRITIONAL INFORMATION PER SERVING:

Calories: 163
Fat: 10.1g
Carbohydrates: 16.1g
Fiber: 5.6g
Sugar: 6g
Protein: 6g
Sodium: 79mg

BROCCOLI WITH BELL PEPPERS

Servings: 6
Preparation Time: 15 minutes
Cooking Time: 10 minutes

INGREDIENTS:

- 2 tablespoons olive oil
- 4 garlic cloves, minced
- 1 large white onion, sliced
- 2 cups small broccoli florets
- 3 red bell peppers, seeded and sliced
- ¼ cup low-sodium vegetable broth
- Salt and ground black pepper, as required

INSTRUCTIONS:

1. In a large wok, heat the oil over medium heat and sauté the garlic for about 1 minute.
2. Add the onion, broccoli and bell peppers and stir fry for about 5 minutes.
3. Add the broth and stir fry for about 4 minutes more.
4. Serve hot.

NUTRITIONAL INFORMATION PER SERVING:

Calories: 84
Fat: 5g
Carbohydrates: 9.6g
Fiber: 2.2g
Sugar: 4.6g
Protein: 2.1g
Sodium: 72mg

3-VEGGIES MEDLEY

Servings: 6
Preparation Time: 25 minutes
Cooking Time: 15 minutes

INGREDIENTS:

- 1 tablespoon olive oil
- 1 small yellow onion, chopped
- 1 teaspoon fresh thyme, chopped
- 1 garlic clove, minced
- 8 ounces fresh mushrooms, sliced
- 1-pound Brussels sprouts
- 3 cups fresh spinach
- Salt and ground black pepper, as required

INSTRUCTIONS:

1. In a large wok, heat the oil over medium heat and sauté the onion for about 3-4 minutes.
2. Add the thyme and garlic and sauté for about 1 minute.
3. Add the mushrooms and cook for about 15 minutes or until caramelized.
4. Add the Brussels sprouts and cook for about 2-3 minutes.
5. Stir in the spinach and cook for about 3-4 minutes.
6. Stir in the salt and black pepper and remove from the heat.
7. Serve hot.

NUTRITIONAL INFORMATION PER SERVING:

Calories: 70
Fat: 2.8g
Carbohydrates: 10g
Fiber: 3.9g
Sugar: 2.8g
Protein: 4.4g
Sodium: 61mg

3 VEGGIES COMBO

Servings: 4
Preparation Time: 15 minutes
Cooking Time: 10 minutes

INGREDIENTS:

- 1 tablespoon olive oil
- ½ cup onion, sliced
- ½ cup red bell pepper, seeded and julienned
- ½ cup orange bell pepper, seeded and julienned
- 1½ cups yellow squash, sliced
- 1½ cups zucchini, sliced
- 1½ teaspoons garlic, minced
- ¼ cup water
- Salt and ground black pepper, as required

INSTRUCTIONS:

1. In a large wok, heat the oil over medium-high heat and sauté the onion, bell peppers and squash for about 4-5 minutes.
2. Add the garlic and sauté for about 1 minute.
3. Add the remaining ingredients and stir to combine.
4. Reduce the heat to medium and cook for about 3-4 minutes, stirring occasionally.
5. Serve hot.

NUTRITIONAL INFORMATION PER SERVING:

Calories: 65
Fat: 3.8g
Carbohydrates: 7.7g
Fiber: 1.7g
Sugar: 3.6g
Protein: 1.7g
Sodium: 50mg

CAULIFLOWER WITH PEAS

Servings: 4
Preparation Time: 15 minutes
Cooking Time: 15 minutes

INGREDIENTS:

- 2 medium tomatoes, chopped
- ¼ cup water
- 2 tablespoons olive oi
- 3 garlic cloves, minced
- ½ tablespoon fresh ginger, minced
- 1 teaspoon ground cumin
- 2 teaspoons ground coriander
- 1 teaspoon cayenne pepper
- ¼ teaspoon ground turmeric
- 2 cups cauliflower, chopped
- 1 cup fresh green peas, shelled
- Salt and ground black pepper, as required
- ½ cup warm water

INSTRUCTIONS:

1. In a blender, add tomato and ¼ cup of water and pulse until a smooth puree forms. Set aside.
2. In a large wok, heat oil over medium heat and sauté the garlic, ginger, green chilies and spices for about 1 minute.
3. Add the cauliflower, peas and tomato puree and cook, stirring for about 3-4 minutes.

4. Add the warm water and bring to a boil.
5. Adjust the heat to medium-low and cook, covered for about 8-10 minutes or until vegetables are done completely.
6. Serve hot.

NUTRITIONAL INFORMATION PER SERVING:

Calories: 60
Fat: 2.9g
Carbohydrates: 8g
Fiber: 2g
Sugar: 1g
Protein: 1,9g
Sodium: 61mg

BOK CHOY & MUSHROOM STIR FRY

Servings: 4
Preparation Time: 15 minutes
Cooking Time: 10 minutes

INGREDIENTS:

- 1 pound baby bok choy
- 4 teaspoons olive oil
- 1 teaspoon fresh ginger, minced
- 2 garlic cloves, chopped
- 5 ounces fresh mushrooms, sliced
- 2 tablespoons red wine
- 2 tablespoons soy sauce
- Ground black pepper, as required

INSTRUCTIONS:

1. Trim bases of bok choy and separate outer leaves from stalks, leaving the smallest inner leaves attached.
2. In a large cast-iron wok, heat the oil over medium-high heat and sauté the ginger and garlic for about 1 minute.
3. Stir in the mushrooms and cook for about 4-5 minutes, stirring frequently.
4. Stir in the bok choy leaves and stalks and cook for about 1 minute, tossing with tongs.
5. Stir in the wine, soy sauce and black pepper and cook for about 2-3 minutes, tossing occasionally.
6. Serve hot.

NUTRITIONAL INFORMATION PER SERVING:

Calories: 77
Fat: 5g
Carbohydrates: 5.3g
Fiber: 1.6g
Sugar: 2.2g
Protein: 3.5g
Sodium: 527mg

BROCCOLI WITH BELL PEPPERS

Servings: 6
Preparation Time: 10 minutes
Cooking Time: 10 minutes

INGREDIENTS:

- 2 tablespoons olive oil
- 4 garlic cloves, minced
- 1 large white onion, sliced
- 2 cups small broccoli florets
- 3 red bell peppers, seeded and sliced
- ¼ cup low-sodium vegetable broth
- Salt and ground black pepper, as required

INSTRUCTIONS:

1. In a large wok, heat oil over medium heat and sauté the garlic for about 1 minute.
2. Add the onion, broccoli and bell peppers and cook for about 5 minutes, stirring frequently.
3. Stir in the broth and cook for about 4 minutes, stirring frequently.
4. Stir in the salt and black pepper and remove from the heat.
5. Serve hot.

NUTRITIONAL INFORMATION PER SERVING:

Calories: 170
Fat: 3g
Carbohydrates: 6g
Fiber: 2g
Sugar: 1g
Protein: 2g
Sodium: 347mg

STUFFED ZUCCHINI

Servings: 8
Preparation Time: 15 minutes
Cooking Time: 18 minutes

INGREDIENTS:

- 4 medium zucchinis, halved lengthwise
- 1 cup red bell pepper, seeded and minced
- ½ cup Kalamata olives, pitted and minced
- ½ cup tomatoes, minced
- 1 teaspoon garlic, minced
- 1 tablespoon dried oregano, crushed
- Salt and ground black pepper, as required
- ½ cup feta cheese, crumbled
- ¼ cup fresh parsley, chopped finely

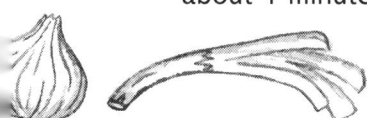

INSTRUCTIONS:

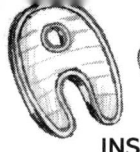

1. Preheat your oven to 350 degrees F.
2. Grease a large baking sheet.
3. With a melon baller, scoop out the flesh of each zucchini half. Discard the flesh.
4. In a bowl, mix together bell pepper, olives, tomato, garlic, oregano and black pepper.
5. Stuff each zucchini half with veggie mixture evenly.
6. Arrange zucchini halves onto the prepared baking sheet and bake for approximately 15 minutes.
7. Now, set the oven to broiler on high.
8. Top each zucchini half with feta cheese and broil for about 3 minutes.
9. Garnish with parsley and serve hot.

Nutritional Information per Serving:

Calories: 60
Fat: 3.2g
Carbohydrates: 6.4g
Fiber: 2g
Sugar: 3.2g
Protein: 3g
Sodium: 209mg

ZUCCHINI & BELL PEPPER CURRY

Servings: 6
Preparation Time: 20 minutes
Cooking Time: 20 minutes

INGREDIENTS:

- 2 medium zucchinis, chopped
- 1 green bell pepper, seeded and cubed
- 1 red bell pepper, seeded and cubed
- 1 yellow onion, sliced thinly
- 2 tablespoons olive oil
- 2 teaspoons curry powder
- Salt and ground black pepper, as required
- ¼ cup homemade low-sodium vegetable broth
- ¼ cup fresh cilantro, chopped

INSTRUCTIONS:

1. Preheat your oven to 375 degrees F.
2. Lightly grease a large baking dish.
3. In a large bowl, add all ingredients except cilantro and mix until well combined.
4. Transfer the vegetable mixture into the prepared baking dish.
5. Bake for approximately 15-20 minutes.
6. Serve immediately with the garnishing of cilantro.

NUTRITIONAL INFORMATION PER SERVING:

Calories: 60
Fat: 3.2g
Carbohydrates: 6.4g
Fiber: 2g
Sugar: 3.2g
Protein: 3g
Sodium: 209mg

ZUCCHINI NOODLES WITH MUSHROOM SAUCE

Servings: 5
Preparation Time: 20 minutes
Cooking Time: 15 minutes

INGREDIENTS:

For Mushroom Sauce:

- 1½ tablespoons olive oil
- 1 large garlic clove, minced
- 1¼ cups fresh button mushrooms, sliced
- ¼ cup homemade low-sodium vegetable broth
- ¼ cup cream
- Salt and ground black pepper, as required

For Zucchini Noodles:

- 3 large zucchinis, spiralized with blade C
- ¼ cup fresh parsley leaves, chopped

INSTRUCTIONS:

1. For mushroom sauce: In a large wok, heat the oil over medium heat and sauté the garlic for about 1 minute.
2. Stir in the mushrooms and cook for about 6-8 minutes.
3. Stir in the broth and cook for about 2 minutes, stirring continuously.
4. Stir in the cream, salt and black pepper and cook for about 1 minute.
5. Meanwhile, for the zucchini noodles: in a large pan of boiling water, add the zucchini noodles and cook for about 2-3 minutes.

6. With a slotted spoon, transfer the zucchini noodles into a colander and immediately rinse under cold running water.
7. Drain the zucchini noodles well and transfer onto a large paper towel-lined plate to drain.
8. Divide the zucchini noodles onto serving plates evenly.
9. Remove the mushroom sauce from the heat and place over zucchini noodles evenly.
10. Serve immediately with the garnishing of parsley.

NUTRITIONAL INFORMATION PER SERVING:

Calories: 77
Fat: 4.6g
Carbohydrates: 7.9g
Fiber: 2.4g
Sugar: 4g
Protein: 3.4g
Sodium: 120mg

SQUASH CASSEROLE

Servings: 8
Preparation Time: 15 minutes
Cooking Time: 55 minutes

INGREDIENTS:

- ¼ cup plus 2 tablespoons olive oil, divided
- 1 small yellow onion, chopped
- 3 summer squashes, sliced
- 4 eggs, beaten
- 3 cups low-fat cheddar cheese, shredded and divided
- 2 tablespoons unsweetened almond milk
- 2-3 tablespoons almond flour
- 2 tablespoons Erythritol
- Salt and ground black pepper, as required

INSTRUCTIONS:

1. Preheat your oven to 375 degrees F.
2. In a large wok, heat 2 tablespoons of oil over medium heat and cook the onion and squash for about 8-10 minutes, stirring occasionally.
3. Remove the wok from the heat.
4. Place the eggs, 1 cup of cheddar cheese, almond milk, almond flour, Erythritol, salt and black pepper in a large bowl and mix until well combined.
5. Add the squash mixture, and remaining oil and stir to combine.
6. Transfer the mixture into a large casserole dish and sprinkle with the remaining cheddar cheese.
7. Bake for approximately 35-45 minutes.
8. Remove the casserole dish from oven and set aside for about 5-10 minutes before serving.
9. Cut into 8 equal-sized portions and serve.

NUTRITIONAL INFORMATION PER SERVING:

Calories: 284
Fat: 22.8g
Carbohydrates: 5g
Fiber: 1.2g
Sugar: 1.9g
Protein: 15.8g
Sodium: 361mg

VEGGIES & WALNUT LOAF

Servings: 10
Preparation Time: 15 minutes
Cooking Time: 1 hour 10 minutes

INGREDIENTS:

- 1 tablespoon olive oil
- 2 yellow onions, chopped
- 2 garlic cloves, minced
- 1 teaspoon dried rosemary, crushed
- 1 cup walnuts, chopped
- 2 large carrots, peeled and chopped
- 1 large celery stalk, chopped
- 1 large green bell pepper, seeded and chopped
- 1 cup fresh button mushrooms, chopped
- 5 large eggs
- 1¼ cups almond flour
- Salt and ground black pepper, as required

INSTRUCTIONS:

1. Preheat your oven to 350-degree F.
2. Line 2 loaf pans with lightly greased parchment papers.
3. In a large wok, heat the olive oil over medium heat and sauté the onion for about 4-5 minutes.
4. Add the garlic and rosemary and sauté for about 1 minute.
5. Add the walnuts and vegetables and cook for about 3–4 minutes.
6. Remove the wok from heat and transfer the mixture into a large bowl.
7. Set aside to cool slightly.

8. In another mixing bowl, add the eggs, flour, sea salt, and black pepper, and beat until well combined.
9. Add the egg mixture into the bowl with vegetable mixture and mix until well combined.
10. Divide the mixture into prepared loaf pans evenly.
11. Bake for approximately 50–60 minutes or until top becomes golden brown.
12. Remove from the oven and set aside to cool slightly.
13. Carefully invert the loaves onto a platter.
14. Cut into desired sized slices and serve.

NUTRITIONAL INFORMATION PER SERVING:

Calories: 195
Fat: 15.5g
Carbohydrates: 9.1g
Fiber: 3.5g
Sugar: 2.5g
Protein: 6.8g
Sodium: 32mg

TOFU & VEGGIE BURGERS

Servings: 2
Preparation Time: 20 minutes
Cooking Time: 8 minutes

INGREDIENTS:

For Patties:

- ½ cup firm tofu, pressed and drained
- 1 medium carrot, peeled and gated
- 1 tablespoon onion, chopped
- 1 tablespoon scallion, chopped
- 1 tablespoon fresh parsley, chopped
- ½ garlic clove, minced
- 2 teaspoons low-sodium soy sauce
- 1 tablespoon arrowroot flour
- 1 teaspoon nutritional yeast flakes
- ½ teaspoon Dijon mustard
- 1 teaspoon paprika
- ¼ teaspoon ground turmeric
- ½ teaspoon ground black pepper
- 2 tablespoons olive oil

For Serving:

- ½ cup cherry tomatoes, halved
- 2 cup fresh baby greens

INSTRUCTIONS:

1. For patties: in a bowl, add the tofu and with a fork, mash well.
2. Add the remaining ingredients except for oil and mix until well combined.
3. Make 4 equal-sized patties from the mixture.
4. Heat the oil in a frying pan over low heat and cook the patties for about 4 minutes per side.
5. Divide the avocado, tomatoes and greens onto serving plates.
6. Top each plate with 2 patties and serve.

NUTRITIONAL INFORMATION PER SERVING:

Calories: 198
Fat: 17g
Carbohydrates: 7.9g
Fiber: 2.7g
Sugar: 2.7g
Protein: 7.2g
Sodium: 341mg

TOFU & VEGGIE LETTUCE WRAPS

Servings: 4
Preparation Time: 15 minutes
Cooking Time: 6 minutes

INGREDIENTS:

For Wraps:

- 1 tablespoon olive oil
- 14 ounces extra-firm tofu, drained, pressed and cut into cubes
- 1 teaspoon curry powder
- Salt, as required
- 8 lettuce leaves
- 1 small carrot, peeled and julienned
- ½ cup radishes, sliced
- 2 tablespoons fresh cilantro, chopped

For Sauce:

- ½ cup creamy peanut butter
- 1 tablespoon maple syrup
- 2 tablespoons low-sodium soy sauce
- 2 tablespoons fresh lime juice
- ¼ teaspoon red pepper flakes, crushed
- ¼ cup water

INSTRUCTIONS:

1. For tofu: in a wok, heat the oil over medium heat and cook the tofu, curry powder and a little salt for about 5-6 minutes or until golden brown, stirring frequently.
2. Remove from the heat and set aside to cool slightly.
3. Meanwhile, for sauce: in a bowl, add all the ingredients and beat until smooth.

4. Arrange the lettuce leaves onto serving plates.
5. Divide the tofu, carrot, radish and peanuts over each leaf evenly.
6. Garnish with cilantro and serve alongside the peanut sauce.

NUTRITIONAL INFORMATION PER SERVING:

Calories: 381
Fat: 28.5g
Carbohydrates: 18g
Fiber: 4.4g
Sugar: 9g
Protein: 19.4g
Sodium: 657mg

TOFU WITH KALE

Servings: 2
Preparation Time: 15 minutes
Cooking Time: 10 minutes

INGREDIENTS:

- 1 tablespoon extra-virgin olive oil
- ½ pound tofu, pressed, drained and cubed
- 1 teaspoon fresh ginger, minced
- 1 garlic clove, minced
- ¼ teaspoon red pepper flakes, crushed
- 6 ounces fresh kale, tough ribs removed and chopped finely
- 1 tablespoon low-sodium soy sauce

INSTRUCTIONS:

1. In a large non-stick wok, heat olive oil over medium-high heat and stir-fry the tofu for about 3-3 minutes.
2. Add the ginger, garlic and red pepper flakes and cook for about 1 minute, stirring continuously.
3. Stir in the kale and soy sauce and stir-fry for about 4-5 minutes.
4. Serve hot.

NUTRITIONAL INFORMATION PER SERVING:

Calories: 190
Fat: 11.8g
Carbohydrates: 11g
Fiber: 3g
Sugar: 1.3g
Protein: 12.8g
Sodium: 487mg

TOFU WITH BROCCOLI

Servings: 4
Preparation Time: 20 minutes
Cooking Time: 25 minutes

INGREDIENTS:

For Tofu:

- 14 ounces firm tofu, drained, pressed and cut into 1-inch slices
- 1/3 cup arrowroot starch, divided
- ¼ cup olive oil
- 1 teaspoon fresh ginger, grated
- 1 medium onion, sliced thinly
- 3 tablespoons low-sodium soy sauce
- 2 tablespoons balsamic vinegar
- 1 tablespoon maple syrup
- ½ cup water

For Steamed Broccoli:

- 2 cups broccoli florets

INSTRUCTIONS:

1. In a shallow bowl, place ¼ cup of the arrowroot starch.
2. Add the tofu cubes and coat with arrowroot starch.
3. In a cast-iron wok, heat the olive oil over medium heat and cook the tofu cubes for about 8-10 minutes or until golden from all sides.
4. With a slotted spoon, transfer the tofu cubes onto a plate. Set aside.
5. In the same wok, add ginger and sauté for about 1 minute.
6. Add the onions and sauté for about 2-3 minutes.
7. Add the soy sauce, vinegar and maple syrup and bring to a gentle simmer.
8. In the meantime, in a small bowl, dissolve the remaining arrowroot starch in water.
9. Slowly, add the arrowroot starch mixture into the sauce, stirring continuously.
10. Stir in the cooked tofu and cook for about 1 minute.
11. Meanwhile, in a large pan of water, arrange a steamer basket and bring to a boil.
12. Adjust the heat to medium-low.
13. Place the broccoli florets in the steamer basket and steam, covered for about 5-6 minutes.
14. Remove from the heat and drain the broccoli completely.
15. Transfer the broccoli into the wok of tofu and stir to combine.
16. Serve hot.

NUTRITIONAL INFORMATION PER SERVING:

Calories: 230
Fat: 17g
Carbohydrates: 11g
Fiber: 2.9g
Sugar: 6g
Protein: 10.9g
Sodium: 692mg

TOFU WITH PEAS

Servings: 5
Preparation Time: 15 minutes
Cooking Time: 20 minutes

INGREDIENTS:

- 2 tablespoons olive oil, divided
- 1 (16-ounce) package extra-firm tofu, drained, pressed and cubed
- 1 cup yellow onion, chopped
- 1 tablespoon fresh ginger, minced
- 2 garlic cloves, minced
- 1 tomato, chopped finely
- 2 cups frozen peas, thawed
- ¼ cup water
- 2 tablespoons fresh cilantro, chopped

INSTRUCTIONS:

1. In a non-stick wok, heat 1 tablespoon of the oil over medium-high heat and cook the tofu for about 4-5 minutes or until browned completely, stirring occasionally.
2. Transfer the tofu into a bowl.
3. In the same wok, heat the remaining oil over medium heat and sauté the onion for about 3-4 minutes.
4. Add the ginger and garlic and sauté for about 1 minute.
5. Add the tomatoes and cook for about 4-5 minutes, crushing with the back of a spoon.
6. Stir in the peas and broth and cook for about 2-3 minutes.
7. Stir in the tofu and cook for about 1-2 minutes.
8. Serve hot with the garnishing of cilantro.

NUTRITIONAL INFORMATION PER SERVING:

Calories: 291
Fat: 11.8g
Carbohydrates: 20g
Fiber: 10g
Sugar: 9g
Protein: 19g
Sodium: 732mg

TOFU WITH BRUSSELS SPROUT

Servings: 3
Preparation Time: 15 minutes
Cooking Time: 15 minutes

INGREDIENTS:

- 1½ tablespoons olive oil, divided
- 8 ounces extra-firm tofu, drained, pressed and cut into slices
- 2 garlic cloves, chopped
- 1/3 cup pecans, toasted and chopped
- 1 tablespoon unsweetened applesauce
- ¼ cup fresh cilantro, chopped
- ½ pound Brussels sprouts, trimmed and cut into wide ribbons
- ¾ pound mixed bell peppers, seeded and sliced

INSTRUCTIONS:

1. In a wok, heat ½ tablespoon of the oil over medium heat and sauté the tofu and for about 6-7 minutes or until golden brown.
2. Add the garlic and pecans and sauté for about 1 minute.
3. Add the applesauce and cook for about 2 minutes.
4. Stir in the cilantro and remove from heat.
5. Transfer tofu into a plate and set aside
6. In the same wok, heat the remaining oil over medium-high heat and cook the Brussels sprouts and bell peppers for about 5 minutes.
7. Stir in the tofu and remove from the heat.
8. Serve immediately.

NUTRITIONAL INFORMATION PER SERVING:

Calories: 238
Fat: 16g
Carbohydrates: 13g
Fiber: 4.8g
Sugar: 4.5g
Protein: 11.8g
Sodium: 26mg

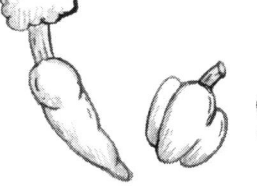

TOFU WITH VEGGIES

Servings: 4
Preparation Time: 20 minutes
Cooking Time: 45 minutes

INGREDIENTS:

- 1 (14-ounce) package extra firm tofu, pressed, drained and cut into small cubes
- 2 tablespoons sesame oil, divided
- 4 tablespoons low-sodium soy sauce
- 3 tablespoons maple syrup
- 2 tablespoons peanut butter
- 2 tablespoons fresh lime juice
- 1-2 teaspoons chili garlic sauce
- 1-pound green beans, trimmed
- 2-3 small red bell peppers, seeded and cubed
- 2 scallion greens, chopped

INSTRUCTIONS:

1. Preheat your oven to 400 degrees F.
2. Line a baking sheet with parchment paper.
3. Arrange the tofu cubes onto the prepared baking sheet in a single layer.
4. Bake for approximately 25-30 minutes.
5. Meanwhile, in a small bowl, add 1 tablespoon of the sesame oil, soy sauce, maple syrup, peanut butter, lime juice, and chili garlic sauce and beat until well combined. Set aside.
6. Remove from the oven and place the tofu cubes into the bowl of sauce.
7. Stir the mixture well and set aside for about 10 minutes, stirring occasionally.
8. With a slotted spoon, remove the tofu cubes from bowl, reserving the sauce.
9. Heat a large cast-iron wok over medium heat and cook the tofu cubes for about 5 minutes, stirring occasionally.
10. With a slotted spoon, transfer the tofu cubes onto a plate. Set aside.
11. In the same wok, add the remaining sesame oil, green beans, bell peppers and 2-3 tablespoons of reserved sauce and cook, covered for about 4-5 minutes.
12. Adjust the heat to medium-high, and stir in the cooked tofu remaining reserved sauce.
13. Cook for about 1-2 minutes, stirring frequently.
14. Stir in the scallion greens and serve hot.

NUTRITIONAL INFORMATION PER SERVING:

Calories: 320
Fat: 19g
Carbohydrates: 22g
Fiber: 6g
Sugar: 10g
Protein: 17.2g
Sodium: 129mg

TOFU & MUSHROOM CURRY

Servings: 4
Preparation Time: 20 minutes
Cooking Time: 25 minutes

INGREDIENTS:

For Tofu:

- 16 ounces extra-firm tofu, pressed, drained and cut into ½-inch cubes
- 1 garlic clove, minced
- 3 tablespoons balsamic vinegar
- 3 tablespoons low-sodium soy sauce
- 3 tablespoons arrowroot starch
- 2 tablespoons sesame oil
- 1 tablespoon Erythritol
- 1 teaspoon red pepper flakes
- 2 tablespoons coconut oil

For Curry:

- ¼ cup water
- 1 small yellow onion, minced
- 3 large garlic cloves, minced
- 1 teaspoon fresh ginger, grated
- 2 cups fresh mushrooms, sliced
- 3 tablespoons red curry paste
- 13 ounces light coconut milk
- 1 tablespoon low-sodium soy sauce
- 2 tablespoons fresh lime juice
- 1 teaspoon lime zest, grated
- 8 fresh basil leaves, chopped

INSTRUCTIONS:

1. For tofu: in a resealable bag, place all ingredients.
2. Seal the bag and shake to coat well.
3. Refrigerate to marinate for 2-4 hours.

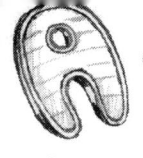

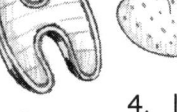

4. In a large wok, melt the coconut oil over medium heat and stir fry the tofu cubes for about 4-5 minutes or until golden brown completely.
5. With a slotted spoon, transfer the tofu cubes into a bowl.
6. For curry: in a large pan, add the water over medium heat and ring to a simmer.
7. Add the minced onion, garlic and ginger and cook for about 5 minutes.
8. Add the mushrooms and curry paste and stir to combine well.
9. Stir in the remaining ingredients except for basil and simmer for about 10 minutes.
10. Stir in the tofu and simmer for about 5 minutes.
11. Garnish with basil and serve.

NUTRITIONAL INFORMATION PER SERVING:

Calories: 399
Fat: 25g
Carbohydrates: 15g
Fiber: 1.6g
Sugar: 4.1g
Protein: 14.4g
Sodium: 940mg

TOFU & VEGGIES CURRY

Servings: 5
Preparation Time: 20 minutes
Cooking Time: 30 minutes

INGREDIENTS:

1. 1 (16-ounce) block firm tofu, drained, pressed and cut into ½-inch cubes
2. 2 tablespoons coconut oil
3. 1 medium yellow onion, chopped
4. 1½ tablespoons fresh ginger, minced
5. 2 garlic cloves, minced
6. 1 tablespoon curry powder
7. Salt and ground black pepper, as required
8. 1 cup fresh mushrooms, sliced
9. 1 cup carrots, peeled and sliced
10. 1 (14-ounce) can unsweetened low-fat coconut milk
11. ½ cup low-sodium vegetable broth
12. 2 teaspoons Erythritol
13. 10 ounces cauliflower florets
14. 1 tablespoon fresh lime juice
15. ¼ cup fresh basil leaves, sliced thinly

INSTRUCTIONS:

1. In a Dutch oven, heat the oil over medium heat and sauté the onion, ginger and garlic for about 5 minutes.
2. Stir in the curry powder, salt and black pepper and cook for about 2 minutes, stirring occasionally.
3. Add the mushrooms and carrot and cook for about 4-5 minutes.
4. Stir in the coconut milk, broth and brown sugar and bring to a boil.
5. Add the tofu and cauliflower and simmer for about 12-15 minutes, stirring occasionally.
6. Stir in the lime juice and remove from the heat.
7. Serve hot.

NUTRITIONAL INFORMATION PER SERVING:

Calories: 330
Fat: 16g
Carbohydrates: 18g
Fiber: 6g
Sugar: 8g
Protein: 17.2g
Sodium: 129mg

TEMPEH WITH BELL PEPPERS

Servings: 3
Preparation Time: 15 minutes
Cooking Time: 15 minutes

INGREDIENTS:

- 2 tablespoons balsamic vinegar
- 2 tablespoons low-sodium soy sauce
- 2 tablespoons tomato sauce
- 1 teaspoon maple syrup
- ½ teaspoon garlic powder
- 1/8 teaspoon red pepper flakes, crushed
- 1 tablespoon vegetable oil
- 8 ounces tempeh, cut into cubes
- 1 medium onion, chopped
- 2 large green bell peppers, seeded and chopped

INSTRUCTIONS:

1. In a small bowl, add the vinegar, soy sauce, tomato sauce, maple syrup, garlic powder and red pepper flakes and beat until well combined. Set aside.
2. Heat 1 tablespoon of oil in a large wok over medium heat and cook the tempeh about 2-3 minutes per side.
3. Add the onion and bell peppers and heat for about 2-3 minutes.
4. Stir in the sauce mixture and cook for about 3-5 minutes, stirring frequently.
5. Serve hot.

NUTRITIONAL INFORMATION PER SERVING:

Calories: 291
Fat: 11.9g
Carbohydrates: 23g
Fiber: 10g
Sugar: 10g
Protein: 19g
Sodium: 732mg

TEMPEH WITH BRUSSEL SPROUT & KALE

Servings: 3
Preparation Time: 15 minutes
Cooking Time: 17 minutes

INGREDIENTS:

- 2 tablespoons olive oil
- 1/3 cup red onion, chopped finely
- 1½ cups tempeh, cubed
- 2 cups Brussels sprout, quartered
- 2 garlic cloves, minced
- ½ teaspoon ground cumin
- ½ teaspoon garlic powder
- Salt and ground black pepper, as required
- 2 cups fresh kale, tough ribs removed and chopped

INSTRUCTIONS:

1. Heat the oil in a wok over medium-high heat and sauté the onion for about 4-5 minutes.
2. Add in remaining ingredients except for kale and cook for about 6-7 minutes, stirring occasionally.
3. Add kale and cook for about 5 minutes, stirring twice.
4. Serve hot.

NUTRITIONAL INFORMATION PER SERVING:

Calories: 291
Fat: 18.8g
Carbohydrates: 18g
Fiber: 3.3g
Sugar: 2g
Protein: 18.g
Sodium: 86mg

TEMPEH WITH VEGGIES

Servings: 3
Preparation Time: 15 minutes
Cooking Time: 17 minutes

INGREDIENTS:

For Sauce:

- 3 tablespoons tahini
- 2 tablespoons low-sodium soy sauce
- 1 tablespoon sesame oil
- 1 tablespoon chili-garlic sauce
- 1 tablespoon maple syrup

For tempeh & Veggies:

- 3 tablespoons olive oil, divided
- 8 ounces tempeh, cut into 1x2-inch rectangular strips
- 8 ounces fresh button mushrooms, sliced thinly
- 8 ounces fresh spinach
- 1 tablespoon fresh ginger, minced
- 1 tablespoon garlic, minced

INSTRUCTIONS:

1. For sauce: in a bowl, add all ingredients and beat until well combined.
2. In a large wok, heat the oil over medium-high heat and cook the tempeh for about 4-5 minutes or until browned.
3. With a slotted spoon, transfer the tempeh into a bowl and set aside.
4. In the same wok, heat the remaining oil over medium-high heat and cook the mushrooms for about 6-7 minutes, stirring frequently.
5. With a slotted spoon, transfer the mushrooms into a bowl and set aside.
6. In the same wok, add the spinach, ginger and garlic and cook for about 2-3 minutes.
7. Stir in the cooked tempeh, mushrooms and sauce and cook for about 1-2 minutes, stirring continuously.
8. Serve hot.

NUTRITIONAL INFORMATION PER SERVING:

Calories: 341
Fat: 26.5g
Carbohydrates: 15g
Fiber: 2.9g
Sugar: 4.8g
Protein: 16.5g
Sodium: 100mg

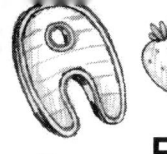

FUELING HACKS RECIPES

BERRY MOJITO

Servings: 2
Preparation Time: 10 minutes

INGREDIENTS:

- 2 tablespoons fresh lime juice
- 6 fresh mint leaves
- 1 packet Mixed Berry Flavor Infuser
- 16 ounces seltzer water
- Ice cubes, as required

INSTRUCTIONS:

1. In the bottom of 2 cocktail glasses, divide the lime juice and mint leaves.
2. With the bottom end of a spoon, gently muddle the mint leaves.
3. Now, divide the Berry Infuser and seltzer water into each glass and stir to combine.
4. Place ice cubes in each glass and serve.

NUTRITIONAL INFORMATION PER SERVING:

Calories: 5
Fat: 12.6g
Carbohydrates: 1.1g
Fiber: 0.5g
Sugar: 0g
Protein: 0g
Sodium: 0mg

COCONUT SMOOTHIE

Servings: 1
Preparation Time: 5 minutes

INGREDIENTS:

- 1 sachet Essential Creamy Vanilla Shake
- 6 ounces unsweetened almond milk
- 6 ounces diet ginger ale
- 2 tablespoons unsweetened coconut, shredded
- ¼ teaspoon rum extract
- ½ cup ice

INSTRUCTIONS:

1. In a small blender, place all ingredients and pulse until smooth.
2. Transfer the smoothie into a serving glass and serve immediately.

NUTRITIONAL INFORMATION PER SERVING:

Calories: 120
Fat: 6.2g
Carbohydrates: 15.9g
Fiber: 5.6g
Sugar: 7.6g
Protein: 15g
Sodium: 124mg

TIRAMISU SHAKE

Servings: 1
Preparation Time: 5 minutes

INGREDIENTS:

- 1 packet cappuccino mix
- 1 tablespoon sugar-free chocolate syrup
- ½ cup water
- ½ cup ice, crushed

INSTRUCTIONS:

1. In a small blender, add all the ingredients and pulse until smooth and creamy.
2. Transfer the shake into a serving glass and serve immediately.

NUTRITIONAL INFORMATION PER SERVING:

Calories: 107
Fat: 0g
Carbohydrates: 15g
Fiber: 4.5g
Sugar: 8g
Protein: 14g
Sodium: 150mg

VANILLA SHAKE

Servings: 1
Preparation Time: 5 minutes

INGREDIENTS:

- ½ packet Vanilla Shake Fueling
- ½ packet Gingerbread Fueling
- ½ cup unsweetened almond milk
- ½ cup water
- 8 ice cubes

INSTRUCTIONS:

1. In a small blender, place all ingredients and pulse until smooth.
2. Transfer the shake into a serving glass and serve immediately.

NUTRITIONAL INFORMATION PER SERVING:

Calories: 130
Fat: 3.3g
Carbohydrates: 15g
Fiber: 4.5g
Sugar: 6g
Protein: 13g
Sodium: 100mg

SHAMROCK SHAKE

Servings: 1
Preparation Time: 5 minutes

INGREDIENTS:

- 1 packet Vanilla Shake
- 6 ounces unsweetened almond milk
- ¼ teaspoon peppermint extract
- 1-2 drops green food coloring
- 1 cup ice cubes

INSTRUCTIONS:

1. In a small blender, place all ingredients and pulse until smooth.
2. Transfer the shake into a serving glass and serve immediately.

Nutritional Information per Serving:

Calories: 120
Fat: 3.9g
Carbohydrates: 13.5g
Fiber: 4.7g
Sugar: 6.1g
Protein: 11.7g
Sodium: 80mg

CHOCOLATE SHAKE

Servings: 1
Preparation Time: 10 minutes

INGREDIENTS:

- 1 packet cappuccino mix
- ½ cup water
- 1 tablespoon sugar-free chocolate syrup
- ½ cup ice, crushed

INSTRUCTIONS:

1. In a small blender, place all ingredients and pulse until smooth.
2. Transfer the shake into a serving glass and serve immediately.

NUTRITIONAL INFORMATION PER SERVING:

Calories: 107
Fat: 0.5g
Carbohydrates: 15g
Fiber: 4.5g
Sugar: 8g
Protein: 13g
Sodium: 121mg

PEPPERMINT MOCHA

Servings: 1
Preparation Time: 5 minutes

INGREDIENTS:

- 1 sachet Essential Velvety Hot Chocolate
- 6 ounces freshly brewed coffee
- ¼ cup warm unsweetened almond milk
- ¼ teaspoon peppermint extract
- 1 tablespoon whipped topping
- Pinch of ground cinnamon

INSTRUCTIONS:

1. In a serving mug, place the Hot Chocolate sachet, coffee, almond milk and peppermint extract and stir until well blended.
2. Top the hot chocolate with whipped topping and sprinkle with cinnamon.
3. Serve immediately.

NUTRITIONAL INFORMATION PER SERVING:

Calories: 133
Fat: 1.1g
Carbohydrates: 15.2g
Fiber: 4.4g
Sugar: 10g
Protein: 14.6g
Sodium: 110mg

PUMPKIN FRAPPE

Servings: 1
Preparation Time: 5 minutes

INGREDIENTS:

- 1 sachet Essential Spiced Gingerbread
- 4 ounces strong brewed coffee
- 4 ounces unsweetened almond milk
- 1/8 teaspoon pumpkin pie spice
- ½ cup ice
- 1 tablespoon whipped topping

INSTRUCTIONS:

1. In a blender, add the Spiced Gingerbread sachet, coffee, almond milk, pumpkin pie spice and ice and pulse until smooth.
2. Transfer the mixture into a glass and top with whipped topping.
3. Serve immediately.

NUTRITIONAL INFORMATION PER SERVING:

Calories: 138
Fat: 4.8g
Carbohydrates: 16.4g
Fiber: 4.5g
Sugar: 5.3g
Protein: 11.7g
Sodium: 54mg

VANILLA FRAPPE

Servings: 1
Preparation Time: 5 minutes

INGREDIENTS:

- 1 sachet Essential Vanilla Shake
- 8 ounces unsweetened almond milk
- ½ cup ice
- 1 tablespoon whipped topping

INSTRUCTIONS:

1. In a blender, add the Vanilla Shake sachet, almond milk and ice and pulse until smooth.
2. Transfer the mixture into a glass and top with whipped topping.
3. Serve immediately.

NUTRITIONAL INFORMATION PER SERVING:

Calories: 155
Fat: 4.5g
Carbohydrates: 15.2g
Fiber: 4.9g
Sugar: 7.2g
Protein: 42.3g
Sodium: 59mg

CHOCOLATE FRAPPE

Servings: 1
Preparation Time: 5 minutes

INGREDIENTS:

- 1 sachet Essential Frosty Mint Chocolate Soft Serve Treat
- 4 ounces strong brewed coffee
- 4 ounces unsweetened almond milk
- 1½ tablespoons sugar-free chocolate syrup, divided
- ¼ teaspoon peppermint extract
- ½ cup ice
- 1 tablespoon whipped topping

INSTRUCTIONS:

1. In a blender, add the Chocolate sachet, coffee, almond milk, 1 tablespoon of chocolate syrup, peppermint extract and ice and pulse until smooth.
2. Transfer the mixture into a glass and top with whipped topping.
3. Drizzle with remaining chocolate syrup and serve immediately.

NUTRITIONAL INFORMATION PER SERVING:

Calories: 148
Fat: 4.8g
Carbohydrates: 18g
Fiber: 4.5g
Sugar: 7.2g
Protein: 11.7g
Sodium: 125mg

CARAMEL MACCHIATO FRAPPE

Servings: 1
Preparation Time: 10 minutes

INGREDIENTS:

- 8 ounces unsweetened cashew milk
- 1 sachet Essential Caramel Macchiato Shake
- ½ cup ice
- 2 tablespoons whipped topping
- 1 tablespoon sugar-free caramel syrup

INSTRUCTIONS:

1. In a blender, add the Macchiato Shake sachet, cashew milk and ice and pulse until smooth.
2. Transfer the mixture into a glass and top with whipped topping.
3. Drizzle with caramel syrup and serve immediately.

NUTRITIONAL INFORMATION PER SERVING:

Calories: 139
Fat: 4.1g
Carbohydrates: 16g
Fiber: 3g
Sugar: 8.5g
Protein: 11.2g
Sodium: 329mg

EGGNOG

Servings: 1
Preparation Time: 10 minutes

INGREDIENTS:

- 1 sachet Essential Vanilla Shake
- 8 ounces unsweetened almond milk
- 1 egg (yolk and white separated)
- ¼ teaspoon rum extract
- Pinch of ground nutmeg

INSTRUCTIONS:

1. In a blender, add the Vanilla Shake sachet, almond milk and egg yolk and pulse until smooth.
2. In the bowl of a stand mixer, place egg white and beat on medium speed until stiff peaks form.
3. Place the whipped egg whites into a serving glass and top with shake mixture.
4. Stir the mixture and sprinkle with nutmeg.
5. Serve immediately.

NUTRITIONAL INFORMATION PER SERVING:

Calories: 211
Fat: 8.2g
Carbohydrates: 15.3g
Fiber: 5g
Sugar: 7.4g
Protein: 20.5g
Sodium: 100mg

PUMPKIN SPICED LATTE

Servings: 1
Preparation Time: 5 minutes
Cooking Time: 1 minute

INGREDIENTS:

- ½ cup unsweetened cashew milk
- 2 tablespoons pumpkin puree
- ½ cup strong brewed coffee
- 1 sachet Essential Spiced Gingerbread

INSTRUCTIONS:

1. In a microwave-safe mug, place cashew milk and pumpkin puree and microwave for 1 minute.
2. Remove from microwave and immediately stir in coffee and Gingerbread sachet until smooth.
3. Serve immediately.

NUTRITIONAL INFORMATION PER SERVING:

Calories: 134
Fat: 3.1g
Carbohydrates: 14g
Fiber: 4.9g
Sugar: 6g
Protein: 11.5g
Sodium: 264mg

HOT CHOCOLATE

Servings: 1
Preparation Time: 10 minutes
Cooking Time: 2 minutes

INGREDIENTS:

- 1 sachet Essential Velvety Hot Chocolate
- ½ teaspoon ground cinnamon
- Pinch of cayenne pepper
- 6 ounces unsweetened almond milk
- 1 tablespoon whipped cream

INSTRUCTIONS:

1. In a serving mug, place all the ingredients except for whipped cream and beat until well blended.
2. Microwave on high for about 2 minutes.
3. Top with whipped cream and serve.

NUTRITIONAL INFORMATION PER SERVING:

Calories: 185
Fat: 7.6g
Carbohydrates: 15.9g
Fiber: 5.3g
Sugar: 10g
Protein: 15.1g
Sodium: 80mg

CHERRY MOCHA POPSICLES

Servings: 6
Preparation Time: 10 minutes
Cooking Time: 45 seconds

INGREDIENTS:

- 1 cup unsweetened almond milk
- 3 sachets Dark Chocolate Covered Cherry Shake
- 1 teaspoon vanilla extract
- 1 tablespoon instant espresso powder
- 2 cups plain low-fat Greek yogurt
- 1-2 packets zero-calorie sugar substitute

INSTRUCTIONS:

1. In a microwave-safe mug, place the almond milk and microwave on High for about 45 seconds.
2. Remove the mug from microwave and immediately stir in the espresso powder until dissolved completely.
3. Set aside to cool completely.
4. In a blender, add the cooled espresso milk and remaining ingredients and pulse until smooth.
5. Divide the mixture into 6 large Popsicle molds and freeze overnight.

NUTRITIONAL INFORMATION PER SERVING:

Calories: 104
Fat: 5.2g
Carbohydrates: 13.7g
Fiber: 2.2g
Sugar: 8.4g
Protein: 10.4g
Sodium: 90mg

YOGURT COOKIE DOUGH

Servings: 1
Preparation Time: 5 minutes

INGREDIENTS:

- 1 sachet Essential Chocolate Chip Cookie
- 1 (5.3-ounce) container low-fat plain Greek yogurt

INSTRUCTIONS:

1. In a bowl add Chocolate Chip Cookie and yogurt and mix until well combined.
2. Refrigerate to chill before serving.

NUTRITIONAL INFORMATION PER SERVING:

Calories: 197
Fat: 3.6g
Carbohydrates: 22g
Fiber: 4g
Sugar: 15g
Protein: 18.5g
Sodium: 345mg

CHOCOLATE COCONUT PIE

Servings: 2
Preparation Time: 10 minutes
Cooking Time: 20 seconds

INGREDIENTS:

- 1 sachet Drizzled Chocolate Fudge Crisp Bar
- Olive oil cooking spray
- 2 tablespoons whipped topping
- 1 sachet Essential Chocolate Fudge Pudding
- ½ cup unsweetened coconut milk
- 1 tablespoon unsweetened coconut, shredded

INSTRUCTIONS:

1. In a microwave-safe bowl, add the Chocolate bar and microwave on High for about 15-20 seconds.
2. Place the melted bar into a lightly greased ramekin and wit the back of a spoon, press it slightly.
3. In a bowl, add the Fudge pudding and milk and mix well.
4. Place the pudding mixture over the bar in ramekin and refrigerate for about 30 minutes.
5. Top with whipped topping and coconut and serve.

NUTRITIONAL INFORMATION PER SERVING:

Calories: 265
Fat: 18.8g
Carbohydrates: 16.1g
Fiber: 5.1g
Sugar: 6.4g
Protein: 12.6g
Sodium: 163mg

CARAMEL CRUNCH PARFAIT

Servings: 1
Preparation Time: 10 minutes

INGREDIENTS:

- 6 ounces low-fat plain Greek yogurt
- ½ packet stevia
- ¼ teaspoon vanilla extract
- 2 tablespoons whipped topping
- 1 sachet Puffed Sweet & Salty Snacks, crushed
- 1 tablespoon sugar-free caramel syrup

INSTRUCTIONS:

1. In a bowl, mix together the yogurt, stevia and vanilla extract.
2. Top with whipped topping Puffed Snack sachet.
3. Drizzle with caramel syrup and serve.

NUTRITIONAL INFORMATION PER SERVING:

Calories: 150
Fat: 6.2g
Carbohydrates: 16.9g
Fiber: 1g
Sugar: 7.9g
Protein: 7.4g
Sodium: 151mg

CHOCOLATE BERRY PARFAIT

Servings: 2
Preparation Time: 10 minutes

INGREDIENTS:

- 1 sachet Chocolate Cherry Ganache Bar
- 1½ cups low-fat plain Greek yogurt
- ¼ cup strawberry-flavored light cream cheese, softened
- 1 tablespoon unsweetened cocoa powder
- 1-2 packets zero-calorie sugar substitute
- 2/3-ounce almonds, sliced

INSTRUCTIONS:

1. In a blender, add all ingredients and pulse until desired consistency is achieved.
2. Serve immediately.

NUTRITIONAL INFORMATION PER SERVING:

Calories: 311
Fat: 18.6g
Carbohydrates: 23g
Fiber: 4.1g
Sugar: 16g
Protein: 15.2g
Sodium: 263mg

BROWNIE PUDDING

Servings: 1
Preparation Time: 5 minutes

INGREDIENTS:

- 1 (5.3-ounce) container low-fat plain Greek yogurt
- 1 sachet Brownie Mix

INSTRUCTIONS:

1. In a bowl, add yogurt and Brownie Mix sachet and mix well.
2. Refrigerate to chill before serving.

NUTRITIONAL INFORMATION PER SERVING:

Calories: 190
Fat: 2g
Carbohydrates: 20g
Fiber: 4g
Sugar: 13g
Protein: 24.7g
Sodium: 223mg

BROWNIE PEANUT BUTTER PUDDING

Servings: 1
Preparation Time: 5 minutes

INGREDIENTS:

- 1 packet Brownie
- 1 (5.3-ounce) container low-fat plain Greek yogurt
- 1 tablespoon peanut butter powder
- Dash of vanilla extract

INSTRUCTIONS:

1. In a bowl add all ingredients and mix until well combined.
2. Refrigerate to chill before serving.

NUTRITIONAL INFORMATION PER SERVING:

Calories: 215
Fat: 2.7g
Carbohydrates: 22g
Fiber: 4.7g
Sugar: 14.4g
Protein: 27.4g
Sodium: 225mg

CHIA SEED PUDDING

Servings: 1
Preparation Time: 10 minutes
Cooking Time: 11 minutes

INGREDIENTS:

- 2 sachets Chia Bliss Smoothie
- 1 cup unsweetened almond milk
- ¼ cup chia seeds

INSTRUCTIONS:

1. In a serving bowl, add all the ingredients and mix until well blended.
2. Refrigerate overnight before serving.

NUTRITIONAL INFORMATION PER SERVING:

Calories: 188
Fat: 17.8g
Carbohydrates: 20g
Fiber: 9g
Sugar: 6g
Protein: 14.5g
Sodium: 90mg

CHOCOLATE CAKE FRIES

Servings: 2
Preparation Time: 10 minutes
Cooking Time: 4 minutes

INGREDIENTS:

- 2 sachets essential Golden Chocolate Chip Pancakes
- ¼ cup liquid egg substitute
- 2 teaspoons vegetable oil

INSTRUCTIONS:

1. In a bowl, add Pancakes sachets and egg substitute and mix until well combined.
2. Place the mixture into a resealable plastic bag.
3. Cut off a small hole on tip of bag.
4. In a wok, heat oil over medium heat.
5. In the wok, pipe mixture in long, straight lines and cook for about 2 minutes per side.
6. Serve warm.

NUTRITIONAL INFORMATION PER SERVING:

Calories: 167
Fat: 6g
Carbohydrates: 11g
Fiber: 4g
Sugar: 4.2g
Protein: 14.8g
Sodium: 304mg

FRENCH TOAST STICKS

Servings: 3
Preparation Time: 15 minutes
Cooking Time: 4 minutes

INGREDIENTS:

- 2 sachets Essential Cinnamon Crunchy Oat Cereal
- 6 tablespoons egg liquid substitute
- 2 tablespoons low-fat cream cheese, softened
- Olive oil cooking spray

INSTRUCTIONS:

1. In a food processor, add the cereal sachets and pulse until fine breadcrumbs like consistency is achieved.
2. Add the egg liquid substitute and cream cheese and pulse until a dough forms.
3. Divide the dough into 6 portions and shape each into a breadstick.
4. Heat a lightly greased wok over medium-high heat and cook the French toast sticks for about 2 minutes per side or until golden brown.
5. Serve warm.

NUTRITIONAL INFORMATION PER SERVING:

Calories: 107
Fat: 3g
Carbohydrates: 10.3g
Fiber: 2.6g
Sugar: 1.5g
Protein: 11.6g
Sodium: 164mg

FUDGE BALLS

Servings: 2
Preparation Time: 10 minutes

INGREDIENTS:

- 1 sachet chocolate pudding
- 1 sachet chocolate shake
- 4 tablespoons peanut butter powder
- ¼ cup unsweetened almond milk
- 2 tablespoons water

INSTRUCTIONS:

1. In a small bowl, add all the ingredients and mix until well combined.
2. Make 8 small equal-sized balls from the mixture.
3. Arrange the balls onto a parchment paper-lined baking sheet and refrigerate until set before serving.

NUTRITIONAL INFORMATION PER SERVING:

Calories: 218
Fat: 5.3g
Carbohydrates: 15.3g
Fiber: 8.3g
Sugar: 7g
Protein: 30g
Sodium: 111mg

PEANUT BUTTER BITES

Servings: 1
Preparation Time: 10 minutes
Cooking Time: 1 minute

INGREDIENTS:

- 2 tablespoons peanut butter powder
- 1 tablespoon water
- 1 sachet Essential Creamy Double Peanut Butter Crisp Bar

INSTRUCTIONS:

1. In a bowl, add the peanut butter powder and water and mix until a smooth paste is formed.
2. In a microwave-safe plate, place the Crisp Bar and microwave for about 15 seconds or until soft.
3. Add the warm bar pieces into the bowl of water mixture and mix until a dough forms.
4. Make small 4 equal-sized balls from the dough and arrange onto a parchment paper-lined plate.
5. Refrigerate until set before serving.

NUTRITIONAL INFORMATION PER SERVING:

Calories: 190
Fat: 5.5g
Carbohydrates: 17g
Fiber: 4g
Sugar: 9g
Protein: 17g
Sodium: 300mg

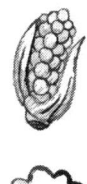

YOGURT CEREAL BARK

Servings: 2
Preparation Time: 10 minutes

INGREDIENTS:

- 12 ounces low-fat plain Greek yogurt
- 1-2 packets zero-calorie sugar substitute
- 1 sachet Essential Red Berry Crunch O's Cereal

INSTRUCTIONS:

1. Line an 8x8-inch baking dish with a piece of foil.
2. In a bowl, add yogurt and sugar substitute and mix well.
3. Place the yogurt mixture into the prepared baking dish and spread in an even layer.
4. Sprinkle the Cereal sachet on top evenly.
5. Freeze overnight or until bark is hard.
6. With a sharp knife, cut the bark into small pieces and serve.

NUTRITIONAL INFORMATION PER SERVING:

Calories: 157
Fat: 2.8g
Carbohydrates: 19.5g
Fiber: 2g
Sugar: 8.5g
Protein: 13g
Sodium: 150mg

CHOCOLATE CRUNCH COOKIES

Servings: 2
Preparation Time: 10 minutes
Cooking Time: 2 min 20 seconds

INGREDIENTS:

- 1 sachet Brownie Mix
- 1 Peanut Butter Chocolate Crunch Bar
- 3 tablespoons water

INSTRUCTIONS:

1. In a bowl, add the brownie mix and water and mix well. Set aside.
2. In a microwave-safe bowl, place the crunch bar and microwave on High for about 20 seconds or until it is slightly melted.
3. Add the crunch bar into the brownie mixture and mix until well combined.
4. Divide the mixture into 2 greased ramekins and microwave on High for about 2 minutes.
5. Remove from microwave and set aside to cool for about 5 minutes before serving.

NUTRITIONAL INFORMATION PER SERVING:

Calories: 110
Fat: 3g
Carbohydrates: 13.5g
Fiber: 4g
Sugar: 6g
Protein: 11g
Sodium: 165mg

OATMEAL COOKIES

Servings: 2
Preparation Time: 10 minutes
Cooking Time: 15 minutes

INGREDIENTS:

- 1 oatmeal raisin crunch bar
- 1 packet oatmeal
- 1/8 teaspoon ground cinnamon
- 1 packet stevia powder
- 1/8 teaspoon baking powder
- ½ teaspoon vanilla extract
- 1/3 cup water

INSTRUCTIONS:

1. Preheat your oven to 350 degrees F. Line a cookie sheet with parchment paper.
2. In a microwave-safe bowl, place the crunch bar and microwave on High for about 15 seconds or until it is slightly melted.
3. In the bowl of bar, add the remaining ingredients and mix until well combined.
4. Set the mixture aside for about 5 minutes.
5. With a spoon, place 4 cookies onto the prepared cookie sheet in a single layer and with your fingers, press ach ball slightly.
6. Bake for approximately 12-15 minutes or until golden brown.
7. Remove from oven and place the cookie sheet onto a wire rack to cool for about 5 minutes.
8. Now, invert the cookies onto the wire rack to cool before serving.

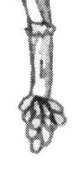

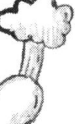

NUTRITIONAL INFORMATION PER SERVING:

Calories: 114
Fat: 2.3g
Carbohydrates: 14.4g
Fiber: 4.1g
Sugar: 3.1g
Protein: 11g
Sodium: 147mg

PEANUT BUTTER COOKIES

Servings: 4
Preparation Time: 10 minutes
Cooking Time: 12 minutes

INGREDIENTS:

- 4 sachets Essential Silky Peanut Butter Shake
- ¼ teaspoon baking powder
- ¼ cup unsweetened almond milk
- 1 tablespoon margarine, softened
- ¼ teaspoon vanilla extract
- 1/8 teaspoon sea salt

INSTRUCTIONS:

1. Preheat your oven to 350 degrees F. Line a cookie sheet with parchment paper.
2. In a bowl, add the Peanut Butter Shake and baking powder and mix well.
3. Add the almond milk, margarine and vanilla extract and mix until well blended.
4. With a spoon, place 8 cookies onto the prepared cookie sheet in a single layer and with a fork, press each ball slightly.
5. Sprinkle each cookie with salt.
6. Bake for approximately 10-12 minutes.
7. Remove from the oven and place the cookie sheet onto a wire rack to cool for about 5 minutes.
8. Now, invert the cookies onto the wire rack to cool before serving.

NUTRITIONAL INFORMATION PER SERVING:

Calories: 57
Fat: 3.4g
Carbohydrates: 4g
Fiber: 0.1g
Sugar: 0.2g
Protein: 2.8g
Sodium: 22mg

MINT COOKIES

Servings: 4
Preparation Time: 15 minutes
Cooking Time: 10 minutes

INGREDIENTS:

- 2 sachet Essential Chocolate Mint Cookie Bars
- 2 sachet Essential Decadent Double Chocolate Brownie
- 2 tablespoons unsweetened almond milk
- 2 egg whites

INSTRUCTIONS:

1. Preheat your oven to 350 degrees F.
2. Line a cookie sheet with parchment paper.
3. In a food processor, add the Chocolate Bars and pulse until crushed.
4. Transfer the crushed bar into a bowl with remaining ingredients and mix until well blended.
5. With a spoon, place 8 cookies onto the prepared cookie sheet in a single layer and with your fingers, press each ball slightly.
6. Bake for approximately 13-15 minutes.
7. Remove from the oven and place the cookie sheet onto a wire rack to cool for about 5 minutes.
8. Now, invert the cookies onto the wire rack to cool before serving.

Nutritional Information per Serving:
Calories: 120
Fat: 2.8g
Carbohydrates: 14.2g
Fiber: 4g
Sugar: .16g
Protein: 12.8g
Sodium: 90mg

GINGERSNAP COOKIES

Serving: 1
Preparation Time: 10 minutes
Cooking Time: 20 minutes

INGREDIENTS:

- 1 sachet Essential Spiced Gingerbread
- 2 tablespoons cold water
- Olive oil cooking spray
- 2 tablespoons low-fat whipped cream cheese spread
- 1/8 teaspoon vanilla tract
- 3-5 drops liquid stevia

INSTRUCTIONS:

1. Preheat your oven to 350 degrees F.
2. Lightly grease a cookie sheet.
3. In a bowl, add Spiced Gingerbread sachet and beat until smooth.

4. With a small spoon, place about 3 cookies onto the prepared cookie sheet in a single layer.
5. Bake for approximately 18-20 minutes or until golden brown.
6. Remove from the oven and place the cookie sheet onto a wire rack to cool for about 5 minutes.
7. Now, invert the cookies onto the wire rack to cool before serving.
8. Meanwhile, in a small bowl, place cream cheese, vanilla extract and stevia and beat until smooth.
9. Spread frosting over cookies and serve.

NUTRITIONAL INFORMATION PER SERVING:

Calories: 262
Fat: 12.6g
Carbohydrates: 19.1g
Fiber: 5g
Sugar: 6.1g
Protein: 12g
Sodium: 270mg

CRUNCH SANDWICH COOKIES

Servings: 1
Preparation Time: 10 minutes
Cooking Time: 15 seconds

INGREDIENTS:

- 1 packet S'more Crunch Bar
- 1 tablespoon whipped topping

INSTRUCTIONS:

1. Line 2 cups of a muffin tin with cupcake liners.
2. Break the Crunch Bar in 2 pieces.
3. In a microwave-safe bowl, place the bar pieces and microwave for about 15 seconds.
4. Place the bar into the prepared muffin cups evenly and with your fingers, press down to form round cookies.
5. Freeze for about 15 minutes.
6. Remove from the freezer and place the cookies onto a plate.
7. Spread whipped topping between both cookies and serve.

NUTRITIONAL INFORMATION PER SERVING:

Calories: 118
Fat: 3.2g
Carbohydrates: 13.4g
Fiber: 4g
Sugar: 6.2g
Protein: 11.1g
Sodium: 174mg

SANDWICH COOKIES

Servings: 1
Preparation Time: 10 minutes
Cooking Time: 12 minutes

INGREDIENTS:

- 1 sachet Chocolate Chip Soft Bake
- 1/8 teaspoon baking powder
- 3 tablespoons water
- 1 tablespoon whipped cream

INSTRUCTIONS:

1. Preheat your oven to 375 degrees F. Line a cookie sheet with parchment paper.
2. In a bowl, mix together the Chocolate Bake sachet and baking powder.
3. Slowly, add the water and mix until well blended.
4. Divide the dough in 2 pieces and place onto the prepared cookie sheet.
5. With your hands, press each dough piece in a cookie shape.
6. Bake for approximately 12 minutes.
7. Remove from the oven and place the cookie sheet onto a wire rack to cool for about 5 minutes.
8. Now, invert the cookies onto the wire rack to cool before serving.
9. Arrange a cookie, smooth side upwards.
10. Place the whipped cream on top of the cookie.
11. Cover with the remaining cookie and lightly press together.
12. Serve.

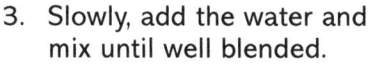

NUTRITIONAL INFORMATION PER SERVING:

Calories: 154
Fat: 6.6g
Carbohydrates: 15.7g
Fiber: 4g
Sugar: 7g
Protein: 11.3g
Sodium: 120mg

SNICKERDOODLES

Servings: 2
Preparation Time: 10 minutes
Cooking Time: 8 minutes

INGREDIENTS:

- 2 packets French Vanilla Shake
- 1 packet Splenda with Fiber
- 1 teaspoon baking powder

- ¼ teaspoon ground cinnamon
- 1 teaspoon vanilla extract
- ¼ cup water

INSTRUCTIONS:

1. Preheat your oven to 350 degrees F. Line a cookie sheet with parchment paper.
2. In a bowl, add the Vanilla Shake packet, Splenda, baking powder and cinnamon and mix well.
3. Add the vanilla extract and mix well.
4. Slowly, add the water and mix until a paste is formed.
5. With a spoon, place 4 cookies onto the prepared cookie sheet in a single layer and with your fingers, press ach ball slightly.
6. Bake for approximately 8 minutes.
7. Remove from oven and place the cookie sheet onto a wire rack to cool for about 5 minutes.
8. Now, invert the cookies onto the wire rack to cool before serving.

NUTRITIONAL INFORMATION PER SERVING:

Calories: 74
Fat: 0.2g
Carbohydrates: 10.2g
Fiber: 2.2g
Sugar: 5.8g
Protein: 7g
Sodium: 111mg

CHOCOLATE WHOOPIE PIES

Servings: 2
Preparation Time: 20 minutes
Cooking Time: 15 minutes

INGREDIENTS:

- 2 sachets Decadent Double Chocolate Brownie
- ¼ teaspoon baking powder
- 6 tablespoons unsweetened almond milk, divided
- 3 tablespoons egg liquid substitute
- 1 teaspoon vegetable oil
- ¼ cup powdered peanut butter

INSTRUCTIONS:

1. Preheat your oven to 350 degrees F. Grease 4 cups of a muffin tin.
2. In a small bowl, add the Chocolate Brownie, ¼ C. of almond milk, egg substitute and oil and mix until well blended.
3. Place the mixture into the prepared muffin cups.
4. Bake for approximately 18-20 minutes or until a toothpick inserted in the center comes out clean.
5. Remove the muffin tin from oven and place onto a wire rack to cool for about 10 minutes.
6. Carefully invert the muffins onto the wire rack to cool completely.
7. Meanwhile, in a bowl, add the remaining almond milk and peanut butter and mix well.
8. After cooling, slice each muffin in half horizontally.
9. Spread the peanut butter powder mixture over the bottom half of each muffin.
10. Cover each bottom half with the remaining muffin halves and serve.

NUTRITIONAL INFORMATION PER SERVING:

Calories: 141
Fat: 5.4g
Carbohydrates: 13.3g
Fiber: 4.2g
Sugar: 5.2g
Protein: 13.6g
Sodium: 120mg

BROWNIE BITES

Servings: 6
Preparation Time: 10 minutes

INGREDIENTS:

- 3 tablespoons peanut butter powder
- 1 cup plus 3 tablespoons water, divided
- 6 sachets Double Chocolate Brownie Mix
- 1 cup water

INSTRUCTIONS:

1. In a small bowl, add the peanut butter powder and 3 tablespoons of water and mix until well combined.
2. In another bowl, add Double Chocolate Brownie sachets and remaining water and mix until well combined.
3. In the bottom of 6 silicon molds, place the peanut butter powder mixture evenly and top with brownie mixture.

4. Freeze the molds until set completely.
5. Remove from the freezer and set aside for about 30-40 minutes before serving.

NUTRITIONAL INFORMATION PER SERVING:

Calories: 137
Fat: 3g
Carbohydrates: 16g
Fiber: 5.1g
Sugar: 8g
Protein: 15g
Sodium: 270mg

CHOCOLATE HAYSTACKS

Servings: 1
Preparation Time: 10 minutes

INGREDIENTS:

- 1 sachet Brownie Mix
- 3 tablespoons water
- 1 tablespoon peanut butter powder
- 1 packet stevia powder
- 1 packet Cinnamon Pretzel Sticks, crushed

INSTRUCTIONS:

1. In a small bowl, add the brownie mix and water and mix until paste forms.
2. Add peanut butter powder and stevia and mix until well combined.
3. Add the crushed pretzels and mix until well combined.
4. With a spoon, place 6 haystacks onto a piece of foil and freeze for about 1 hour or until set.

NUTRITIONAL INFORMATION PER SERVING:

Calories: 127
Fat: 3.1g
Carbohydrates: 15.5g
Fiber: 5g
Sugar: 4.5g
Protein: 15g
Sodium: 141mg

PEANUT BUTTER BITES

Servings: 1
Preparation Time: 10 minutes
Cooking Time: 15 seconds

INGREDIENTS:

- 2 tablespoons peanut butter powder
- 1 tablespoon water
- 1 sachet Essential Creamy Double Peanut Butter Crisp Bar

INSTRUCTIONS:

1. In a bowl, add the peanut butter powder and water and mix until a smooth paste is formed.
2. In a microwave-safe plate, place the Crisp Bar and microwave for about 15 seconds or until soft.
3. Add the warm bar pieces into the bowl of water mixture and mix until a dough forms.
4. Make small 4 equal-sized balls from the dough and arrange onto a parchment paper-lined plate.
5. Refrigerate until set before serving.

NUTRITIONAL INFORMATION PER SERVING:

Calories: 190
Fat: 5.5g
Carbohydrates: 17g
Fiber: 4g
Sugar: 9g
Protein: 27g
Sodium: 300mg

MARSHMALLOW CEREAL TREAT

Servings: 1
Preparation Time: 5 minutes
Cooking Time: 1 minutes

INGREDIENTS:

- 1 packet Meal Mixed Berry Cereal Crunch
- 2 tablespoons marshmallow dip

INSTRUCTIONS:

1. In a small bowl, add the Cereal Crunch and marshmallow dip and mix well.
2. Place the mixture into a microwave-safe mini loaf pan and with the back of a spoon, press slightly.
3. Microwave for about 1 minute.
4. Remove from the microwave and set aside to cool completely before serving.

NUTRITIONAL INFORMATION PER SERVING:

Calories: 100
Fat: 0.5g
Carbohydrates: 15g
Fiber: 4g
Sugar: 3g
Protein: 11g
Sodium: 150mg

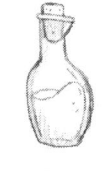

BLUEBERRY SCONES

Servings: 6
Preparation Time: 15 minutes
Cooking Time: 20 minutes

INGREDIENTS:

- 4 sachets Blueberry Almond Hot Cereal
- ¼ cup ground flaxseed
- 1-2 packets zero-calorie sugar substitute
- ½ teaspoon baking powder
- 3 tablespoons frozen unsalted butter, cut into ½-inch pieces
- 3 tablespoons low-fat plain Greek yogurt
- ¼ teaspoon almond extract
- ¼ teaspoon ground cinnamon

INSTRUCTIONS:

1. Preheat your oven to 400 degrees F. Line a baking sheet with parchment paper.
2. In a food processor, add the Hot Cereal sachet, flaxseed, sugar substitute and baking powder and pulse until well blended.
3. Add the butter and pulse until a coarse meal-like mixture is formed.
4. Add the yogurt and almond extract and pulse until just blended.
5. Place the dough onto the prepared baking sheet and shape into a 6-inch circle.
6. Sprinkle the top of the dough circle with cinnamon.
7. Bake for approximately 15-20 minutes or until top becomes golden brown.
8. Remove the baking sheet from oven and set aside to cool.
9. Cut the dough circle into 6 wedges and serve.

NUTRITIONAL INFORMATION PER SERVING:

Calories: 198
Fat: 10.1g
Carbohydrates: 16.5g
Fiber: 5.1g
Sugar: 2.7g
Protein: 12.3g
Sodium: 160mg

GINGERBREAD BISCOTTI

Servings: 4
Preparation Time: 15 minutes
Cooking Time: 45 minutes

INGREDIENTS:

- 1 sachet Essential Spiced Gingerbread
- ¼ teaspoon baking powder
- 2 tablespoons sugar-free maple syrup
- 2 egg whites

INSTRUCTIONS:

1. Preheat your oven to 350 degrees F. Line a baking sheet with parchment paper.
2. In a bowl, mix together the gingerbread sachet and baking powder.
3. In the bowl, add the maple syrup and egg whites and mix until well blended.
4. With lightly greased hands, place the dough onto the prepared baking sheet.
5. With your hands, shape the dough into an 8-inch long log.
6. Bake for approximately 25-30 minutes or until the top is firm.
7. Remove the baking sheet from oven and set aside to cool for about 5-10 minutes.
8. Cut the log into 8 (1-inch thick) slices.
9. Arrange the biscotti slices onto the baking sheet in a single layer, cut side down.
10. Now, set the temperature of the oven to 325 degrees F and Bake for approximately 15 minutes.
11. Remove the baking sheet from oven and place the baking sheet onto a wire rack to cool for about 5 minutes.
12. Now, invert the biscotti sticks onto the wire rack to cool before serving.

NUTRITIONAL INFORMATION PER SERVING:

Calories: 63
Fat: 0.7g
Carbohydrates: 10.7g
Fiber: 1g
Sugar: 7.3g
Protein: 5.3g
Sodium: 77mg

YOGURT BERRY DONUTS

Servings: 2
Preparation Time: 10 minutes
Cooking Time: 15 minutes

INGREDIENTS:

- 2 sachets Yogurt Berry Blast Smoothie
- 2 tablespoons liquid egg substitute
- 1/3 cup unsweetened almond milk

- ½ teaspoon baking powder
- Olive oil cooking spray

INSTRUCTIONS:

1. Preheat your oven to 350 degrees F.
2. Lightly grease 4 holes of a donut pan.
3. In a bowl, add the Smoothie sachets, milk, egg substitute and baking powder and mix well.
4. Divide the mixture into the prepared donut holes.
5. Bake for approximately 12-15 minutes.
6. Remove from the oven and set aside to cool slightly before serving.

NUTRITIONAL INFORMATION PER SERVING:

Calories: 106
Fat: 0.6g
Carbohydrates: 14g
Fiber: 5.2g
Sugar: 6.1g
Protein: 13.1g
Sodium: 282mg

CHOCOLATE DONUTS

Servings: 4
Preparation Time: 15 minutes
Cooking Time: 27 ½ minutes

INGREDIENTS:

- 2 sachets Essential Decadent Double Brownie
- 2 sachets Essential Chocolate Chip Pancakes
- 6 tablespoons liquid egg substitute
- ¼ cup unsweetened almond milk
- ½ teaspoon vanilla extract
- ½ teaspoon baking powder

INSTRUCTIONS:

1. Preheat your oven to 350 degrees F. Lightly grease 4 holes of a donut pan.
2. In a bowl, add all ingredients and mix until well blended.
3. Place the mixture into the prepared donut pan evenly.
4. Bake for approximately 12-15 minutes or until donuts are set completely.
5. Remove from the oven and set aside to cool slightly.
6. Serve warm.

NUTRITIONAL INFORMATION PER SERVING:

Calories: 127
Fat: 2g
Carbohydrates: 15.2g
Fiber: 4.1g
Sugar: 6.2g
Protein: 13.9g
Sodium: 100mg

BLUEBERRY MUFFINS

Servings: 6
Preparation Time: 10 minutes
Cooking Time: 10 minutes

INGREDIENTS:

- 6 packets Wild Blueberry Almond Hot Cereal
- 1 ½ tablespoons baking powder
- ¾ cup water
- ¾ cup liquid egg substitute

INSTRUCTIONS:

1. Preheat your oven to 350 degrees F.
2. Grease 6 holes of a mini muffin tin.
3. In a bowl, place all ingredients and mix well.
4. Place the mixture into the prepared muffin cups evenly.
5. Bake for approximately 10 minutes or until a toothpick inserted in the center comes out clean.
6. Remove the muffin tin from oven and place onto a wire rack to cool for about 10 minutes.
7. Carefully invert the muffins onto the wire rack to cool completely before serving.

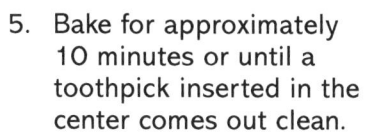

NUTRITIONAL INFORMATION PER SERVING:

Calories: 130
Fat: 2g
Carbohydrates: 17g
Fiber: 4.1g
Sugar: 2.2g
Protein: 14.8g
Sodium: 194mg

MOCHA MUFFIN

Servings: 4
Preparation Time: 10 minutes
Cooking Time: 15 minutes

INGREDIENTS:

For Muffins:

- 1 packet Chocolate Chip Pancakes
- 1 packet Cappuccino
- 1 tablespoon egg beaters
- 1 packet stevia powder
- ¼ teaspoon baking powder
- ¼ cup water

For Frosting:

- 2 tablespoons light cream cheese, softened
- ½ packet stevia powder

INSTRUCTIONS:

1. Preheat your oven to 350 degrees F. Lightly grease 8 cups of a mini muffin tin.
2. For muffins: in a small bowl, add all the ingredients and mix until well combined.
3. Place the mixture into the prepared muffin cups evenly.
4. Bake for approximately 15 minutes or until a toothpick inserted in the center comes out clean.
5. Remove from the oven and place the muffin tin onto a wire rack to cool for about 10 minutes.
6. Carefully invert the muffins onto the wire rack to cool completely before frosting.
7. For frosting: in a small bowl, add the cream cheese and stevia and beat until smooth.
8. Place a dollop of frosting over each muffin and serve.

NUTRITIONAL INFORMATION PER SERVING:

Calories: 72
Fat: 12.6g
Carbohydrates: 5.8g
Fiber: 1.2g
Sugar: 2.7g
Protein: 8.1g
Sodium: 111mg

SWEET POTATO MUFFINS

Servings: 1
Preparation Time: 10 minutes
Cooking Time: 15 minutes

INGREDIENTS:

- 1 sachet Honey Sweet Potatoes
- ½ cup water
- 2 tablespoons eggbeaters
- ¼ teaspoon baking powder
- Pinch of ground cinnamon

INSTRUCTIONS:

1. Preheat your oven to 350 degrees F.
2. Lightly grease 2 cups of a standard-sized muffin tin.
3. In a bowl, add all ingredient except for cinnamon and mix until well combined.
4. Place the mixture into the prepared muffin cups evenly and sprinkle with cinnamon.
5. Bake for approximately 15 minutes or until a toothpick inserted in the center comes out clean.
6. Remove the muffin tin from oven and place onto a wire rack to cool for about 10 minutes.
7. Carefully invert the muffins onto the wire rack to cool completely before serving.

NUTRITIONAL INFORMATION PER SERVING:

Calories: 152
Fat: 3.4g
Carbohydrates: 16.5g
Fiber: 4.3g
Sugar: 3.4g
Protein: 14.9g
Sodium: 200mg

SWEET POTATO & CHEESE MUFFINS

Servings: 12
Preparation Time: 10 minutes
Cooking Time: 31 ½ minutes

INGREDIENTS:

- 4 sachets Honey Sweet Potatoes
- 1 cup unsweetened almond milk
- 4 eggs
- 2/3 cups part-skim ricotta cheese
- 1 ounce goat cheese, crumbled
- ¼ cup yellow onion, chopped
- 1 tablespoon fresh rosemary, chopped
- 1/8 teaspoon ground nutmeg

INSTRUCTIONS:

1. Preheat your oven to 350 degrees F.
2. Lightly grease a 12 cups standard-sized muffin tin.
3. In a large microwave-safe bowl, add the Honey Sweet Potatoes sachets and almond milk and mix well.
4. Microwave on High for about 1 ½ minutes.
5. Remove from the microwave and stir the mixture well.
6. Set aside to cool.
7. After cooling, add the remaining ingredients and mix until well blended.
8. Place the mixture into the prepared muffin cups evenly.
9. Bake for approximately 25-30 minutes or until a toothpick inserted in the center comes out clean.

10. Remove the muffin tin from oven and place onto a wire rack to cool for about 10 minutes.
11. Carefully invert the muffins onto the wire rack to cool completely before serving.

NUTRITIONAL INFORMATION PER SERVING:

Calories: 85
Fat: 3.4g
Carbohydrates: 6.5g
Fiber: 1.6g
Sugar: 1.4g
Protein: 7.1g
Sodium: 172mg

PEANUT BUTTER CREAM CUPCAKES

Servings: 4
Preparation Time: 15 minutes
Cooking Time: 15 minutes

INGREDIENTS:

- 2 packets Original Pancakes
- 1 packet Original Style Eggs
- ½ teaspoon baking powder
- ½ cup unsweetened vanilla almond milk
- 4 teaspoons canola oil
- 2 tablespoons low-fat cream cheese
- 1 packet calorie-free sweetener
- 2 teaspoons powdered peanut butter
- ¼ teaspoon vanilla extract
- 1 packet Peanut Butter Soft Serve

INSTRUCTIONS:

1. Preheat your oven to 350 degrees F.
2. Lightly grease 4 cups of a standard-sized muffin tin.
3. In a bowl, add Original Pancakes sachet, Original Style Eggs sachet and baking powder and mix well.
4. Add almond milk and oil and mix until well combined.
5. Place the mixture into the prepared muffin cups evenly.
6. Bake for approximately 15 minutes or until a toothpick inserted in the center comes out clean.
7. Remove from the oven and place the muffin tin onto a wire rack to cool for about 10 minutes.
8. Carefully invert the muffins onto the wire rack to cool completely before filling.
9. With a paring knife, cut a large circle in the top of each cupcake, cutting down almost to the bottom.
10. Cut the bottom off of each of the cut-out cupcake pieces, leaving thin tops for each cupcake.
11. Prepare Peanut Butter Soft Serve packet according to package's instructions.
12. Immediately fill each cupcake with Peanut Butter Soft Serve.
13. Place cupcake tops on top and freeze for about 1 hour.
14. For frosting: in a bowl, add cream cheese, sweetener, powdered peanut butter and vanilla extract and beat until well combined.
15. Spread frosting over cupcakes and serve.

NUTRITIONAL INFORMATION PER SERVING:

Calories: 164
Fat: 8g
Carbohydrates: 13.6g
Fiber: 4.3g
Sugar: 4.1g
Protein: 12.7g
Sodium: 173mg

MERINGUE CUPS

Servings: 2
Preparation Time: 10 minutes
Cooking Time: 2¼ minutes

INGREDIENTS:

- 2 Essential Zesty Lemon Crisp Bars, crushed roughly
- 1 ½ cups low-fat plain Greek yogurt
- 1 (0.3-ounce) box sugar-free lemon gelatin
- ½ teaspoon lime zest, grated

INSTRUCTIONS:

1. Line 6 cups of a muffin tin with paper liners.
2. In a microwave-safe bowl, place Crisp Bar sachets and microwave for about 10-15 seconds.
3. Divide the crisp bar pieces into the prepared muffin cups evenly.
4. In another microwave-safe bowl, place yogurt and gelatin and microwave for about 2 minutes, stirring

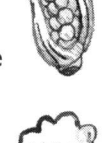

after every 40 seconds.

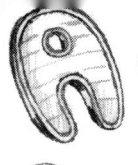

5. Remove from microwave and stir until smooth.
6. Place the yogurt mixture over crunch bar I each muffin cup.
7. Refrigerate for at least 1 hour before serving.
8. Garnish with lime zest and serving.

NUTRITIONAL INFORMATION PER SERVING:

Calories: 213
Fat: 4.5g
Carbohydrates: 20g
Fiber: 5.1g
Sugar: 12g
Protein: 19g
Sodium: 256mg

PEANUT BUTTER CUPS

Servings: 4
Preparation Time: 15 minutes

INGREDIENTS:

- 2 sachets Essential Decadent Double Chocolate Brownie
- 9-10 tablespoons unsweetened almond milk, divided
- ¼ cup powdered peanut butter

INSTRUCTIONS:

1. In a small bowl, add the brownie sachet and 6 tablespoons of almond milk and mix well.
2. In another bowl, add the remaining milk and peanut butter powder and mix well.
3. In 2 different pipping bags, place the brownie mixture and peanut butter powder mixture respectively.

4. In the bottom of 20 silicone baking molds, place the brownie mixture about 1/3 way of full.
5. Top each mold with a little peanut butter powder mixture.
6. Place the remaining brownie mixture on top evenly.
7. Freeze for at least 2 hours before serving.

NUTRITIONAL INFORMATION PER SERVING:

Calories: 85
Fat: 2.2g
Carbohydrates: 16.6g
Fiber: 2.8g
Sugar: 4.3g
Protein: 13.8g
Sodium: 138mg

MINI CHOCOLATE CAKES

Servings: 2
Preparation Time: 10 minutes
Cooking Time: 18 minutes

INGREDIENTS:

- 1 packet Chocolate Chip Pancakes
- 1 sachet Brownie Mix
- ¼ teaspoon baking powder
- ¼ cup water

INSTRUCTIONS:

1. Preheat your oven to 350 degrees F. Grease 2 cups of a muffin tin.
2. In a bowl, add all the ingredients and mix until well combined.
3. Place the mixture into the prepared muffin cups evenly.

4. Bake for approximately 18 minutes or until a toothpick inserted in the center comes out clean.
5. Remove from the oven and place the muffin tin onto a wire rack to cool for about 10 minutes.
6. Carefully invert the muffins onto the wire rack to cool completely before serving.

NUTRITIONAL INFORMATION PER SERVING:

Calories: 106
Fat: 1.7g
Carbohydrates: 14.3g
Fiber: 4g
Sugar: 5.5g
Protein: 11.5g
Sodium: 166mg

MOCHA CAKE

Servings: 2
Preparation Time: 5 minutes
Cooking Time: 2 minutes

INGREDIENTS:

- 1 packet Calorie Burn Cappuccino
- 1 packet Chocolate Chip Pancakes
- 1 packet Splenda
- 1 tablespoon egg beaters
- ¼ teaspoon baking powder
- ¼ cup water

INSTRUCTIONS:

1. In a bowl, add all ingredients and stir until well blended.
2. Place the mixture into a greased 4-inch round microwave-safe dish and microwave on High for about 1¾-2 minutes.

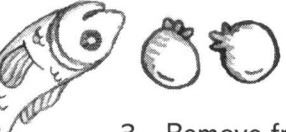

3. Remove from the microwave and divide in 2 portions.
4. Serve warm.

NUTRITIONAL INFORMATION PER SERVING:

Calories: 105
Fat: 0.7g
Carbohydrates: 14.4g
Fiber: 4g
Sugar: 3g
Protein: 13.5g
Sodium: 128mg

SHAKE CAKE

Servings: 1
Preparation Time: 10 minutes
Cooking Time: 15 minutes

INGREDIENTS:

- 1 packet Shake
- ¼ teaspoon baking powder
- 2 tablespoons water
- 2 tablespoons egg beaters

INSTRUCTIONS:

1. Preheat your oven to 350 degrees F. Lightly grease a ramekin.
2. In a bowl, add all the ingredients and mix until well combined.
3. Place the mixture into the prepared ramekin.
4. Bake for approximately 15 minutes.
5. Remove the ramekin from oven and place onto a wire rack to cool for about 10 minutes.
6. Carefully invert the cake onto the wire rack to cool completely before serving.

NUTRITIONAL INFORMATION PER SERVING:

Calories: 118
Fat: 1g
Carbohydrates: 13.8g
Fiber: 4g
Sugar: 6.2g
Protein: 17.8g
Sodium: 63mg

MARSHMALLOW CEREAL CAKE

Servings: 1
Preparation Time: 5 minutes
Cooking Time: 1 minute

INGREDIENTS:

- 1 packet Meal Mixed Berry Cereal Crunch
- 2 tablespoons marshmallow dip

INSTRUCTIONS:

1. In a small bowl, add the Cereal Crunch and marshmallow dip and mix well.
2. Place the mixture into a microwave-safe mini loaf pan and with the back of a spoon, press slightly.
3. Microwave for about 1 minute.
4. Remove from the microwave and set aside to cool completely before serving.

NUTRITIONAL INFORMATION PER SERVING:

Calories: 100
Fat: 0.5g
Carbohydrates: 15g
Fiber: 4g
Sugar: 3g
Protein: 11g
Sodium: 150mg

CINNAMON BUNS

Servings: 1
Preparation Time: 5 minutes
Cooking Time: 1 minute

INGREDIENTS:

- 1 Pancake Mix
- 1 packet Splenda
- ¼ teaspoon ground cinnamon
- 1/8 teaspoon baking powder
- 2 tablespoons water
- ¼ teaspoon vanilla extract

INSTRUCTIONS:

1. In a bowl, add all ingredients and mix until well combined.
2. Place the mixture into a greased microwave-safe bowl and sprinkle with extra cinnamon.
3. Microwave for about 50-60 seconds.
4. Serve warm.

NUTRITIONAL INFORMATION PER SERVING:

Calories: 105
Fat: 0.5g
Carbohydrates: 15.9g
Fiber: 4.3g
Sugar: 6.1g
Protein: 11g
Sodium: 242mg

CHOCOLATE CREPE

Servings: 1
Preparation Time: 10 minutes
Cooking Time: 4 minutes

INGREDIENTS:

- 1 packet Chocolate Chip Pancakes
- ¼ cup water
- ¼ cup part-skim ricotta cheese
- ½ packet stevia powder
- 1/8 teaspoon vanilla extract
- 1 teaspoon sugar-free chocolate syrup

INSTRUCTIONS:

1. In a bowl, add the pancake and water and mix well.
2. Heat a lightly greased wok over medium heat.
3. Place the mixture and spread in a thin circle.
4. Cook for about 1-2 minutes per side or until golden brown.
5. Remove from the heat and place the crepe onto a plate.
6. In a small bowl, add the ricotta cheese, stevia and vanilla extract and mix until well combined.
7. Place the mixture inside the crepe.
8. Drizzle with chocolate syrup and serve.

Nutritional Information per Serving:
Calories: 195
Fat: 6.4g
Carbohydrates: 18g
Fiber: 4g
Sugar: 4.9g
Protein: 19.1g
Sodium: 267mg

PUMPKIN WAFFLES

Servings: 2
Preparation Time: 10 minutes
Cooking Time: 8 minutes

INGREDIENTS:

- 1 sachet Golden Pancake
- 1 tablespoon 100% canned pumpkin
- ¼ teaspoon pumpkin pie spice
- Pinch of ground cinnamon
- ¼ cup water
- 2 tablespoons sugar-free pancake syrup

INSTRUCTIONS:

1. Preheat a mini waffle iron and then grease it.
2. In a bowl, add all ingredients except for pancake syrup and mix until well blended.
3. Place ½ of the mixture into the preheated waffle iron and cook for about 3-4 minutes or until golden brown.
4. Repeat with the remaining mixture.
5. Serve warm with the topping of pancake syrup.

NUTRITIONAL INFORMATION PER SERVING:

Calories: 48
Fat: 0.6g
Carbohydrates: 8.3g
Fiber: 2.3g
Sugar: 1.8g
Protein: 5.6g
Sodium: 126mg

OATMEAL WAFFLES

Servings: 1
Preparation Time: 5 minutes
Cooking Time: 12 minutes

INGREDIENTS:

- 1 packet oatmeal
- ½ teaspoon baking powder
- 2 tablespoons egg whites
- ½ teaspoon vanilla extract
- Pinch of Molly McButter
- Pinch of ground cinnamon
- ½ cup cold water
- 2 tablespoons sugar-free maple syrup

INSTRUCTIONS:

1. Preheat a waffle iron and then grease it.
2. In a bowl, add all ingredients except for maple syrup and mix until well blended.
3. Place the mixture into the preheated waffle iron and cook for 6-7 minutes.
4. Carefully flip the waffle and cook for about 5 minutes or until golden brown.
5. Repeat with the remaining mixture.
6. Serve warm with the topping of maple syrup.

NUTRITIONAL INFORMATION PER SERVING:

Calories: 171
Fat: 1.6g
Carbohydrates: 22g
Fiber: 5.2g
Sugar: 1.5g
Protein: 14.3g
Sodium: 330mg

CHOCOLATE WAFFLES

Servings: 2
Preparation Time: 10 minutes
Cooking Time: 8 minutes

INGREDIENTS:

- 1 packet Chocolate Chip Pancakes
- ¼ teaspoon pumpkin pie spice
- 1 tablespoon 100% canned pumpkin
- ¼ cup water
- 2 teaspoons sugar-free pancake syrup

INSTRUCTIONS:

1. Preheat a mini waffle iron and then grease it.
2. In a bowl, add all the ingredients except for pancake syrup and mix until well combined.
3. Place ½ of the mixture into preheated waffle iron and cook for about 3-4 minutes or until golden brown.
4. Repeat with the remaining mixture.
5. Serve warm with the topping of pancake syrup

NUTRITIONAL INFORMATION PER SERVING:

Calories: 54
Fat: 0.7g
Carbohydrates: 7.3g
Fiber: 1.7g
Sugar: 1.6g
Protein: 6.1g
Sodium: 132mg

MAC & CHEESE WAFFLES

Servings: 2
Preparation Time: 10 minutes
Cooking Time: 9½ minutes

INGREDIENTS:

- 2 packets Chipotle Mac & Cheese
- 6 tablespoons liquid egg whites
- 4 ounces cold water
- 2 tablespoons sugar-free maple syrup

INSTRUCTIONS:

1. In a microwave-safe bowl, place Mac & Cheese packets and water and mix well.
2. Microwave on high for about 1-1½ minutes. Remove from microwave and stir well.
3. Set aside for about 1 minute.
4. Microwave on high for about 1 minute.
5. Remove from microwave and stir well. Set aside until cooled.
6. Add liquid egg whites and stir to combine.
7. Preheat a waffle iron and then grease it.
8. Place the mixture into the preheated waffle iron and cook for about 5-7 minutes or until golden brown.
9. Repeat with the remaining mixture.
10. Serve warm with the topping of maple syrup.

NUTRITIONAL INFORMATION PER SERVING:

Calories: 158
Fat: 1.5g
Carbohydrates: 22g
Fiber: 4g
Sugar: 1g
Protein: 16g
Sodium: 536mg

MAPLE PANCAKES

Servings: 1
Preparation Time: 10 minutes
Cooking Time: 6 minutes

INGREDIENTS:

- 1 Maple Brown Sugar Oatmeal
- ¼ teaspoon baking powder
- 1 tablespoon egg beaters
- 1 packet stevia
- ¼ teaspoon ground cinnamon
- ¼ cup water
- 1 tablespoon sugar-free pancake syrup

INSTRUCTIONS:

1. In a bowl, add all the ingredients except for pancake syrup and mix until well blended.
2. Heat a lightly greased cast-iron wok over medium-high heat.
3. Place the mixture and with the back of a spoon, spread into a circle.
4. Cook for about 2-3 minutes per side or until golden brown.
5. Serve warm with the topping of pancake syrup.

NUTRITIONAL INFORMATION PER SERVING:

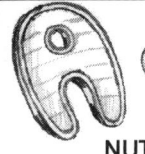

Calories: 111
Fat: 1.5g
Carbohydrates: 15.2g
Fiber: 5.3g
Sugar: 1.1g
Protein: 12.9g
Sodium: 90mg

MASHED POTATO PANCAKE

Servings: 2
Preparation Time: 10 minutes
Cooking Time: 12 minutes

INGREDIENTS:

- 1 Garlic Mashed Potatoes
- ¼ cup low-fat cheddar cheese, shredded
- ¼ teaspoon baking powder
- ½ cup water
- 2 tablespoons low-fat sour cream

INSTRUCTIONS:

1. In a bowl, add all the ingredients except for sour cream and mix until well combined.
2. Set the mixture aside for about 5 minutes.
3. Heat a lightly greased cast-iron wok over medium heat.
4. Place half of the mixture and spread into a circle.
5. Cook for about 2-3 minutes per side or until golden brown.
6. Repeat with the remaining mixture.
7. Serve warm with the topping of sour cream.

NUTRITIONAL INFORMATION PER SERVING:

Calories: 138
Fat: 7.4g
Carbohydrates: 8.5g
Fiber: 2g
Sugar: 1.1g
Protein: 9.4g
Sodium: 290mg

MINI BISCUIT PIZZA

Servings: 1
Preparation Time: 10 minutes
Cooking Time: 14 minutes

INGREDIENTS:

- 1 sachet Buttermilk Cheddar and Herb Biscuits
- 2 tablespoons water
- 1 tablespoon tomato sauce
- 1 tablespoon low-fat cheddar cheese, shredded

INSTRUCTIONS:

1. Preheat your oven to 350 degrees F.
2. In a small bowl, add the biscuit and water and mix well.
3. Place the biscuit mixture onto parchment paper and with a spoon, spread into a thin circle.
4. Bake for approximately 10 minutes.
5. Remove from the oven and spread the tomato sauce over the biscuit circle.
6. Sprinkle with cheddar cheese.
7. Bake for approximately 2-4 minutes or until cheese is melted.
8. Remove from the oven and set aside for about 3-5 minutes.
9. Serve warm.

NUTRITIONAL INFORMATION PER SERVING:

Calories: 142
Fat: 5.4g
Carbohydrates: 13.9g
Fiber: 4.2g
Sugar: 2.7g
Protein: 13g
Sodium: 474mg

PIZZA BREAD

Servings: 1
Preparation Time: 10 minutes
Cooking Time: 10 minutes

INGREDIENTS:

- 1 packet Cream of Tomato Soup
- ¼ teaspoon baking powder
- Salt and ground black pepper, as required
- 2 tablespoons water
- ¼ cup low-fat cheddar cheese, shredded

INSTRUCTIONS:

1. Preheat your oven to 425 degrees F. Grease a small baking sheet.
2. In a bowl, add the soup, baking powder, salt, black pepper and water and mix until well combined.
3. Place the mixture onto the prepared baking sheet and shape into a circle.
4. Bake for approximately 5 minutes.
5. Remove from the oven and with a spatula, flip the bread.
6. Top with the cheese and Bake for approximately 5 minutes more.
7. Serve warm.

NUTRITIONAL INFORMATION PER SERVING:

Calories: 225
Fat: 11.4g
Carbohydrates: 14g
Fiber: 4g
Sugar: 6.2g
Protein: 19g
Sodium: 723mg

MASHED POTATO TORTILLA

Servings: 1
Preparation Time: 10 minutes
Cooking Time: 14 minutes

INGREDIENTS:

- 4 large egg whites
- 1 tablespoon water
- 1 teaspoon baking powder
- 1 packet Mashed Potatoes

INSTRUCTIONS:

1. Preheated the oven to 350 degrees F.
2. Grease a pizza pan.
3. In a bowl, add egg whites and water and beat well.
4. Sprinkle with baking powder and set aside for about 30-60 seconds or until foamy.
5. With a fork, mix until well combined.
6. Add the Mashed Potatoes packet and mix until well combined.
7. Set aside for about 2 minutes.
8. Again stir the mixture well.
9. Place the mixture onto the prepared pizza pan sheet with a spoon, spread in a thin layer.
10. Bake for approximately 12-14 minutes.
11. Serve warm.

NUTRITIONAL INFORMATION PER SERVING:

Calories: 183
Fat: 0.7g
Carbohydrates: 18.3g
Fiber: 1.1g
Sugar: 2.9g
Protein: 24.4g
Sodium: 528mg

POTATO BAGELS

Servings: 1
Preparation Time: 10 minutes
Cooking Time: 12 minutes

INGREDIENTS:

- 2 egg whites
- 1 sachet Mashed Potatoes
- 1 teaspoon baking powder

INSTRUCTIONS:

1. Preheat your oven to 350 degrees F.
2. Lightly grease 1 hole of a donut pan.
3. In a bowl, add the egg whites and beat until foamy.
4. Add the baking powder and mashed potatoes and beat until well blended.
5. Place the mixture into the prepare donut hole.
6. Bake for approximately 10-12 minutes or until done.
7. Serve warm.

NUTRITIONAL INFORMATION PER SERVING:

Calories: 149
Fat: 0.6g
Carbohydrates: 16.8g
Fiber: 2.9g
Sugar: 4.1g
Protein: 19.2g
Sodium: 50mg

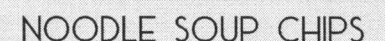

NOODLE SOUP CHIPS

Servings: 1
Preparation Time: 15 minutes
Cooking Time: 18 minutes

INGREDIENTS:

- 1 packet Chicken Noodle Soup
- 3 tablespoons water
- Olive oil cooking spray

INSTRUCTIONS:

1. Preheat your oven to 375 degrees F.
2. In a small blender, add the soup sachet and pulse powdered finely.
3. In a small bowl, add the powdered soup and water and mix until dough ball forms.
4. Set aside for about 3-5 minutes.
5. Arrange the dough ball between 2 grease parchment papers and with your hands, flatten into a thinner circle.
6. Carefully remove the parchment paper from the top of the dough.
7. Carefully place the parchment paper with dough onto a baking sheet.
8. Bake for approximately 10 minutes.
9. Remove the baking sheet from the oven and with a sharp knife, cut into chips.
10. Arrange the chips onto the baking sheet in a single layer and Bake for approximately 6-8 minutes or until crispy.
11. Remove from the oven and set aside to cool before serving.

NUTRITIONAL INFORMATION PER SERVING:

Calories: 100
Fat: 1g
Carbohydrates: 15g
Fiber: 6g
Sugar: 1g
Protein: 12g
Sodium: 360mg

MAC & CHEESE CHIPS

Servings: 1
Preparation Time: 10 minutes
Cooking Time: 10 minutes

INGREDIENTS:

- 1 packet Mac & Cheese
- 2 tablespoons water

INSTRUCTIONS:

1. Preheat your oven to 350 degrees F.
2. In a blender, add the Mac & Cheese packet and pulse until finely powdered.
3. Transfer the powder into a bowl with water and mix until well blended.
4. Set aside for about 5 minutes.
5. Arrange the dough ball between 2 greased parchment papers and with your hands, flatten into a thin circle.
6. Gently remove the top parchment paper from the dough.
7. Carefully place the dough alongside the parchment paper onto a baking sheet.
8. Bake for approximately 10 minutes.
9. Remove the baking sheet from the oven and with a sharp knife, cut into chips.
10. Arrange the chips onto the baking sheet in a single layer and Bake for approximately 10 minutes or until crispy.
11. Remove the baking sheet of chips from the oven and set aside to cool before serving.

NUTRITIONAL INFORMATION PER SERVING:

Calories: 110
Fat: 1.5g
Carbohydrates: 15g
Fiber: 4g
Sugar: 1g
Protein: 11g
Sodium: 66mg

TORTILLA CHIPS

Servings: 2
Preparation Time: 10 minutes
Cooking Time: 25 minutes

INGREDIENTS:

- 2 sachets Hearty Red Bean & Vegetable Chili
- ¼ cup water

INSTRUCTIONS:

1. Preheat your oven to 350 degrees F.
2. Line a rimmed baking sheet with lightly greased parchment paper.
3. In a food processor, add the Vegetable Chili sachet and pulse until finely powdered.
4. Transfer the Vegetable Chili powder into a bowl with water and beat until smooth.
5. Arrange the dough onto the prepared baking sheet and with your hands, smooth the top surface.
6. With a knife, cut the dough into chips pieces.
7. Bake for approximately 10 minutes.
8. Carefully flip the dough pieces and Bake for approximately 10-15 minutes.
9. Remove the baking sheet of chips from the oven and set aside to cool before serving.

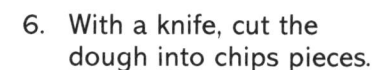

NUTRITIONAL INFORMATION PER SERVING:

Calories: 110
Fat: 1g
Carbohydrates: 15g
Fiber: 4g
Sugar: 4g
Protein: 12g
Sodium: 125mg

MAC & CHEESE DORITOS

Servings: 1
Preparation Time: 15 minutes
Cooking Time: 15 minutes

INGREDIENTS:

- 1 packet Macaroni & Cheese
- ¼ teaspoon garlic salt
- ¼ teaspoon red pepper flakes, crushed
- 2 tablespoons water
- Pinch of red chili powder
- cooking spray

INSTRUCTIONS:

1. Preheat your oven to 350 degrees F.
2. In a food processor, add mac & cheese packet, garlic salt and red pepper flakes and pulse until finely powdered.

3. Transfer into a bowl with water and stir to combine.
4. Set aside for about 2 minutes.
5. Place the dough between 2 greased pieces of parchment and with your hands, spread into a thin circle.
6. Carefully peel off the top layer of parchment.
7. Arrange the dough onto a baking sheet alongside the parchment paper.
8. Sprinkle the dough with chili powder.
9. Bake for approximately 10 minutes.
10. Remove from the oven and with a pizza cutter, cut into chip-size pieces.
11. Flip the chips and Bake for approximately 3-5 minutes.
12. Remove from the oven and set aside to cool completely before serving.

NUTRITIONAL INFORMATION PER SERVING:

Calories: 115
Fat: 1.2g
Carbohydrates: 15.9g
Fiber: 4.3g
Sugar: 1.2g
Protein: 11.2g
Sodium: 395mg

CHICKEN NUGGETS

Servings: 4
Preparation Time: 10 minutes
Cooking Time: 20 minutes

INGREDIENTS:

- 1 egg
- 12 ounce boneless, skinless chicken breast, cubed
- Olive oil cooking spray
- 2 sachets Essential Honey Mustard & Onion Sticks, crushed finely

INSTRUCTIONS:

1. Preheat your oven to 400 degrees F.
2. Line a rimmed baking sheet with a lightly greased piece of foil.
3. In a shallow bowl, crack the egg and beat well.
4. In another shallow bowl, place the crushed Onion Sticks.
5. Dip the chicken cubes in beaten egg and then coat with crushed sticks.
6. Arrange the coated chicken cubes onto the prepared baking sheet in a single layer and spray with cooking spray.
7. Bake for approximately 18-20 minutes, flipping once halfway through.
8. Serve warm.

NUTRITIONAL INFORMATION PER SERVING:

Calories: 162
Fat: 3g
Carbohydrates: 6.6g
Fiber: 2g
Sugar: 1.1g
Protein: 26.6g
Sodium: 170mg

SMASHED POTATO GRILL CHEESE

Servings: 2
Preparation Time: 10 minutes
Cooking Time: 14 minutes

INGREDIENTS:

- 2 sachets Essential Smashed Potatoes
- 1 cup water
- 1 cup low-fat cheddar cheese, shredded

INSTRUCTIONS:

1. In a medium microwave-safe bowl, add the Smashed Potato sachet and water and mix well.
2. Microwave on High for about 1½ minutes.
3. Remove from the microwave and stir well.
4. Preheat the waffle iron and then grease it.
5. Place the mixture into heated all 4 triangles of the waffle iron and cook for about 10-12 minutes.
6. Open the lid and sprinkle the cheddar cheese on 2 triangles of the waffle.
7. Cover with the remaining waffle triangles.

NUTRITIONAL INFORMATION PER SERVING:

Calories: 290
Fat: 12.5g
Carbohydrates: 17g
Fiber: 1g
Sugar: 2g
Protein: 27g
Sodium: 787mg

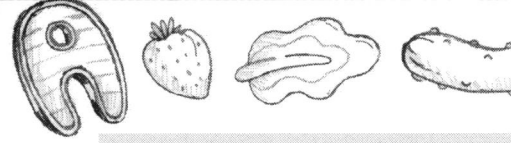

BUFFALO CAULIFLOWER POPPERS

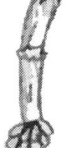

Servings: 3
Preparation Time: 15 minutes
Cooking Time: 30 minutes

INGREDIENTS:
- 1 sachet Select Cheddar Herb Biscuit
- ¼ cup hot buffalo sauce
- ½ cup water
- 3 cups cauliflower florets
- ½ tablespoons butter, melted

INSTRUCTIONS:
1. Preheat your oven to 425 degrees F.
2. Line a large baking sheet a lightly greased piece of foil.
3. In a bowl, add the Biscuit sachet and water and mix until well combined.
4. Add the cauliflower florets and toss to coat well.
5. Arrange the cauliflower florets onto the prepared baking sheet in a single layer.
6. Bake for approximately 20 minutes.
7. Meanwhile, in a bowl, add the buffalo sauce and butter and mix well.
8. Remove the baking sheet from oven.
9. In the bowl of sauce mixture, add the cauliflower florets and toss to coat well.
10. Again arrange the cauliflower florets onto the same baking sheet in a single layer.
11. Bake for approximately 7-10 minutes. Serve warm.

NUTRITIONAL INFORMATION PER SERVING:

Calories: 116
Fat: 4g
Carbohydrates: 13.9g
Fiber: 5.1g
Sugar: 3.7g
Protein: 9.3g
Sodium: 315mg

PARMESAN CHICKEN BITES

Servings: 3
Preparation Time: 15 minutes
Cooking Time: 30 minutes

INGREDIENTS:
- 2 packets Parmesan Cheese Puffs, crushed finely
- 2 ounces boneless, skinless chicken breast, cubed
- 2 tablespoons low-fat Parmesan cheese, grated
- 2 tablespoons hot sauce

INSTRUCTIONS:
1. Preheat your oven to 350 degrees F.
2. Line a baking sheet with parchment paper.
3. In a plastic Ziploc bag, place the crushed Parmesan puffs and Parmesan cheese and mix well.
4. In a bowl, add chicken cubes and hot sauce and toss to coat well.
5. Place the coated chicken cubes in Ziploc bag with Parmesan mixture.
6. Seal the bag and shake to coat well.
7. Arrange the coated chicken cubes onto the prepared baking sheet in a single layer.
8. Bake for approximately 25-30 minutes.
9. Serve warm.

NUTRITIONAL INFORMATION PER SERVING:

Calories: 104
Fat: 3.2g
Carbohydrates: 9.5g
Fiber: 2.6g
Sugar: 1g
Protein: 12g
Sodium: 527mg

MOZZARELLA PIZZA BITES

Servings: 4
Preparation Time: 15 minutes
Cooking Time: 12 minutes

INGREDIENTS:
- 4 packets Buttermilk Cheddar Herb Biscuit
- Olive oil cooking spray
- 3 plum tomatoes, sliced thinly
- 1 cup fresh basil leaves, julienned
- ½ cup unsweetened almond milk
- 2 teaspoons olive oil
- 4 ounces fresh mozzarella cheese, cut into small pieces
- 2 tablespoons balsamic vinegar

INSTRUCTIONS:
1. Preheat your oven to 450 degrees F.
2. Lightly grease a 12 cups muffin tin.
3. In a bowl, add the Biscuit sachet, almond milk and oil and mix until well combined.
4. Place the biscuit mixture into the prepared muffin cups evenly.
5. Place a mozzarella piece over the biscuit mixture, followed by the 1 tomato slice and basil pieces.

6. Bake for approximately 10-12 minutes or until cheese is bubbly.
7. Remove from the oven and set aside to cool slightly.
8. Serve warm with the drizzling of vinegar.

NUTRITIONAL INFORMATION PER SERVING:

Calories: 229
Fat: 11g
Carbohydrates: 19g
Fiber: 5.2g
Sugar: 5.7g
Protein: 20.4g
Sodium: 555mg

TACO SALAD

Servings: 1
Preparation Time: 10 minutes

INGREDIENTS:

- 5 ounces cooked extra-lean ground turkey
- 2 cups romaine lettuce, shredded
- ½ of medium orange bell pepper, seeded and chopped
- ¼ cup low-fat Mexican blend cheese, shredded
- 2 tablespoons pico de gallo
- 2 tablespoons lime vinaigrette
- 1 sachet Puffed Ranch Snack

INSTRUCTIONS:

1. In a bowl, place turkey, lettuce, bell pepper, cheese and pico de gallo and mix well.
2. Drizzle with vinaigrette.
3. Top with Ranch Snack sachet and serve.

NUTRITIONAL INFORMATION PER SERVING:

Calories: 327
Fat: 15.5g
Carbohydrates: 11.4g
Fiber: 2.3g
Sugar: 3.5g
Protein: 34g
Sodium: 584mg

SNACK MIX

Servings: 1
Preparation Time: 5 minutes

INGREDIENTS:

- ½ sachet Puffed Sweet & salty Snacks
- ½ sachet Sharp Cheddar & Sour Cream popcorn
- 1 teaspoon Parmesan cheese, grated
- 1 teaspoon sugar-free caramel syrup

INSTRUCTIONS:

1. In a zip lock bag, place all ingredients.
2. Seal the bag and shake to coat well.
3. Serve immediately.

NUTRITIONAL INFORMATION PER SERVING:

Calories: 64
Fat: 4g
Carbohydrates: 6g
Fiber: 1g
Sugar: 1g
Protein: 1.3g
Sodium: 107mg

SRIRACHA POPCORN

Servings: 1
Preparation Time: 5 minutes

INGREDIENTS:

- 1 1 teaspoon unsalted butter, melted
- ¾ teaspoon Sriracha
- Pinch of stevia powder
- 1 sachet Sharp Cheddar & Sour Cream Popcorn

INSTRUCTIONS:

1. In a zip lock bag, place all ingredients.
2. Seal the bag and shake to coat well.
3. Serve immediately.

NUTRITIONAL INFORMATION PER SERVING:

Calories: 109
Fat: 8g
Carbohydrates: 7g
Fiber: 1g
Sugar: 0g
Protein: 1g
Sodium: 132mg

PUMPKIN PIE TRAIL MIX

Servings: 1
Preparation Time: 10 minutes

INGREDIENTS:

- 1 sachet Olive Oil & Sea Salt Popcorn
- ½ tablespoon pumpkin seeds
- ½ tablespoon slivered almonds
- ½ tablespoon sugar-free pancake syrup
- ¼ teaspoon pumpkin pie spice

INSTRUCTIONS:

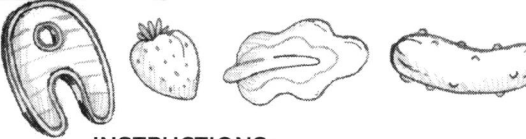

1. In a zip lock bag, place all ingredients.
2. Seal the bag and shake to coat well.
3. Serve immediately.

NUTRITIONAL INFORMATION PER SERVING:

Calories: 112
Fat: 8g
Carbohydrates: 7.7g
Fiber: 1.6g
Sugar: 0.2g
Protein: 2.7g
Sodium: 121mg

SHOPPING LIST

MEAT

Boneless, skinless chicken breasts
Skinless, boneless chicken tenders
Turkey breast
Ground turkey
Extra-lean ground turkey
Flank steak
Ground pork
Salmon
Grouper
Shrimp
Scallops

EGG & DAIRY

Eggs
Unsalted butter
Low-fat plain yogurt
Low-fat plain Greek yogurt
Light sour cream
Whipped cream
Whipped topping
Low-fat cream cheese
Strawberry-flavored light cream cheese
Low-fat cheddar cheese
Cottage cheese
Low-fat Mexican cheese
Low-fat Parmesan cheese
Part-skim ricotta cheese
Fresh mozzarella cheese

FRUIT

Apple
Orange
Fresh strawberries
Avocados
Canned peaches

VEGETABLES & FRESH HERBS

Zucchini
Broccoli
Cauliflower
Fresh mushrooms
Fresh button mushrooms
Asparagus
Red bell peppers
Yellow bell pepper
Green bell pepper
Fresh kale
Fresh baby kale
Fresh spinach
Fresh baby spinach
Carrots
Frozen peas
Celery stalks
Tomatoes
Cherry tomatoes
Cucumber
Radishes
Scallions
Onion
Garlic
Fresh ginger
Lettuce
Jalapeño pepper
Pepperoni pepper
Lime
Lemon
Fresh chives
Fresh parsley
Fresh rosemary
Fresh mint
Fresh cilantro
Fresh thyme
Fresh basil

SEASONING & DRIED HERBS

Salt
Ground cinnamon
Ground nutmeg
Ground cumin
Cayenne pepper
Red pepper flakes
Red chili powder
Ground black pepper
Garlic salt
Garlic powder
Pumpkin pie spice
Taco seasoning
Curry powder
Curry paste
Dried parsley
Dried thyme
Dried oregano

EXTRA:

Olive oil cooking spray
Olive oil
Extra-virgin olive oil
Coconut oil
Vegetable oil
Sesame oil
Unsweetened almond milk
Unsweetened cashew milk
Diet ginger ale
Tahini
Chili garlic sauce
Low-sodium soy sauce
Fish sauce
Hot sauce
Hot buffalo sauce
Sriracha
White vinegar
Balsamic vinegar
Marshmallow dip
Sugar-free caramel syrup

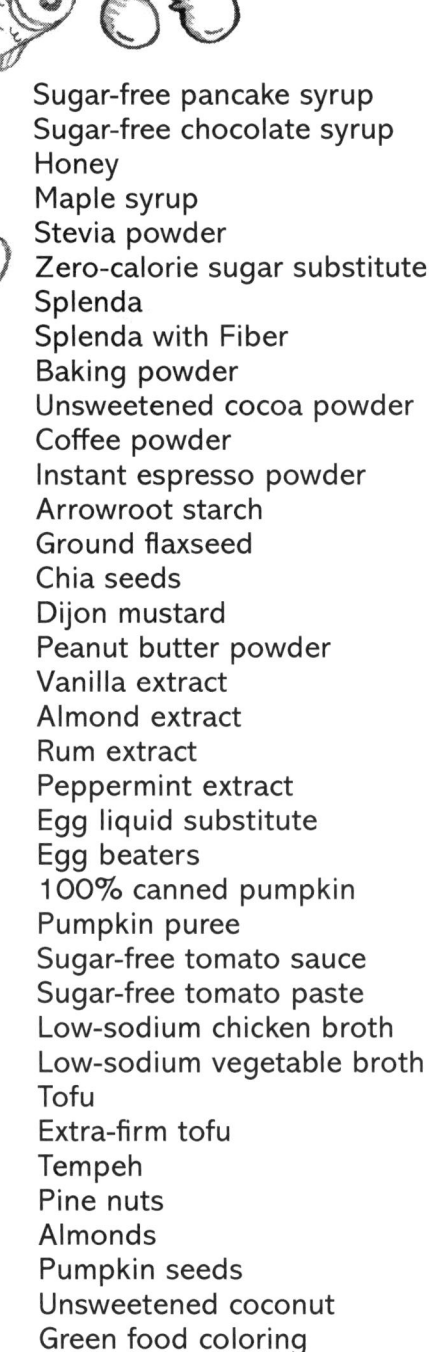

- Sugar-free pancake syrup
- Sugar-free chocolate syrup
- Honey
- Maple syrup
- Stevia powder
- Zero-calorie sugar substitute
- Splenda
- Splenda with Fiber
- Baking powder
- Unsweetened cocoa powder
- Coffee powder
- Instant espresso powder
- Arrowroot starch
- Ground flaxseed
- Chia seeds
- Dijon mustard
- Peanut butter powder
- Vanilla extract
- Almond extract
- Rum extract
- Peppermint extract
- Egg liquid substitute
- Egg beaters
- 100% canned pumpkin
- Pumpkin puree
- Sugar-free tomato sauce
- Sugar-free tomato paste
- Low-sodium chicken broth
- Low-sodium vegetable broth
- Tofu
- Extra-firm tofu
- Tempeh
- Pine nuts
- Almonds
- Pumpkin seeds
- Unsweetened coconut
- Green food coloring

FUELING HACKS PRODUCTS

- Double Chocolate Brownie Mix
- Wild Blueberry Almond Hot Cereal
- Blueberry Almond Hot Cereal
- Essential Creamy Vanilla Shake
- Essential Honey Mustard & Onion Sticks
- Chia Bliss Smoothie
- Essential Cinnamon Crunchy Oat Cereal
- Essential Velvety Hot Chocolate
- Oatmeal raisin crunch bar
- Oatmeal
- Mashed Potatoes
- Essential Smashed Potatoes
- Brownie Mix
- Puffed Sweet & salty Snacks
- Sharp Cheddar & Sour Cream popcorn
- Golden Pancake
- Olive Oil & Sea Salt Popcorn
- Chicken Noodle Soup
- Cream of Tomato Soup
- Essential Spiced Gingerbread
- Essential Decadent Double Brownie
- Essential Chocolate Chip Pancakes
- Brownie Mix
- Peanut Butter Chocolate Crunch Bar
- Hearty Red Bean & Vegetable Chili
- Essential Red Berry Crunch O's Cereal
- Essential Chocolate Chip Cookie
- Honey Sweet Potatoes
- Essential Frosty Mint Chocolate Soft Serve Treat
- Chocolate Cherry Ganache Bar
- Buttermilk Cheddar Herb Biscuit
- Select Cheddar Herb Biscuit
- Essential Creamy Double Peanut Butter Crisp Bar
- Essential Golden Chocolate Chip Pancakes
- Yogurt Berry Blast Smoothie
- Essential Caramel Macchiato Shake
- Olive Oil & Sea Salt Popcorn
- Dark Chocolate Covered Cherry Shake
- French Vanilla Shake
- Chocolate Chip Pancakes
- Parmesan Cheese Puffs, crushed finely
- Meal Mixed Berry Cereal Crunch
- Cinnamon Pretzel Sticks
- Macaroni & Cheese
- Chocolate pudding
- Chocolate shake
- Calorie Burn Cappuccino
- Maple Brown Sugar Oatmeal
- Mixed Berry Flavor Infuser Brownie
- Cappuccino mix
- Chocolate Chip Pancakes
- S'more Crunch Bar

MEAL PLAN 1

The Plan 1 is the commonly prescribed for Lean and Green diet plan because it is quite effective one. The 5 and 1 recommend you to take six small meals in a day. The meals should be divided in such a way that there should be "5 Fuelings" meals and "1 lean and green" meal in a day. For this, you can select any of the fuelings and add to the diet; when to consume the six meals is the dieter's personal choice. You can have 3 fuelings in the morning and afternoon then have a "Lean and green" meal in the evening and end the day with 2 fuelings. Remember, there should be 2-3 hours of the gap between two consecutive meals in a day. Since you will be using more of the fueling and less of the food on this plan, the weight loss is quickly achieved using this plan. And it is often suggested for the early stage of the Lean and Green weight loss program because it helps activates the fat burn.

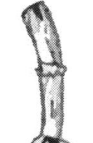

DAY 1:

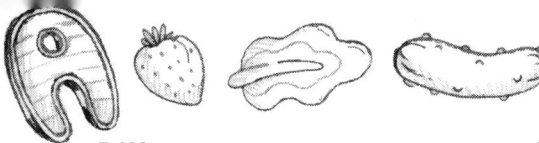

Fueling Hacks:
Hot Chocolate
Oatmeal Cookies
French Toast Sticks
Mac & Cheese Chips
Cheddar Pancakes

Lean & Green Meal:
Turkey & Veggie Casserole

DAY 2:

Fueling Hacks:
Vanilla Shake
Chocolate Haystacks
Potato Bagels
Pumpkin Waffles
Snickerdoodles

Lean & Green Meal:
Pork Stuffed Avocado

DAY 3:

Fueling Hacks:
Eggnog
Soup Chips
Brownie Bites
Marshmallow Cereal Treat
Chicken Nuggets

Lean & Green Meal:
Shrimp & Scallops with Veggies

DAY 4:

Fueling Hacks:
Peppermint Mocha
Blueberry Scones
Chocolate Crepes
Pizza Bread
Mocha Cake

Lean & Green Meal:
Chicken with Bell Peppers

DAY 5:

Fueling Hacks:
Vanilla Frappe
Parmesan Chicken Bites
Chocolate Waffles
Gingerbread Biscotti
Chia Seed Pudding

Lean & Green Meal:
Tofu with Kale

DAY 6:

Fueling Hacks:
Coconut Smoothie
Fudge Balls
Biscuit Pizza
Blueberry Muffins
Maple Pancakes

Lean & Green Meal:
Steak & Veggie Salad

DAY 7:

Fueling Hacks:
Shamrock Shake
Chia Seed Pudding
Chocolate Donuts
Brownie Cookies
Tortilla Chips

Lean & Green Meal:
Turkey & Spinach Stew

MEAL PLAN 2

This is second plan is comparatively easier and simpler than the first plan. This approach recommends the use of 4 fuelings in a day along with 2 lean and green meals and 1 snack. The snack, in this case, should be healthy, and it should be free of carbs and sugars. Sure, this plan is relatively easy, but it does not guarantee quick results. It is overall healthy and can be used as a beginner's approach to starting with.

DAY 1:

Fueling Hacks:
Berry Mojito
Yogurt Cereal Bar
Brownie Peanut Butter Pudding
Taco Salad

Lean & Green Meals:
Chicken & Veggies Stir Fry
Tofu with Peas

Snack:
½ cup canned peaches (packed in water or natural juices)

DAY 2:

Fueling Hacks:
Tiramisu Shake
Yogurt Cookie Dough
Sweet Potato Muffins
Sriracha Popcorn

Lean & Green Meals:
Salmon with Cauliflower Mash
Turkey Chili

Snack:
¾ cup low-fat plain yogurt

DAY 3:

Fueling Hacks:
Chocolate Frappe
Chocolate Berry Parfait
Blueberry Scones
Mozzarella Pizza Bites

Lean & Green Meals:
Shrimp with Zucchini Noodles
Beef Taco Bowl

Snack:
4 ounces apple

DAY 4:

Fueling Hacks:
Peppermint Mocha
Peanut Butter Bites
Mocha Muffin
Mashed Potato Tortilla

Lean & Green Meals:
Veggie Stuffed Steak
Turkey, Apple & Veggie Burgers

Snack:
3 celery stalks

DAY 5:

Fueling Hacks:
Pumpkin Spice Latte
Crunch Sandwich Cookies
Chocolate Cake Fries
Mac & Cheese Doritos

Lean & Green Meals:
Fish & Spinach Curry
Steak, Egg & Veggie Salad

Snack:
½ cup fresh strawberries

DAY 6:

Fueling Hacks:
Eggnog
Chocolate Haystacks
Yogurt Berry Donuts
Buffalo Cauliflower Poppers

Lean & Green Meals:
Chicken & Veggie Quiche
Tofu with Broccoli

Snack:
1 cup unsweetened cashew milk

DAY 7:

Fueling Hacks:
Caramel Macchiato Frappe
Cherry Mocha Popsicles
Smashed Potato Grill Cheese
Pumpkin Pie Trail Mix

Lean & Green Meals:
Stuffed Chicken Breast
Tempeh with Veggies

Snack:
4 ounces orange

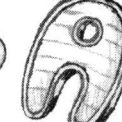

CONCLUSION

It is always great to have a long list of options available at hand when you are about to start a new dietary regime! It is always difficult to jump from a full meal diet to a fuel-based one and to have open choices help you create an interesting menu to stick to. This cookbook is also designed with the sole purpose of providing the Lean and Green wannabe's a whole world of options with our hundreds of recipes so they won't feel missing out on much. So, pick your favorite meals, select one of the two dietary plans, get all the Fuelings, and start your weight loss journey right away!

Made in the USA
Columbia, SC
12 May 2021